SHAPES AND COLORS

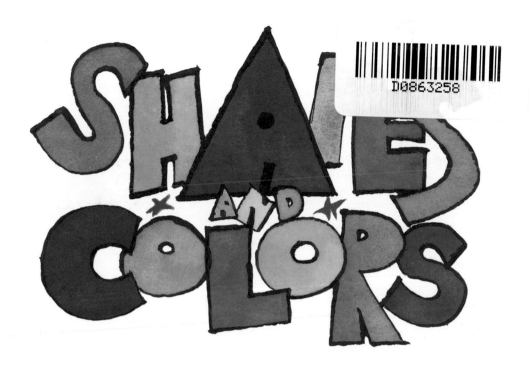

Other *Cul de Sac* Books by Richard Thompson

Cul de Sac
Children at Play
Cul de Sac Golden Treasury: A Keepsake Garland of Classics

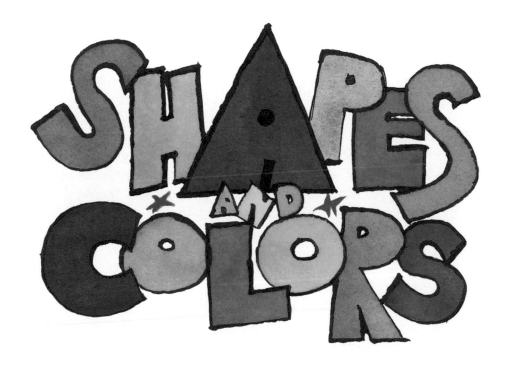

A *Cul de Sac* Collection

by Richard Thompson

**Andrews McMeel
Publishing, LLC**
Kansas City • Sydney • London

——— **ATTENTION: SCHOOLS AND BUSINESSES** ———

Andrews McMeel books are available at quantity discounts with bulk purchase for educational, business, or sales promotional use. For information, please write to: Special Sales Department, Andrews McMeel Publishing, LLC, 1130 Walnut Street, Kansas City, Missouri 64106.

To Pop, with love

Foreword

Cul de Sac is not my favorite comic strip. It's OK, but it's not my favorite (comic strip) and I didn't finish reading this book. All I got to was page 32 and I figured it wouldn't get better. There's too much talking and running and small kids and yelling and the colors are too bright. My favorite comic strip is *Little Neuro*. I like it because there's a lot less talking and running and the colors are not so bright. *Little Neuro* jokes are better than *Cul de Sac* jokes too. *Cul de Sac* has things like jokes but without the funny part at the end.

Also the back of my head doesn't look like that, so *Cul de Sac* is not an accurate comic strip.

—Peter (Petey) Otterloop, Jr.

Ah! You've made your selection?

Well, the top is a little weird.

We could wire on a new top quite easily.

You can?

Really?

We offer many tasteful cosmetic options on our trees.

Oh!

Is it extra?

EW.

We'll do a top replacement and bolt on a few more limbs. A simple procedure.

It'll be like Frankenstein if he was a tree!

It's leaking glue.

It looks so natural.

- And when they plug in the tree, it comes back to life and seeks revenge, leaving its victims smothered in glue.

Thanks. I was wondering what to dream about tonight.

R. Thompson

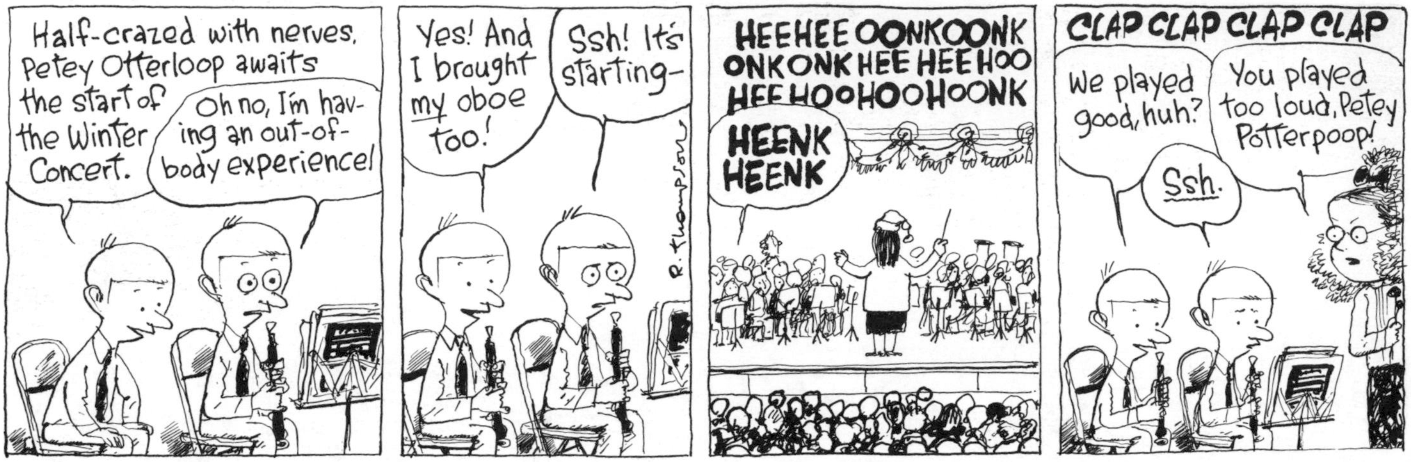
Half-crazed with nerves, Petey Otterloop awaits the start of the Winter Concert.
Oh no, I'm having an out-of-body experience!
Yes! And I brought my oboe too!
Ssh! It's starting–
R. Thompson
HEEHEE OONKOONK ONKONK HEE HEE HOO HEE HOOHOOHOONK
HEENK HEENK
CLAP CLAP CLAP CLAP
We played good, huh?
You played too loud, Petey Potterpoop!
Ssh.

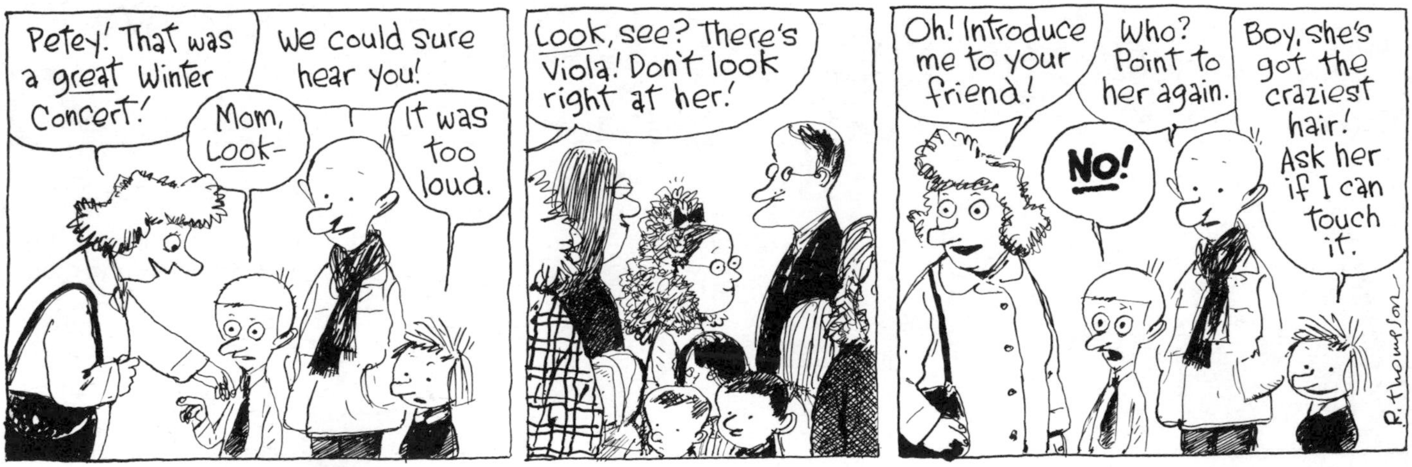
Petey! That was a great Winter Concert!
We could sure hear you!
Mom, Look–
It was too loud.
Look, see? There's Viola! Don't look right at her!
Oh! Introduce me to your friend!
Who? Point to her again.
NO!
Boy, she's got the craziest hair! Ask her if I can touch it.
R. Thompson

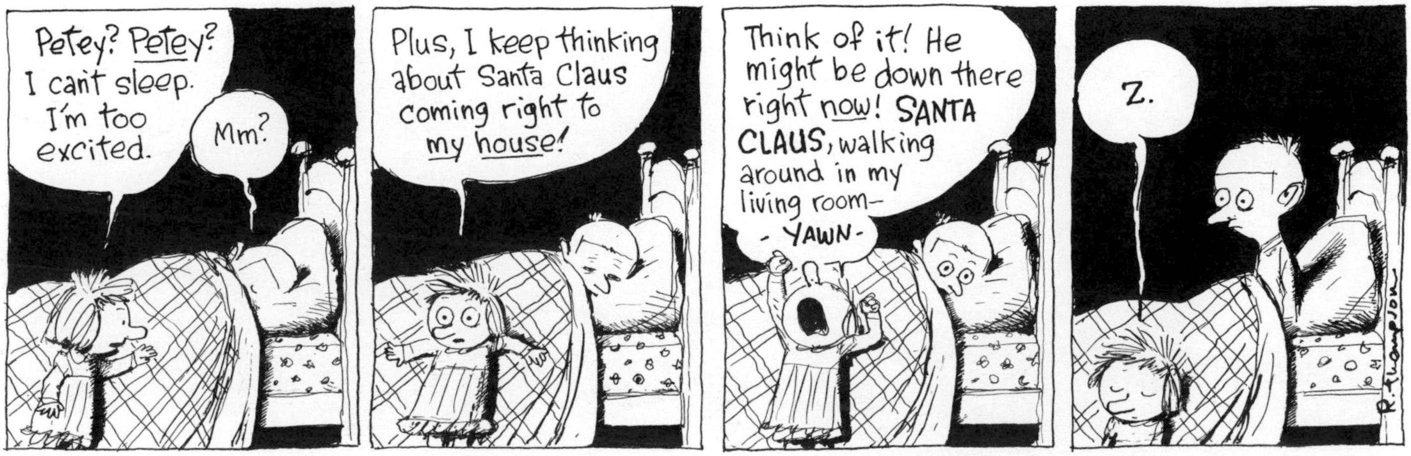
Petey? Petey? I can't sleep. I'm too excited.
Mm?
Plus, I keep thinking about Santa Claus coming right to my house!
Think of it! He might be down there right now! SANTA CLAUS, walking around in my living room–
-YAWN-
Z.
R. Thompson

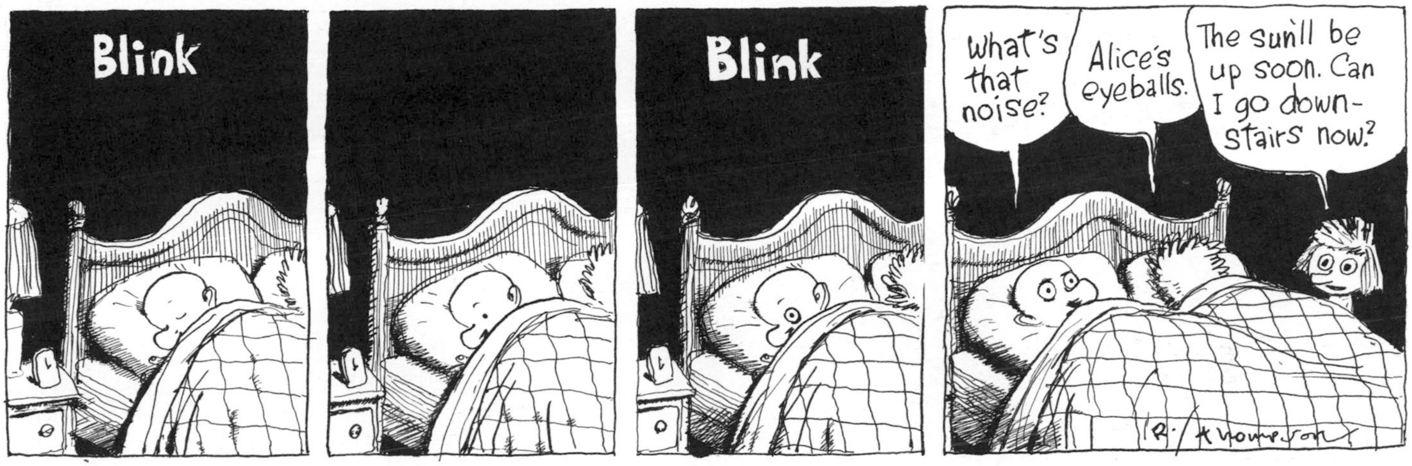
Blink
Blink
What's that noise?
Alice's eyeballs.
The sun'll be up soon. Can I go down-stairs now?

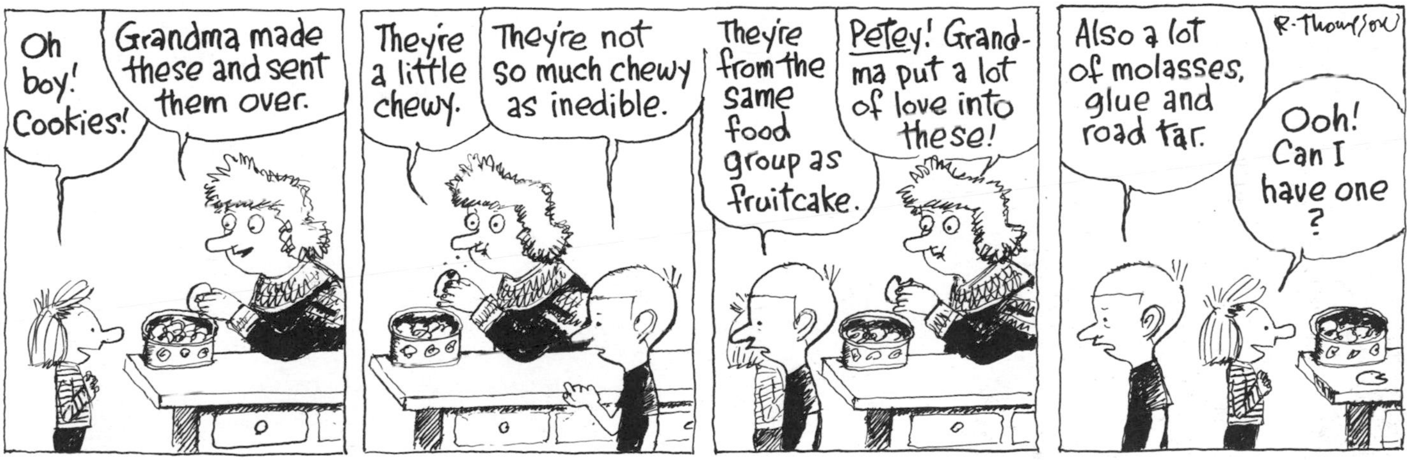
Oh boy! Cookies!
Grandma made these and sent them over.
They're a little chewy.
They're not so much chewy as inedible.
They're from the same food group as fruitcake.
Petey! Grandma put a lot of love into these!
Also a lot of molasses, glue and road tar.
Ooh! Can I have one ?

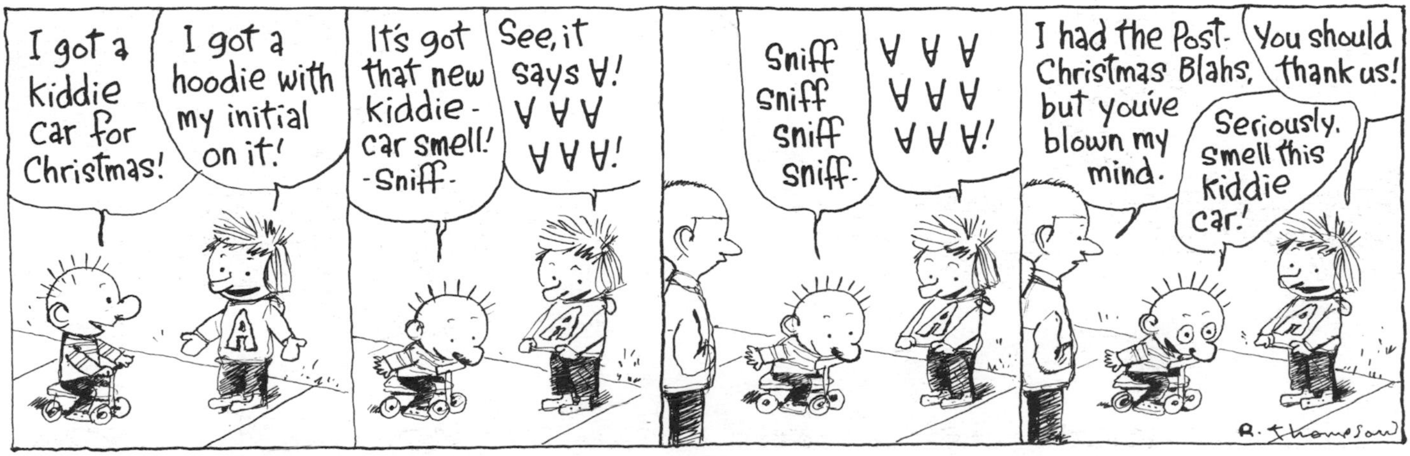
I got a kiddie car for Christmas!
I got a hoodie with my initial on it!
It's got that new kiddie-car smell! -Sniff-
See, it says ∀! ∀ ∀ ∀ ∀ ∀ ∀!
Sniff sniff sniff sniff.
∀ ∀ ∀ ∀ ∀ ∀ ∀ ∀ ∀!
I had the Post-Christmas Blahs, but you've blown my mind.
You should thank us!
Seriously. Smell this kiddie car!

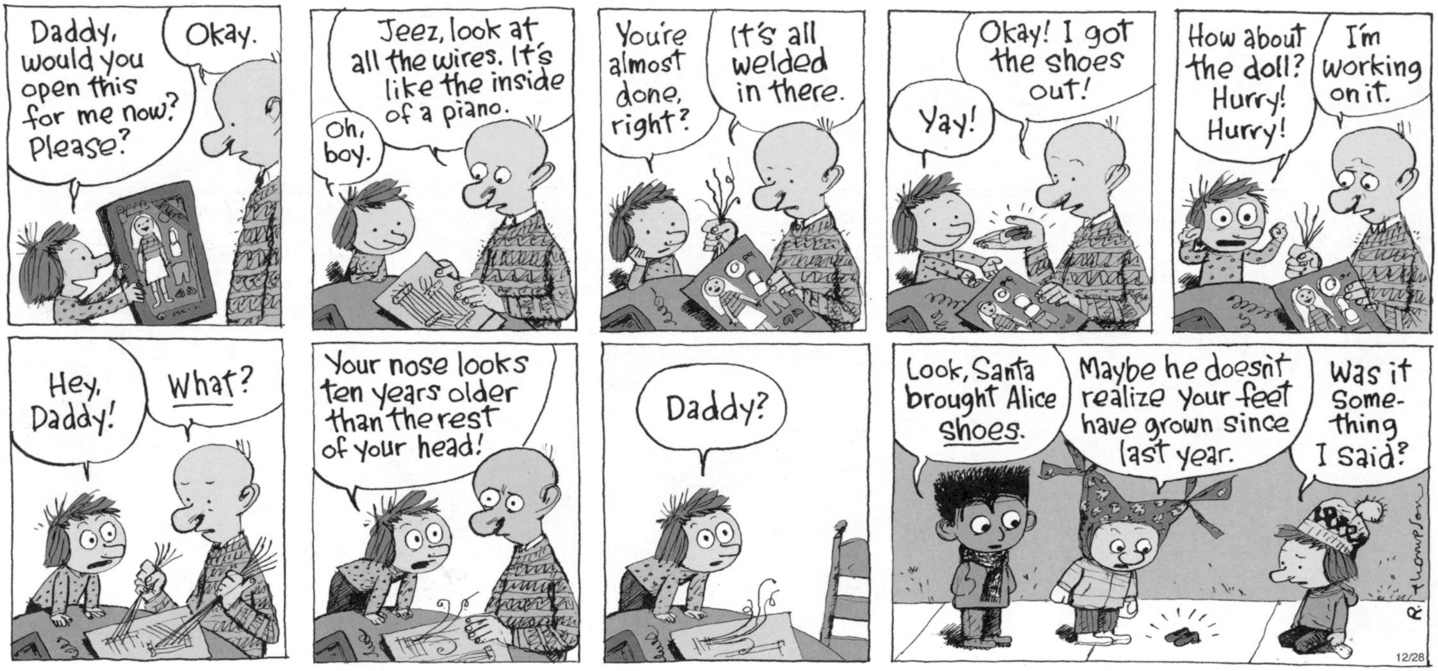
Daddy, would you open this for me now? Please?
Okay.
Jeez, look at all the wires. It's like the inside of a piano.
Oh, boy.
You're almost done, right?
It's all welded in there.
Okay! I got the shoes out!
Yay!
How about the doll? Hurry! Hurry!
I'm working on it.
Hey, Daddy!
What?
Your nose looks ten years older than the rest of your head!
Daddy?
Look, Santa brought Alice shoes.
Maybe he doesn't realize your feet have grown since last year.
Was it some-thing I said?
Thompson
12/28

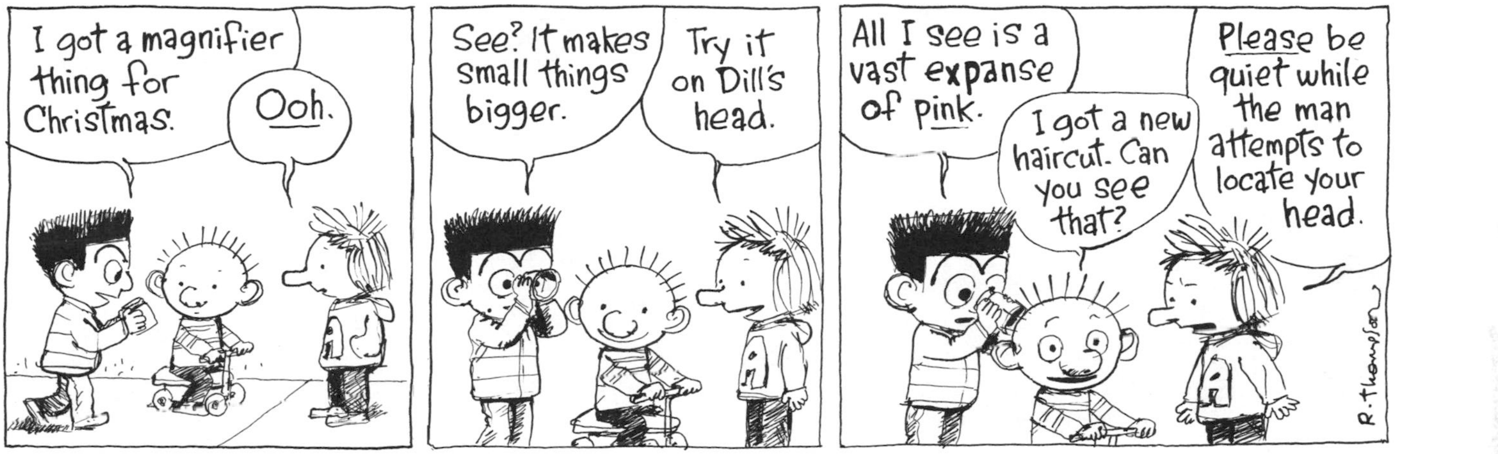
I got a magnifier thing for Christmas.
Ooh.
See? It makes small things bigger.
Try it on Dill's head.
All I see is a vast expanse of pink.
I got a new haircut. Can you see that?
Please be quiet while the man attempts to locate your head.

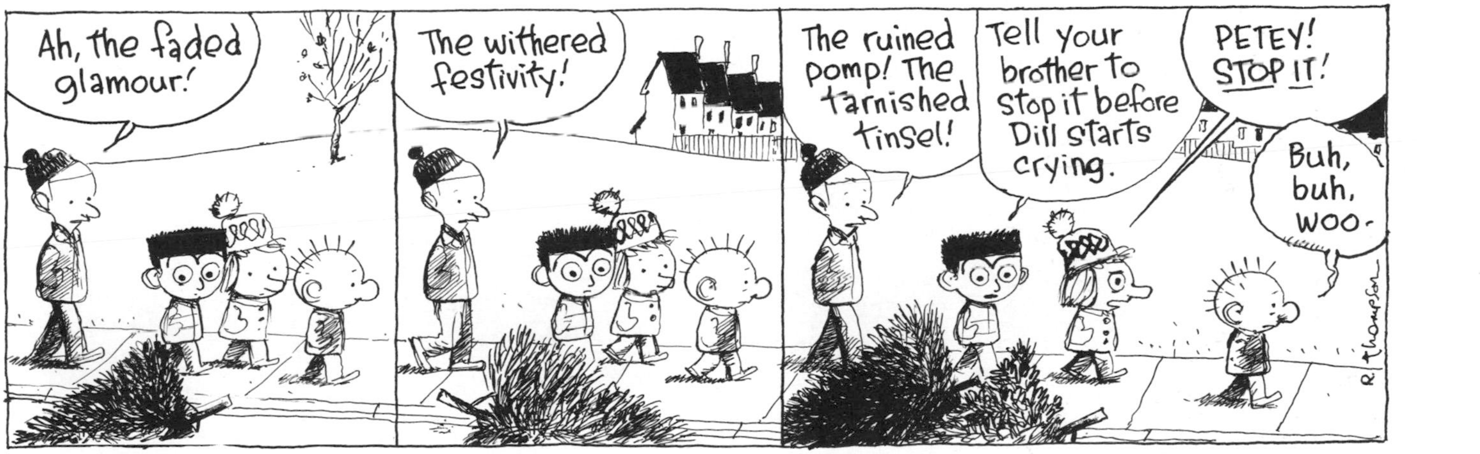
Ah, the faded glamour!
The withered festivity!
The ruined pomp! The tarnished tinsel!
Tell your brother to stop it before Dill starts crying.
PETEY! STOP IT!
Buh, buh, woo-

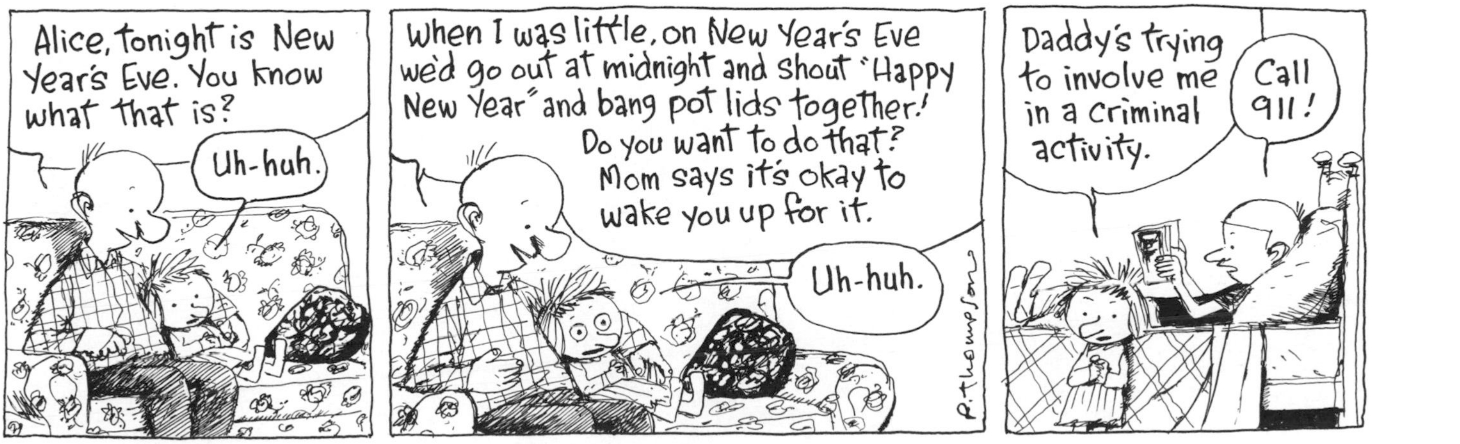
Alice, tonight is New Year's Eve. You know what that is?
Uh-huh.
When I was little, on New Year's Eve we'd go out at midnight and shout "Happy New Year" and bang pot lids together! Do you want to do that? Mom says it's okay to wake you up for it.
Uh-huh.
Daddy's trying to involve me in a criminal activity.
Call 911!

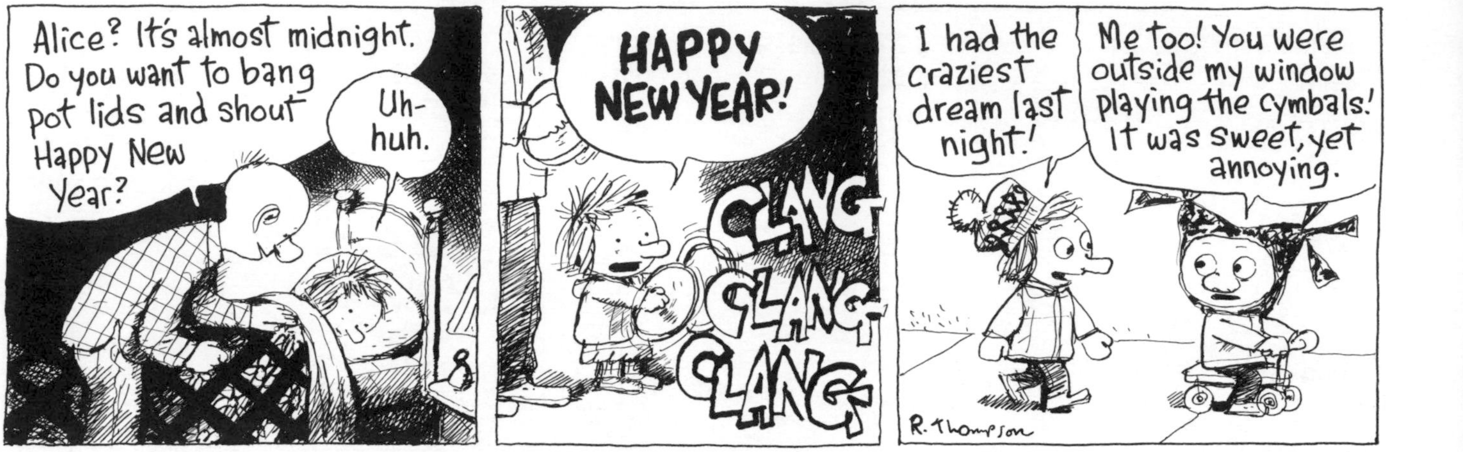
Alice? It's almost midnight. Do you want to bang pot lids and shout Happy New Year?
Uh-huh.
HAPPY NEW YEAR!
CLANG
CLANG
CLANG
I had the craziest dream last night!
Me too! You were outside my window playing the cymbals! It was sweet, yet annoying.
R. Thompson

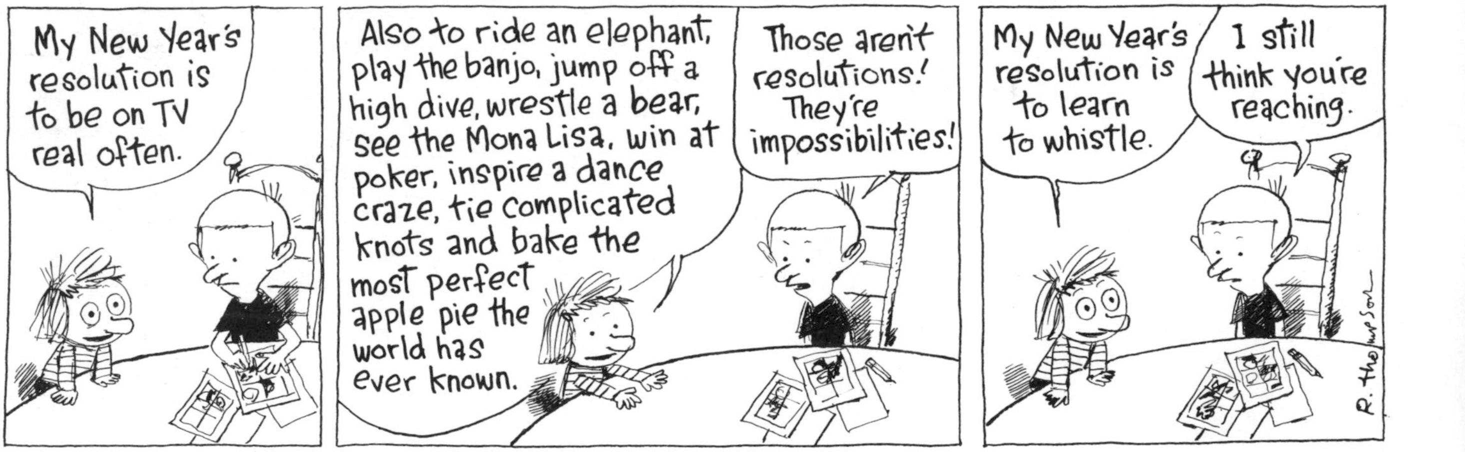
My New Year's resolution is to be on TV real often.
Also to ride an elephant, play the banjo, jump off a high dive, wrestle a bear, see the Mona Lisa, win at poker, inspire a dance craze, tie complicated knots and bake the most perfect apple pie the world has ever known.
Those aren't resolutions! They're impossibilities!
My New Year's resolution is to learn to whistle.
I still think you're reaching.
R. Thompson

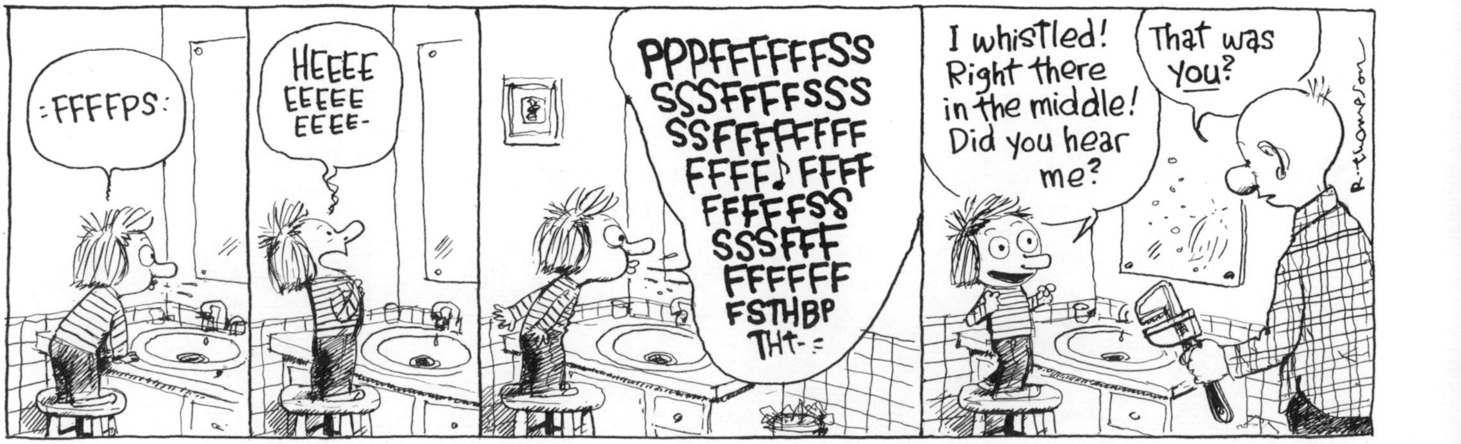
FFFFPS
HEEEE EEEEE EEEE-
PPPFFFFFFFSS SSSFFFFSSS SSFFFFFFFF FFFF FFFF FFFFFSS SSSFFF FFFFFF FSTHBP THT-
I whistled! Right there in the middle! Did you hear me?
That was YOU?
R. Thompson

I don't get it. Why do dining room chairs have ladders on the back?
The cavemen invented them.
Huh?
It used to be sometimes they didn't cook the food very well and it'd come back to life and chase them.
And they'd climb up the ladder to escape.
MOM!
Don't ask Mom about it! You'll awaken painful memories!
R. thompson

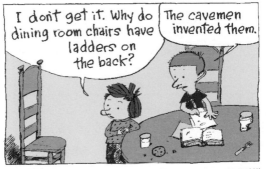

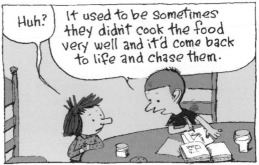

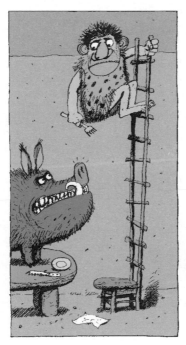

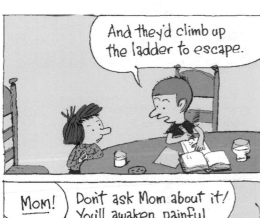

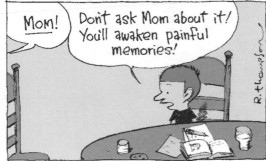

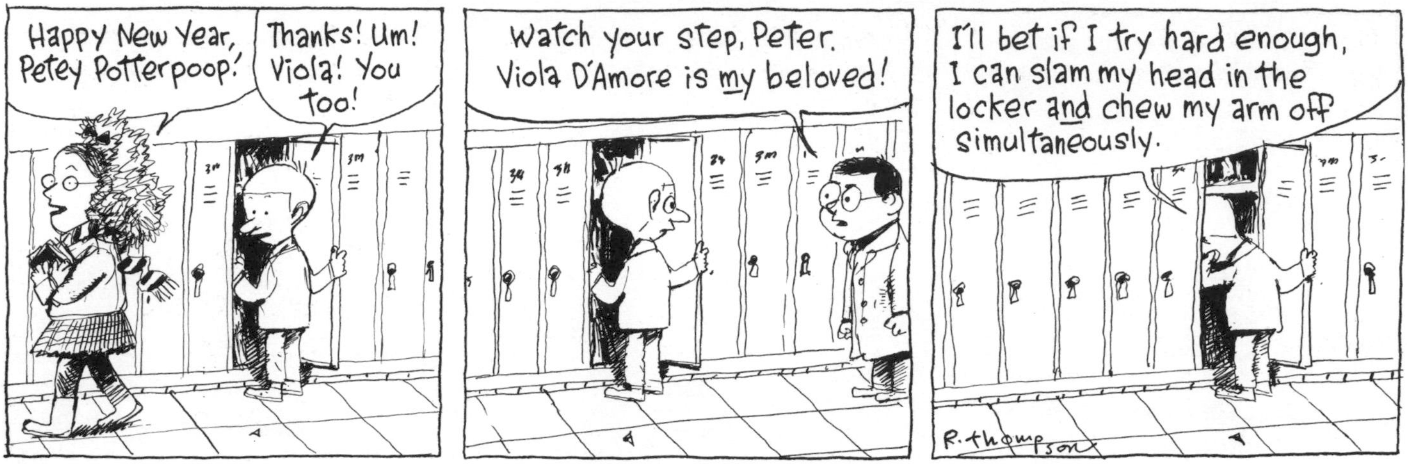
Happy New Year, Petey Potterpoop!
Thanks! Um! Viola! You too!
Watch your step, Peter. Viola D'Amore is my beloved!
I'll bet if I try hard enough, I can slam my head in the locker and chew my arm off simultaneously.
R. Thompson

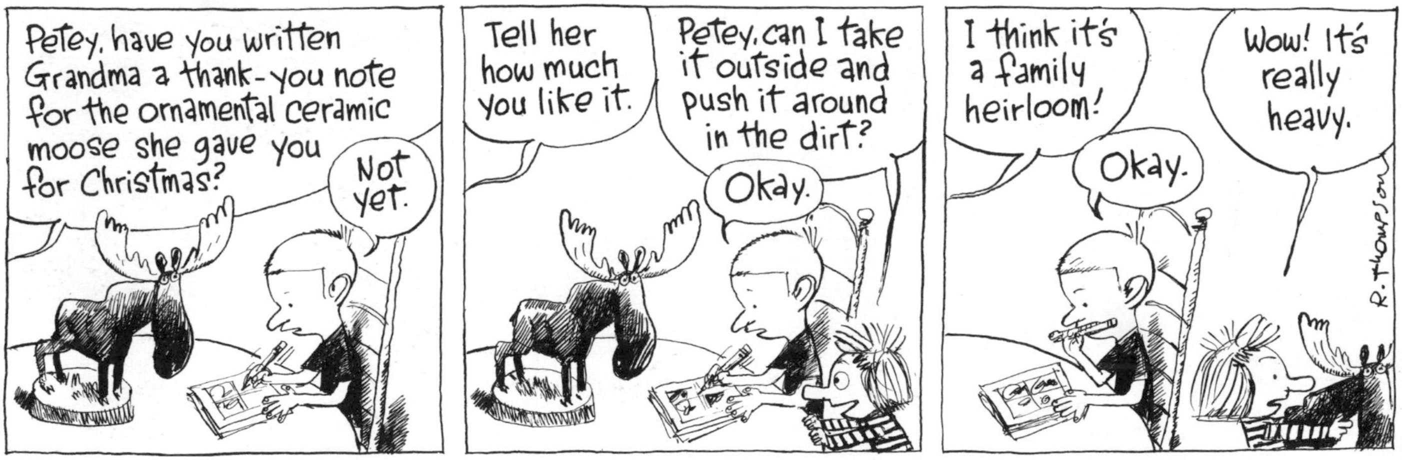
Petey, have you written Grandma a thank-you note for the ornamental ceramic moose she gave you for Christmas?
Not yet.
Tell her how much you like it.
Petey, can I take it outside and push it around in the dirt?
Okay.
I think it's a family heirloom!
Okay.
Wow! It's really heavy.
R. Thompson

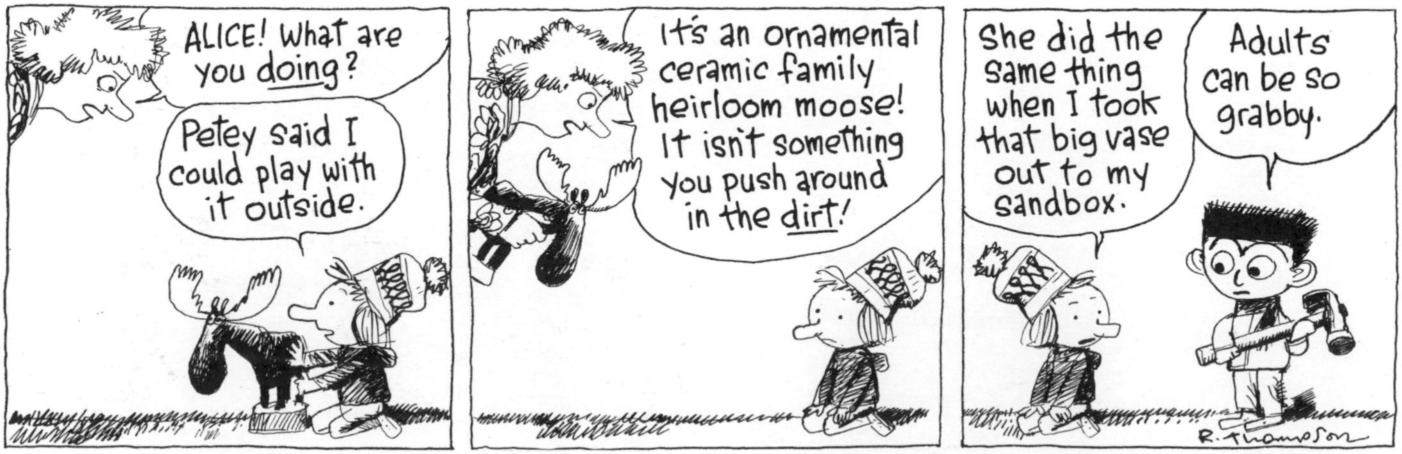
ALICE! What are you doing?
Petey said I could play with it outside.
It's an ornamental ceramic family heirloom moose! It isn't something you push around in the dirt!
She did the same thing when I took that big vase out to my sandbox.
Adults can be so grabby.
R. Thompson

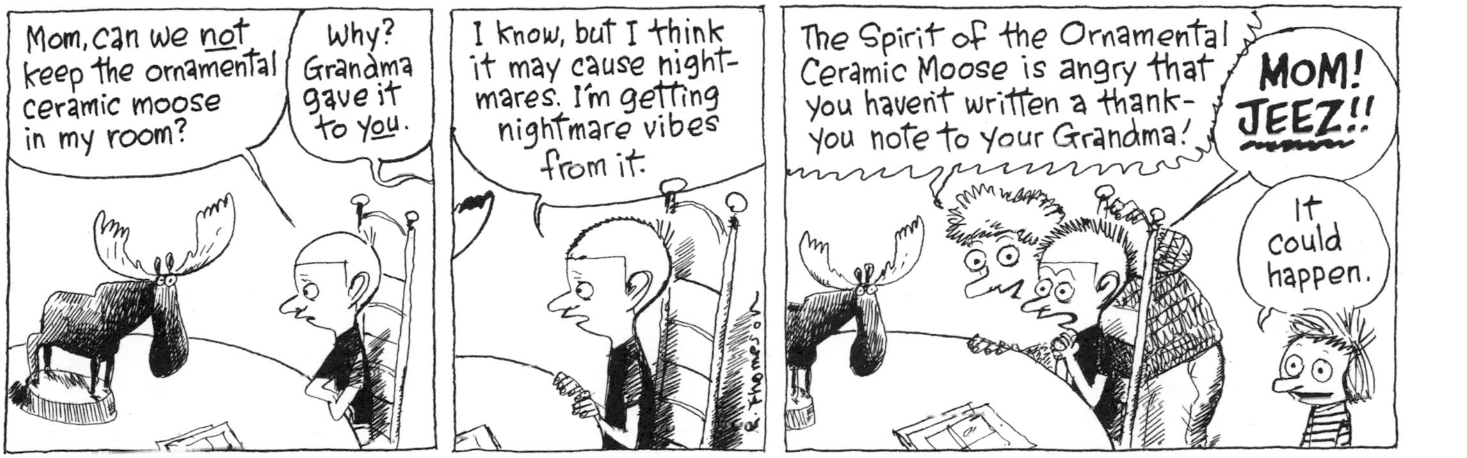

Mom, can we not keep the ornamental ceramic moose in my room?
Why? Grandma gave it to you.
I know, but I think it may cause nightmares. I'm getting nightmare vibes from it.
The Spirit of the Ornamental Ceramic Moose is angry that you haven't written a thank-you note to your Grandma!
MOM! JEEZ!!
It could happen.

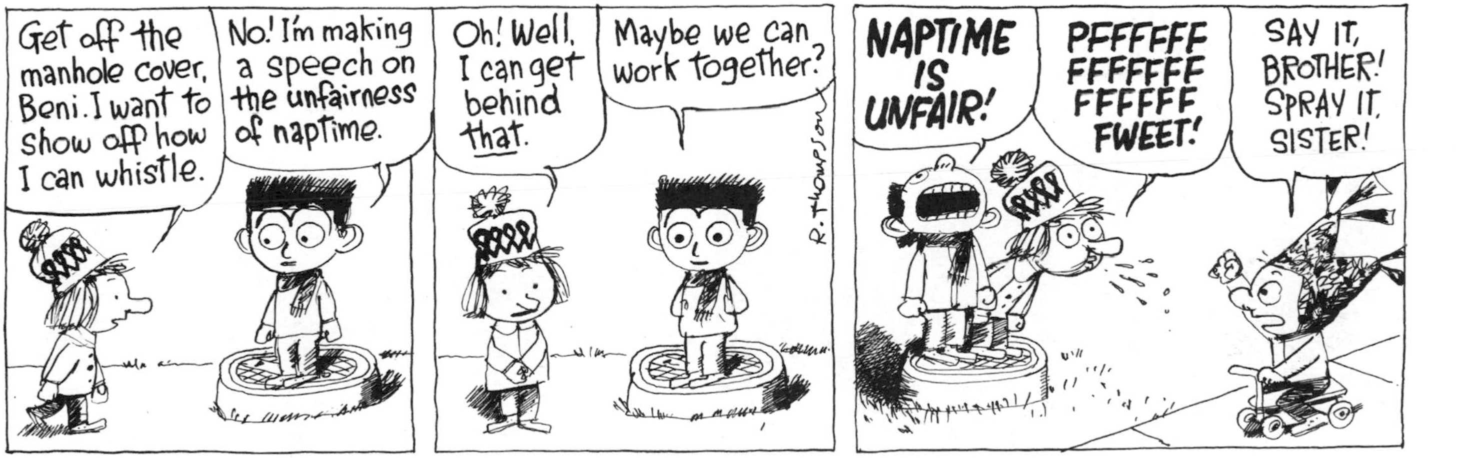

Get off the manhole cover, Beni. I want to show off how I can whistle.
No! I'm making a speech on the unfairness of naptime.
Oh! Well, I can get behind that.
Maybe we can work together?
NAPTIME IS UNFAIR!
PFFFFFF FFFFFFF FFFFFF FWEET!
SAY IT, BROTHER! SPRAY IT, SISTER!

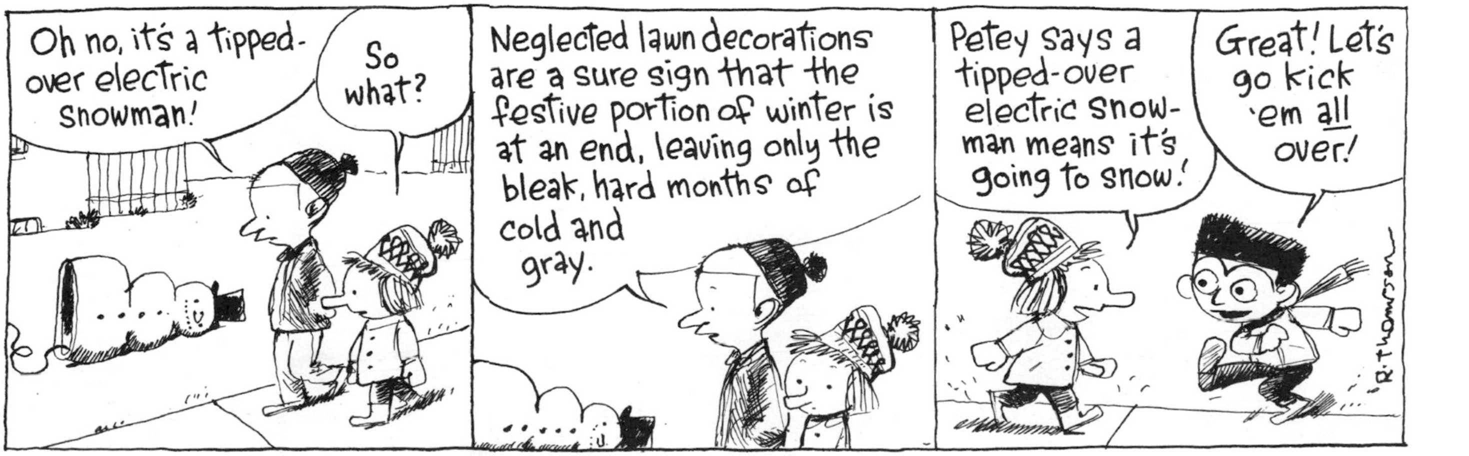

Oh no, it's a tipped-over electric snowman!
So what?
Neglected lawn decorations are a sure sign that the festive portion of winter is at an end, leaving only the bleak, hard months of cold and gray.
Petey says a tipped-over electric snowman means it's going to snow!
Great! Let's go kick 'em all over!

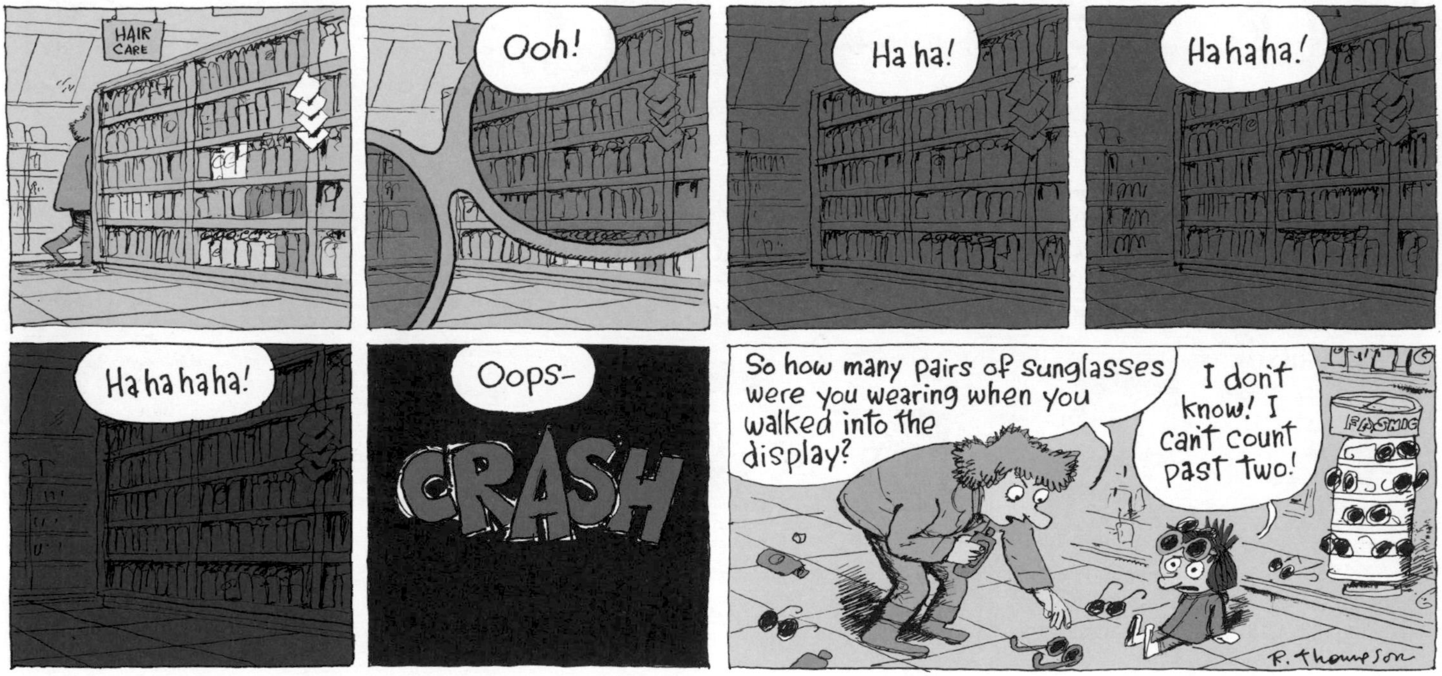
HAIR CARE
Ooh!
Ha ha!
Hahaha!
Hahahaha!
Oops-
CRASH
So how many pairs of sunglasses were you wearing when you walked into the display?
I don't know! I can't count past two!
R. thompson

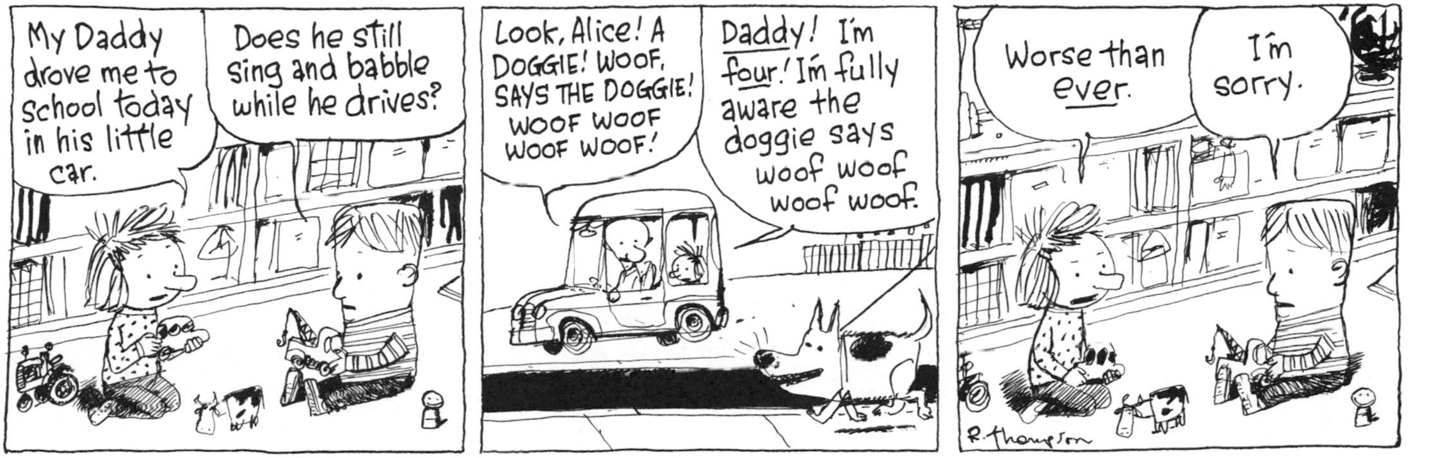
My Daddy drove me to school today in his little car.
Does he still sing and babble while he drives?
Look, Alice! A DOGGIE! WOOF, SAYS THE DOGGIE! WOOF WOOF WOOF WOOF!
Daddy! I'm four! I'm fully aware the doggie says woof woof woof woof.
Worse than ever.
I'm sorry.
R. Thompson

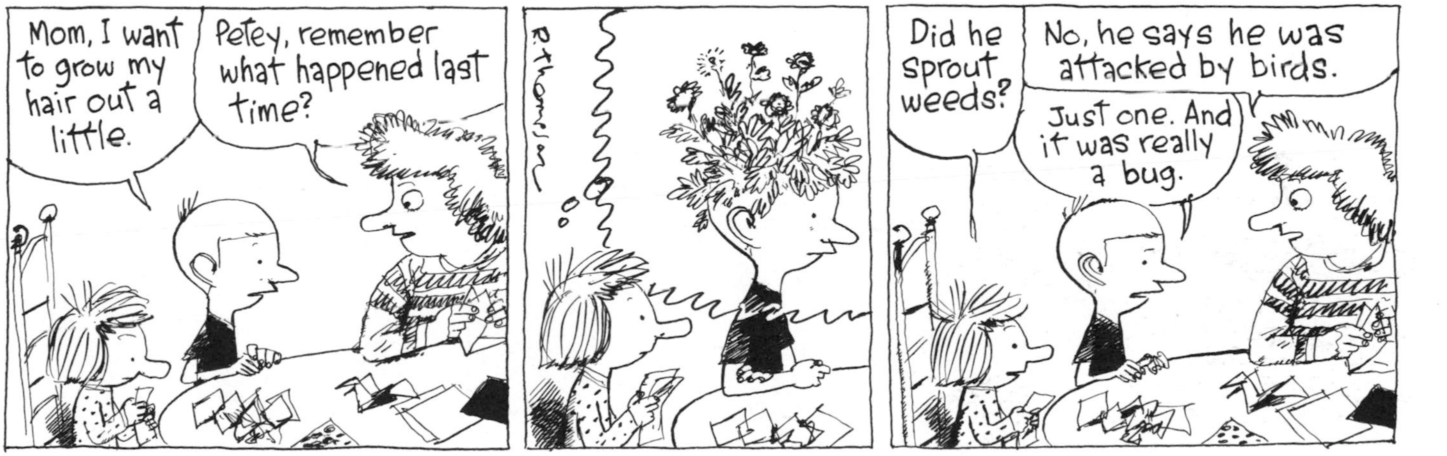
Mom, I want to grow my hair out a little.
Petey, remember what happened last time?
R. Thompson
Did he sprout weeds?
No, he says he was attacked by birds.
Just one. And it was really a bug.

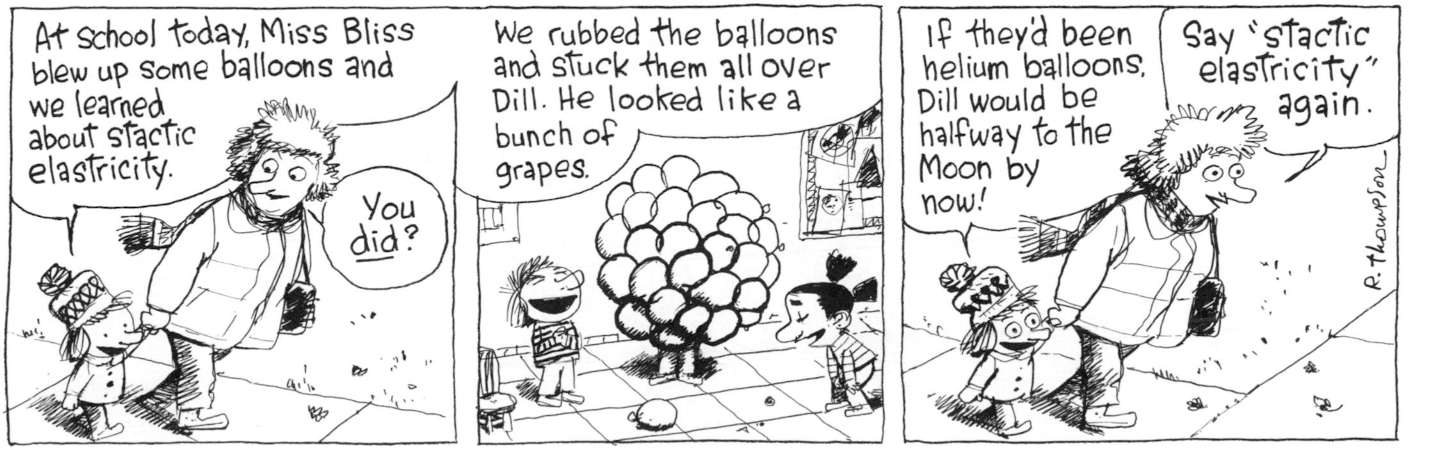
At school today, Miss Bliss blew up some balloons and we learned about stactic elastricity.
You did?
We rubbed the balloons and stuck them all over Dill. He looked like a bunch of grapes.
If they'd been helium balloons, Dill would be halfway to the Moon by now!
Say "stactic elastricity" again.
R. Thompson

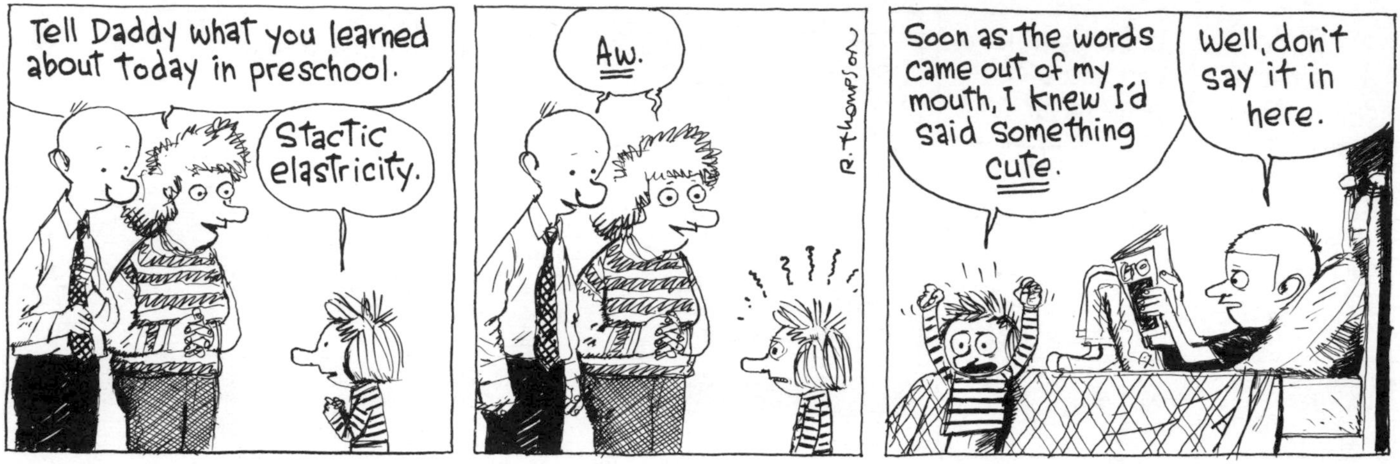
Tell Daddy what you learned about today in preschool.
Stactic elastricity.
Aw.
Soon as the words came out of my mouth, I knew I'd said something cute.
Well, don't say it in here.

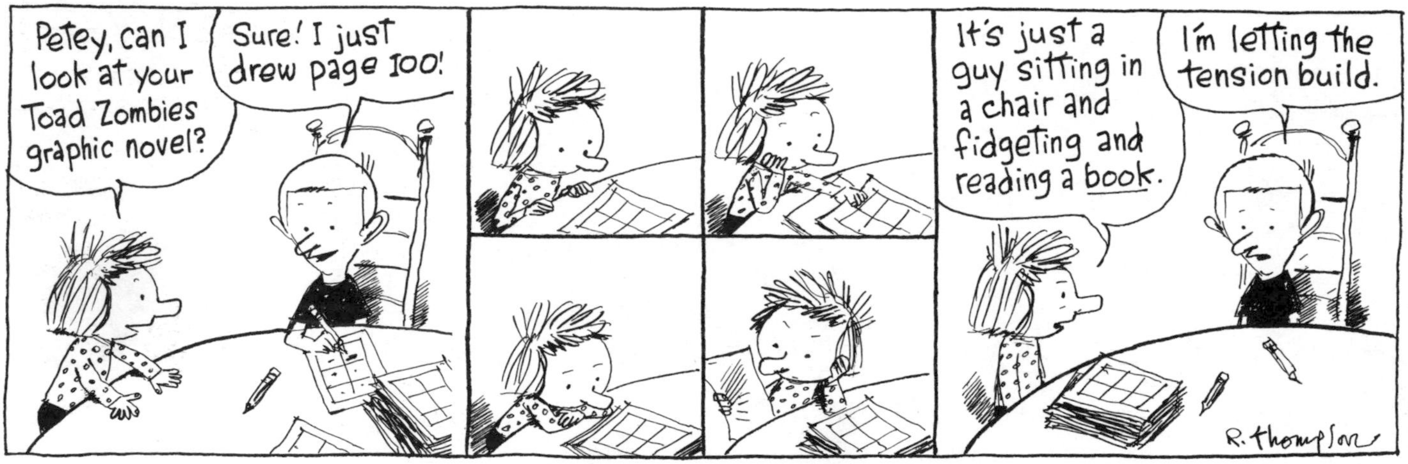
Petey, can I look at your Toad Zombies graphic novel?
Sure! I just drew page 100!
It's just a guy sitting in a chair and fidgeting and reading a book.
I'm letting the tension build.

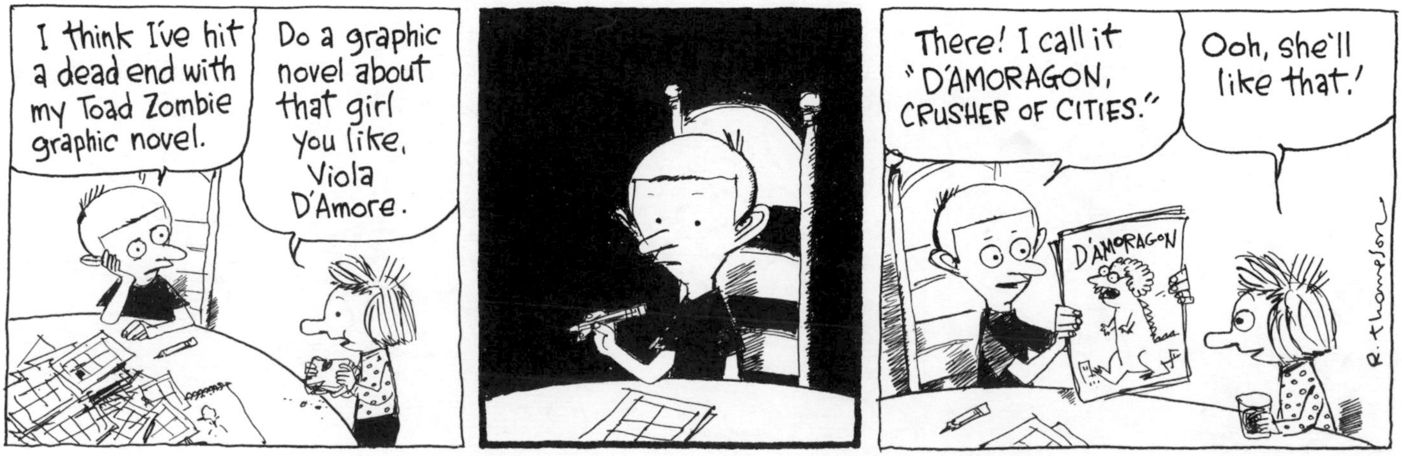
I think I've hit a dead end with my Toad Zombie graphic novel.
Do a graphic novel about that girl you like, Viola D'Amore.
There! I call it "D'AMORAGON, CRUSHER OF CITIES."
D'AMORAGON
Ooh, she'll like that!

SHUFF
SHUFF
SHUFF
Ha ha!
SHUFF
SHUFF
SHUFF
SHUFF
SHUFF
SHUFF
Ha ha ha
ha ha!
Daddy! Look at my hair!
It's crazy! Look, Daddy!
BLAM
YOW
You'd think Daddy'd warn me when he's wearing exploding socks.
He's a dangerous man, I keep telling you.
R. Thompson

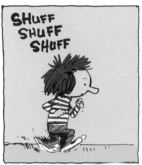

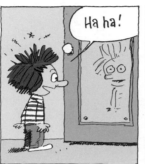

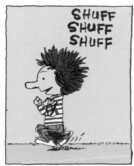

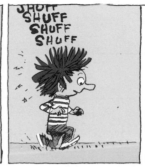

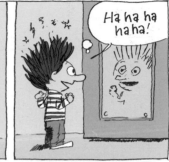

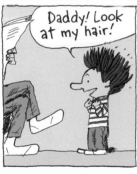

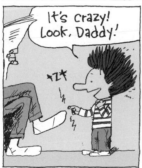

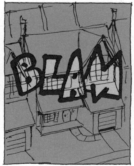

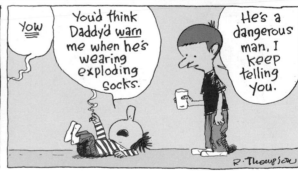

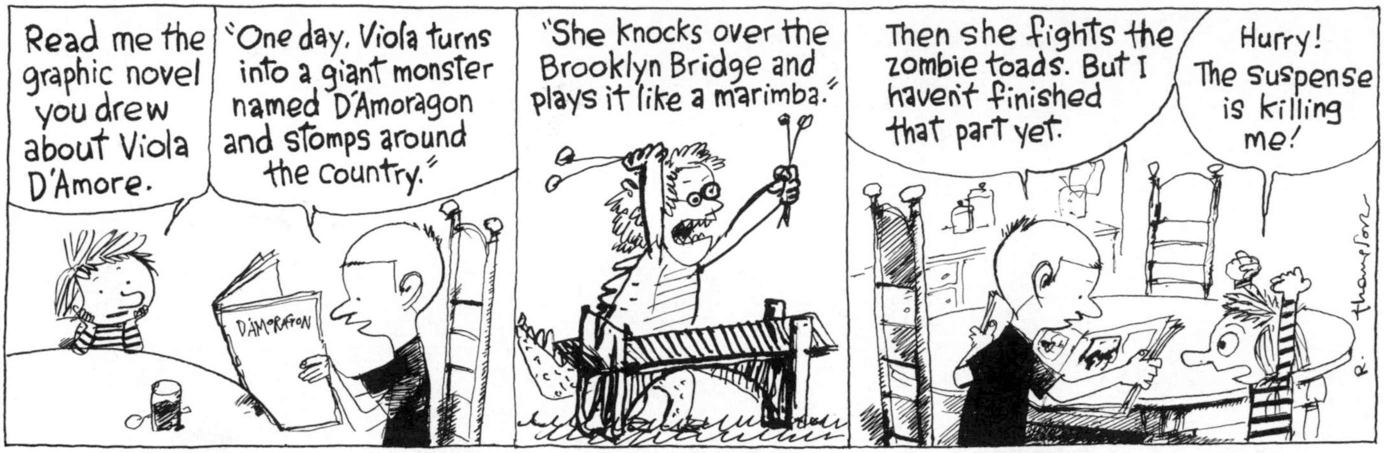
Read me the graphic novel you drew about Viola D'Amore.
"One day, Viola turns into a giant monster named D'Amoragon and stomps around the country."
D'AMORAGON
"She knocks over the Brooklyn Bridge and plays it like a marimba."
Then she fights the zombie toads. But I haven't finished that part yet.
Hurry! The suspense is killing me!

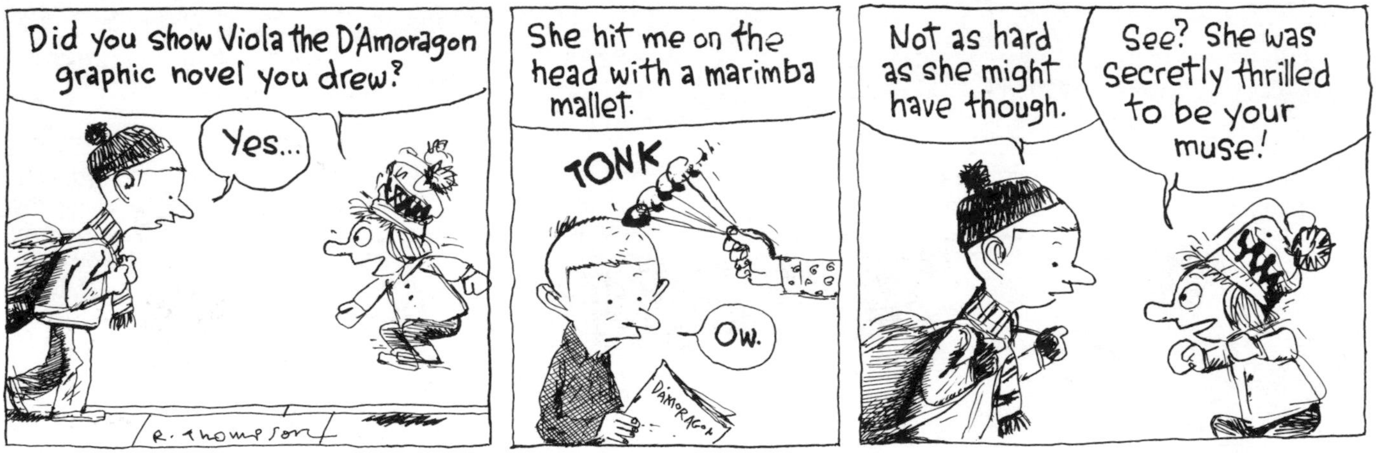
Did you show Viola the D'Amoragon graphic novel you drew?
Yes...
She hit me on the head with a marimba mallet.
TONK
Ow.
D'AMORAGON
Not as hard as she might have though.
See? She was secretly thrilled to be your muse!

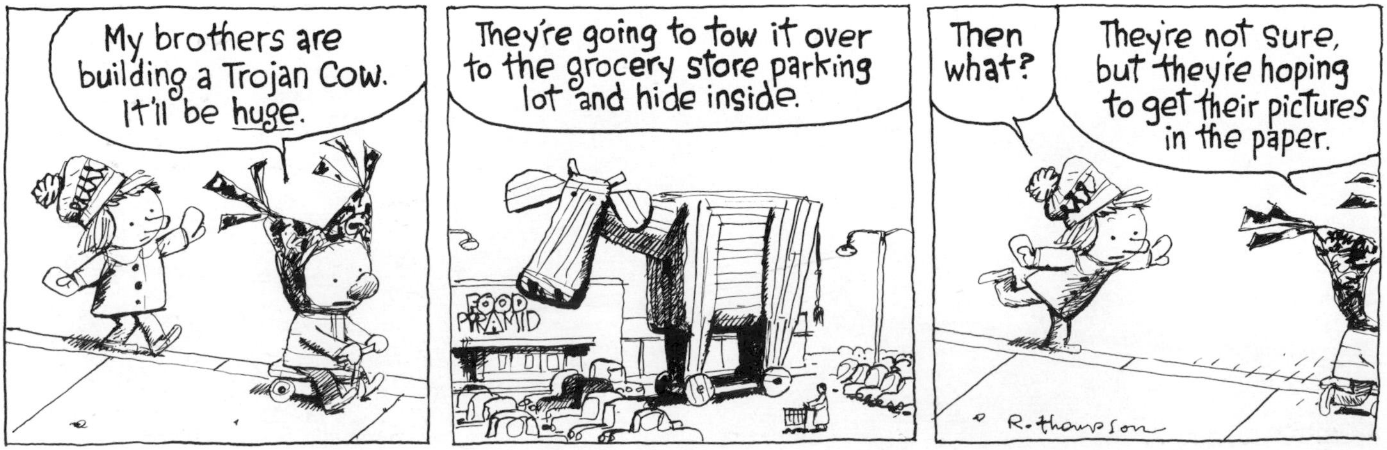
My brothers are building a Trojan Cow. It'll be huge.
They're going to tow it over to the grocery store parking lot and hide inside.
FOOD PYRAMID
Then what?
They're not sure, but they're hoping to get their pictures in the paper.

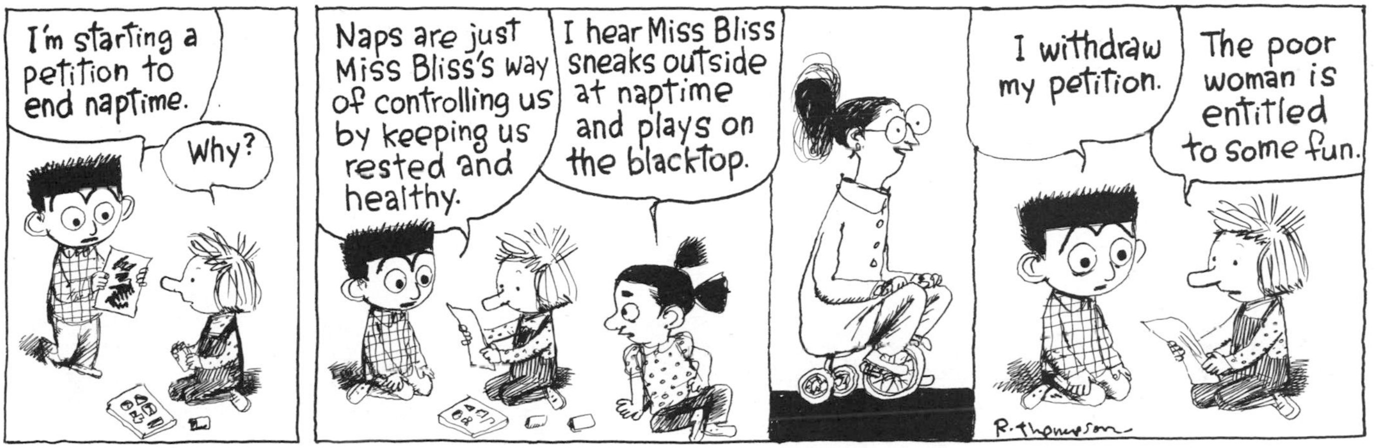
I'm starting a petition to end naptime.
Why?
Naps are just Miss Bliss's way of controlling us by keeping us rested and healthy.
I hear Miss Bliss sneaks outside at naptime and plays on the blacktop.
I withdraw my petition.
The poor woman is entitled to some fun.
R. Thompson

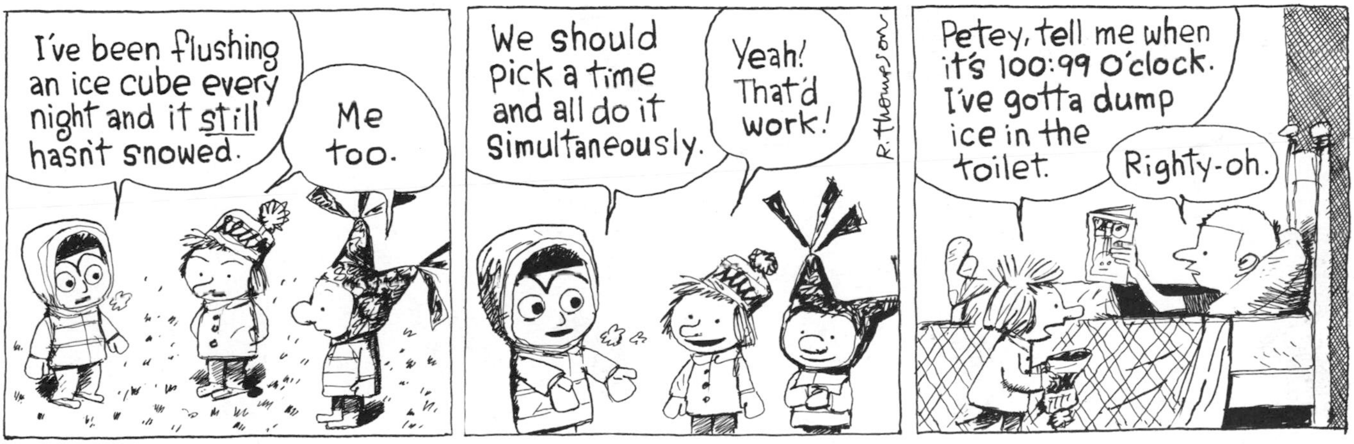
I've been flushing an ice cube every night and it still hasn't snowed.
Me too.
We should pick a time and all do it simultaneously.
Yeah! That'd work!
R. Thompson
Petey, tell me when it's 100:99 O'clock. I've gotta dump ice in the toilet.
Righty-oh.

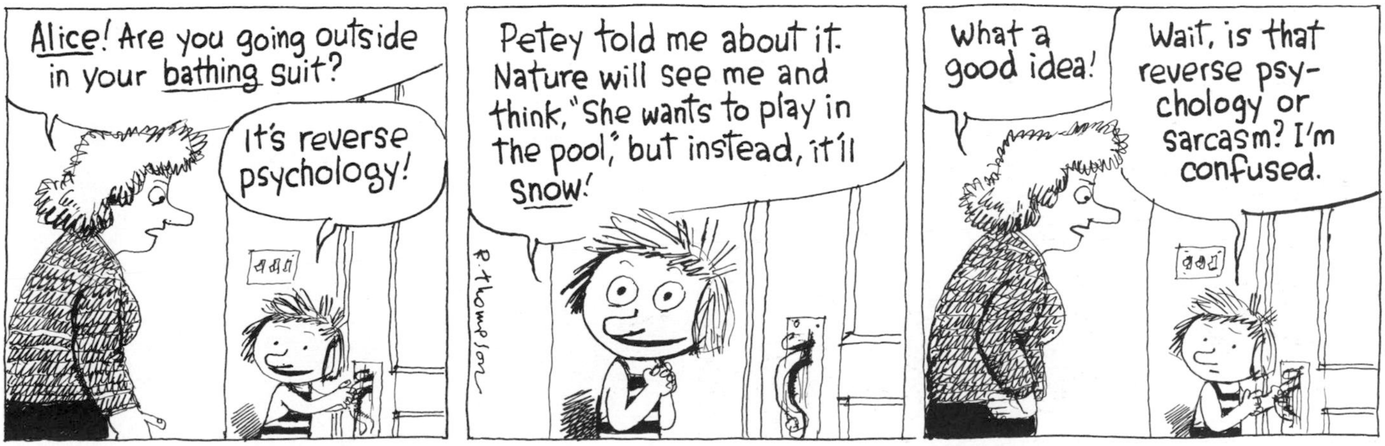
Alice! Are you going outside in your bathing suit?
It's reverse psychology!
Petey told me about it. Nature will see me and think, "She wants to play in the pool," but instead, it'll snow!
R. Thompson
What a good idea!
Wait, is that reverse psychology or sarcasm? I'm confused.

Dill, why do you wear that silly hat? Try mine on-
It won't work.
Of course it'll work.
My head is too round. It won't stay on-
POP
Ha ha! Do it again!
Ha ha!
POP
Pull it way down over your face!
Okay, stand back...
This happened how?
Dill's big dumb head. I took his silly clown hat so we'd be even.
R. Thompson

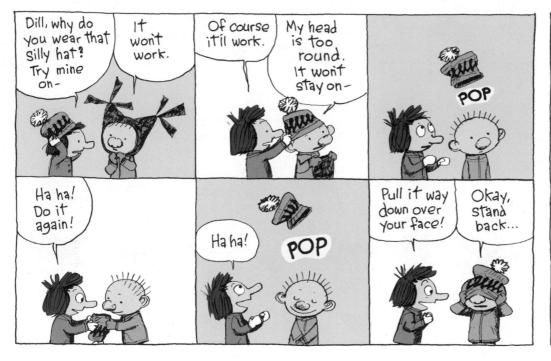

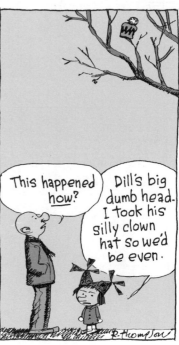

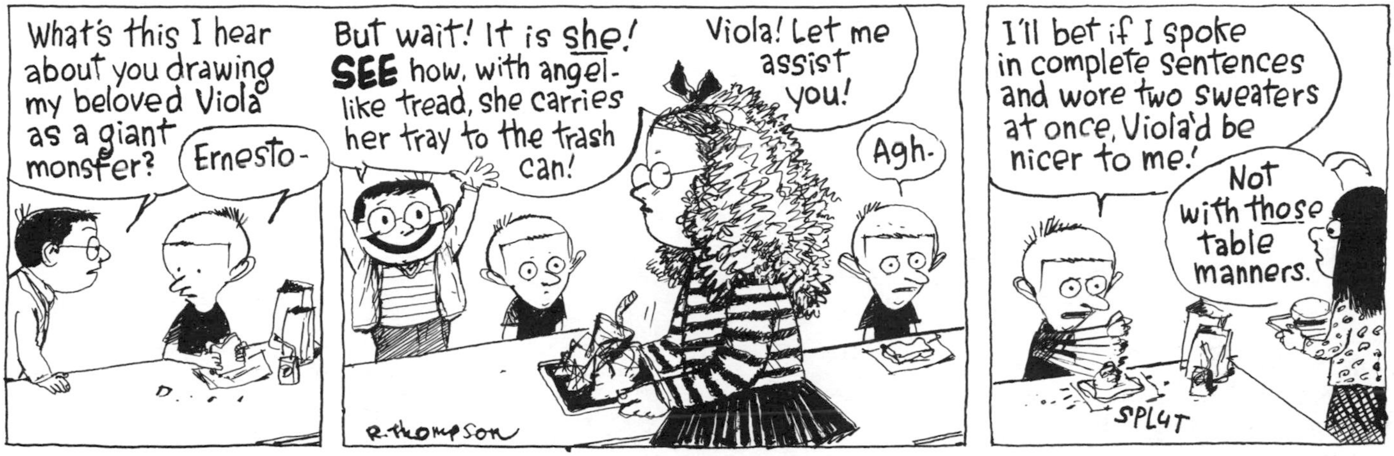
What's this I hear about you drawing my beloved Viola as a giant monster?
Ernesto-
But wait! It is she! SEE how, with angel-like tread, she carries her tray to the trash can!
Viola! Let me assist you!
Agh.
I'll bet if I spoke in complete sentences and wore two sweaters at once, Viola'd be nicer to me!
Not with those table manners.
SPLUT
R. Thompson

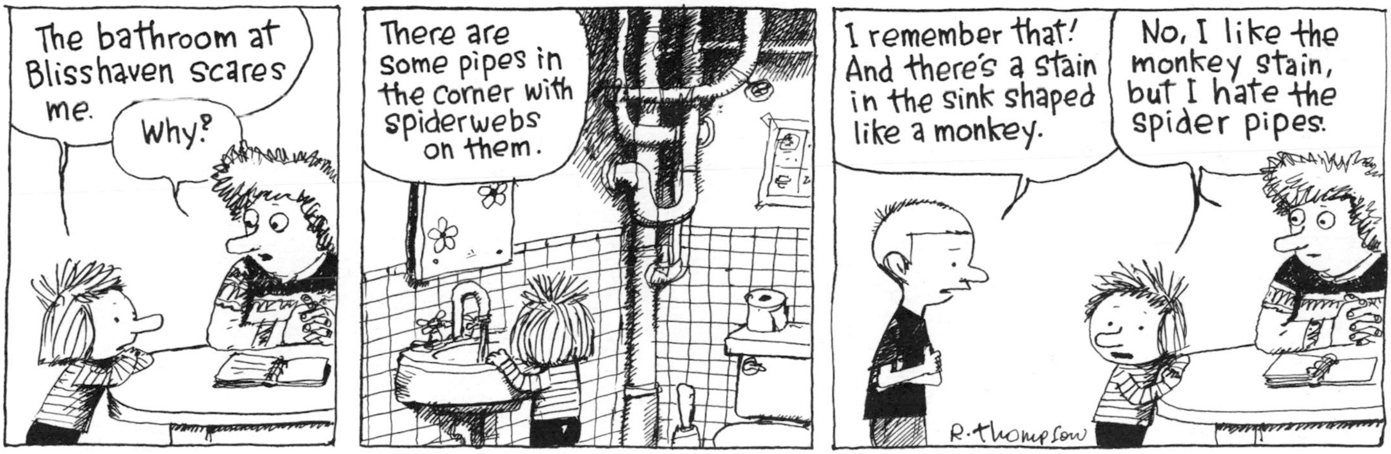
The bathroom at Blisshaven scares me.
Why?
There are some pipes in the corner with spiderwebs on them.
I remember that! And there's a stain in the sink shaped like a monkey.
No, I like the monkey stain, but I hate the spider pipes.
R. Thompson

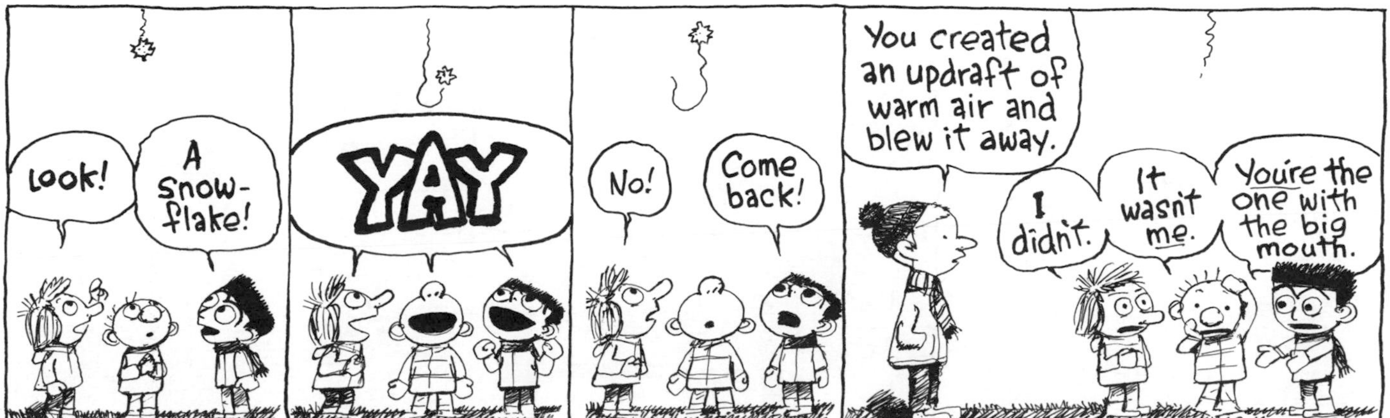
Look!
A snow-flake!
YAY
No!
Come back!
You created an updraft of warm air and blew it away.
I didn't.
It wasn't me.
You're the one with the big mouth.
R. Thompson

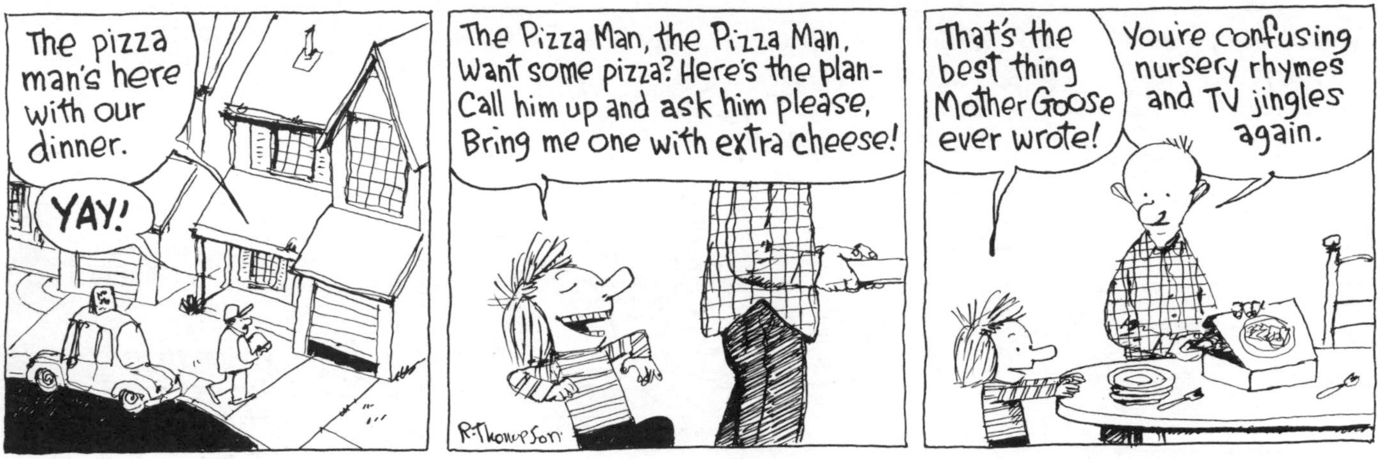
The pizza man's here with our dinner.
YAY!
The Pizza Man, the Pizza Man, Want some pizza? Here's the plan- Call him up and ask him please, Bring me one with extra cheese!
R. Thompson
That's the best thing Mother Goose ever wrote!
You're confusing nursery rhymes and TV jingles again.

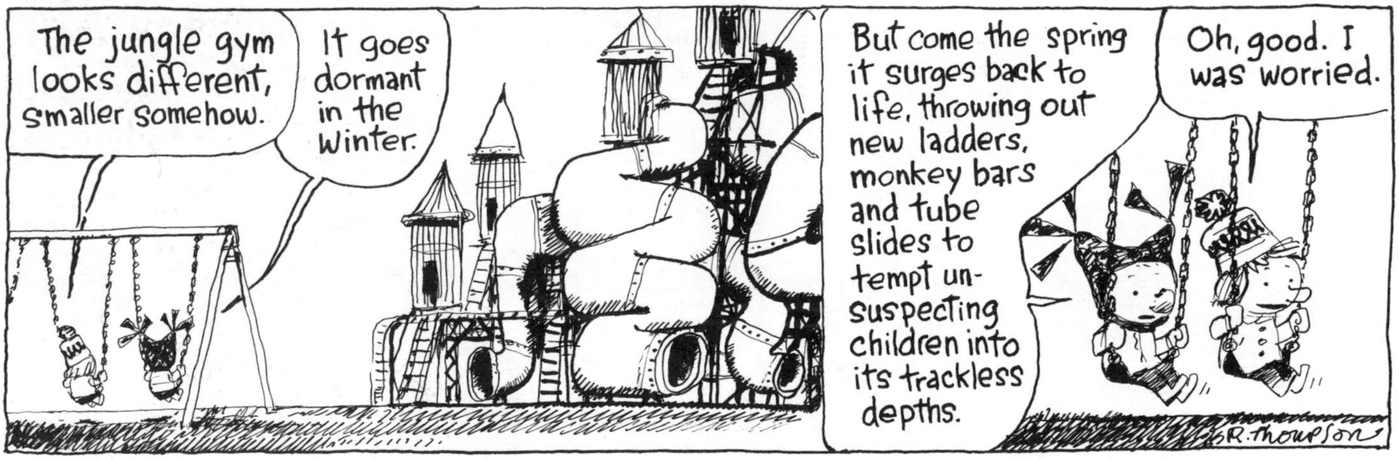
The jungle gym looks different, smaller somehow.
It goes dormant in the winter.
But come the spring it surges back to life, throwing out new ladders, monkey bars and tube slides to tempt unsuspecting children into its trackless depths.
Oh, good. I was worried.
R. Thompson

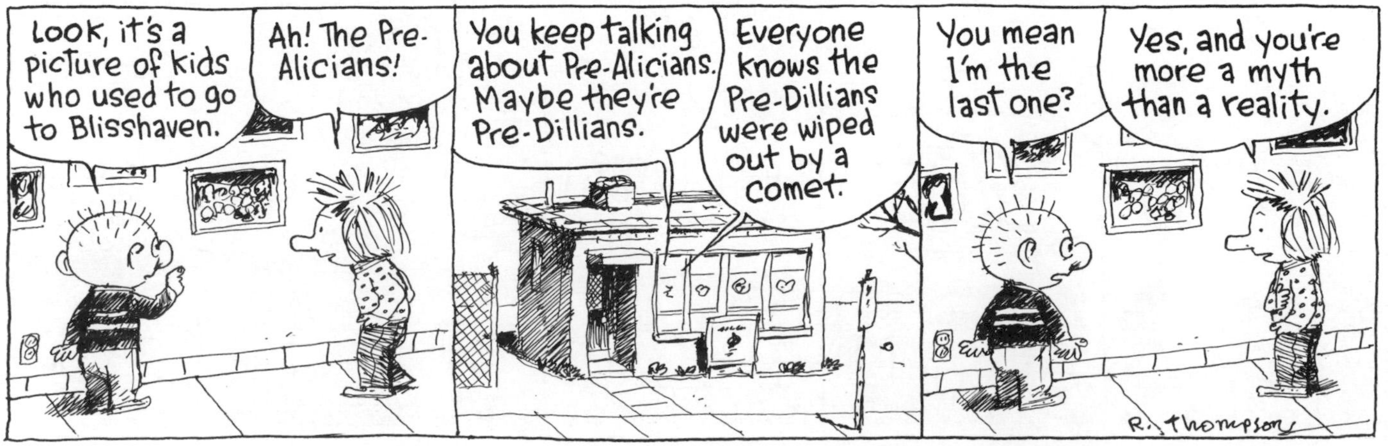
Look, it's a picture of kids who used to go to Blisshaven.
Ah! The Pre-Alicians!
You keep talking about Pre-Alicians. Maybe they're Pre-Dillians.
Everyone knows the Pre-Dillians were wiped out by a comet.
You mean I'm the last one?
Yes, and you're more a myth than a reality.
R. Thompson

That's Orion.
Huh?
It's a constellation, like a big dot-to-dot with stars. Ancient cultures invented them.
Oh.
I see.
It's one reason ancient cultures aren't around anymore.
R. Thompson

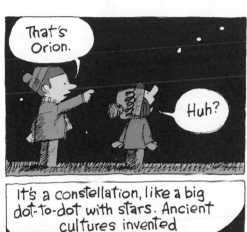

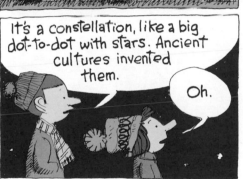

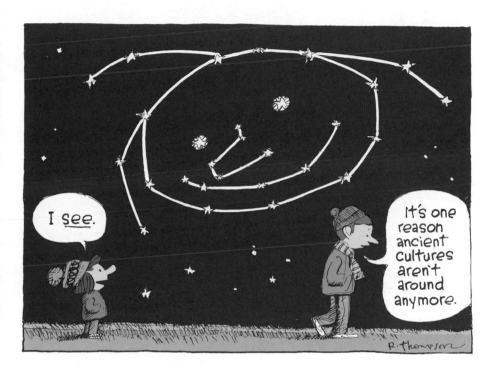

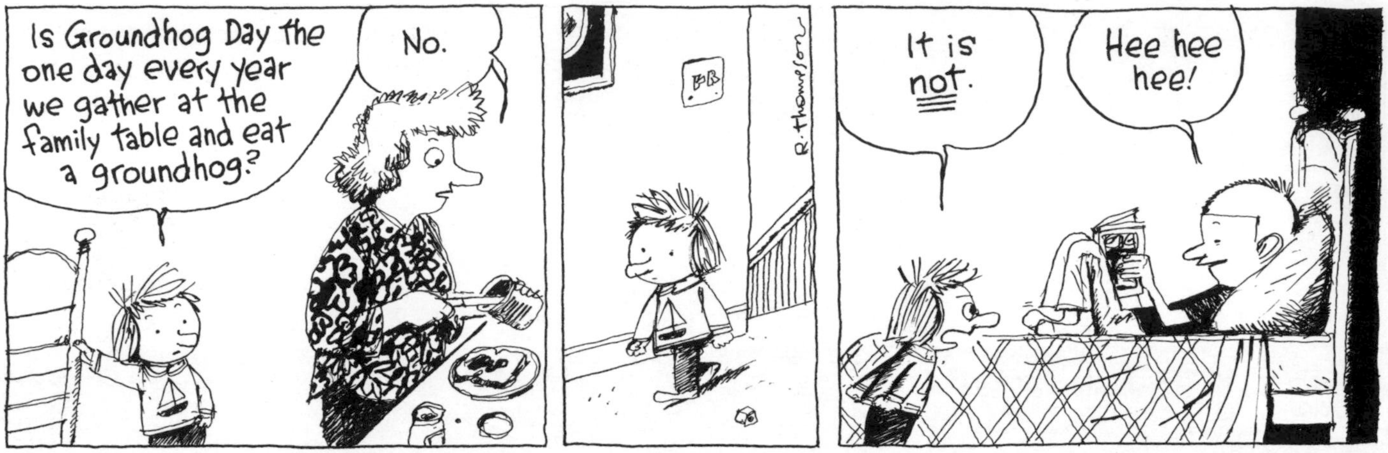
Is Groundhog Day the one day every year we gather at the family table and eat a groundhog?
No.
R. Thompson
It is not.
Hee hee hee!

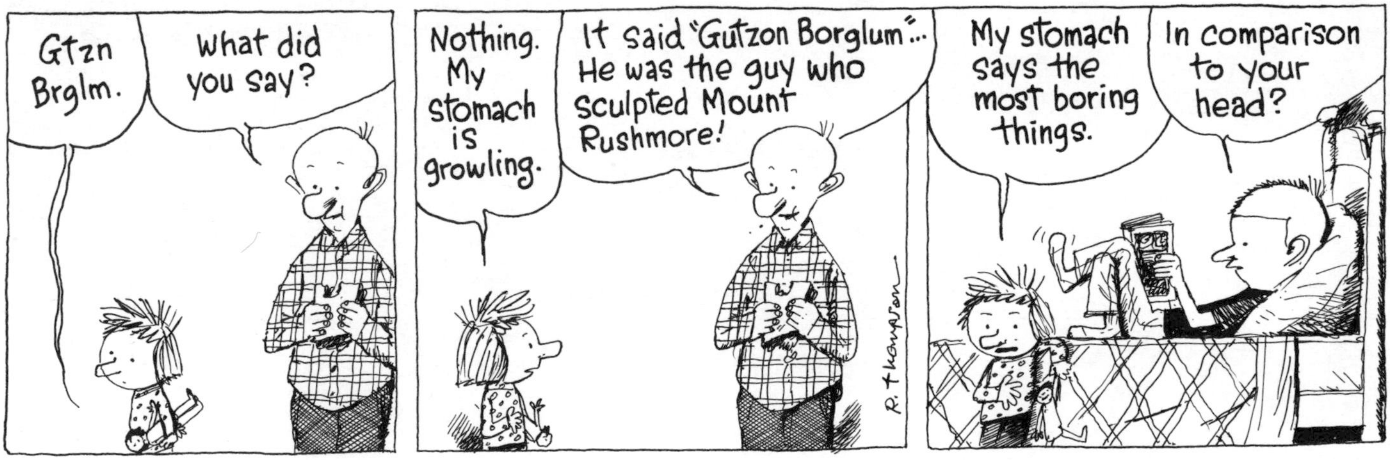
Gtzn Brglm.
What did you say?
Nothing. My stomach is growling.
It said "Gutzon Borglum"... He was the guy who sculpted Mount Rushmore!
R. Thompson
My stomach says the most boring things.
In comparison to your head?

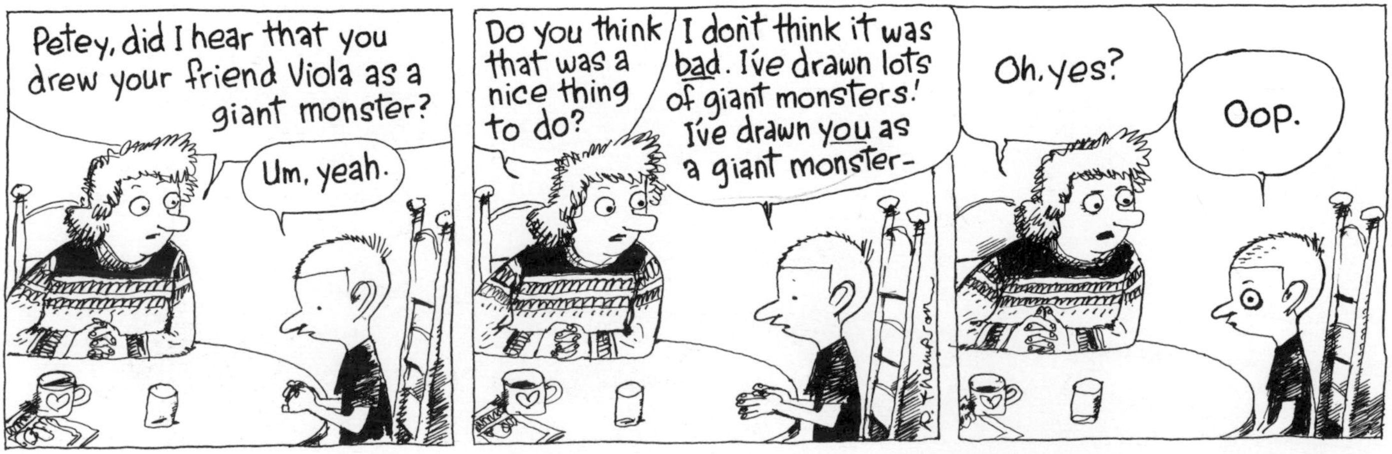
Petey, did I hear that you drew your friend Viola as a giant monster?
Um, yeah.
Do you think that was a nice thing to do?
I don't think it was bad. I've drawn lots of giant monsters! I've drawn you as a giant monster-
R. Thompson
Oh, yes?
Oop.

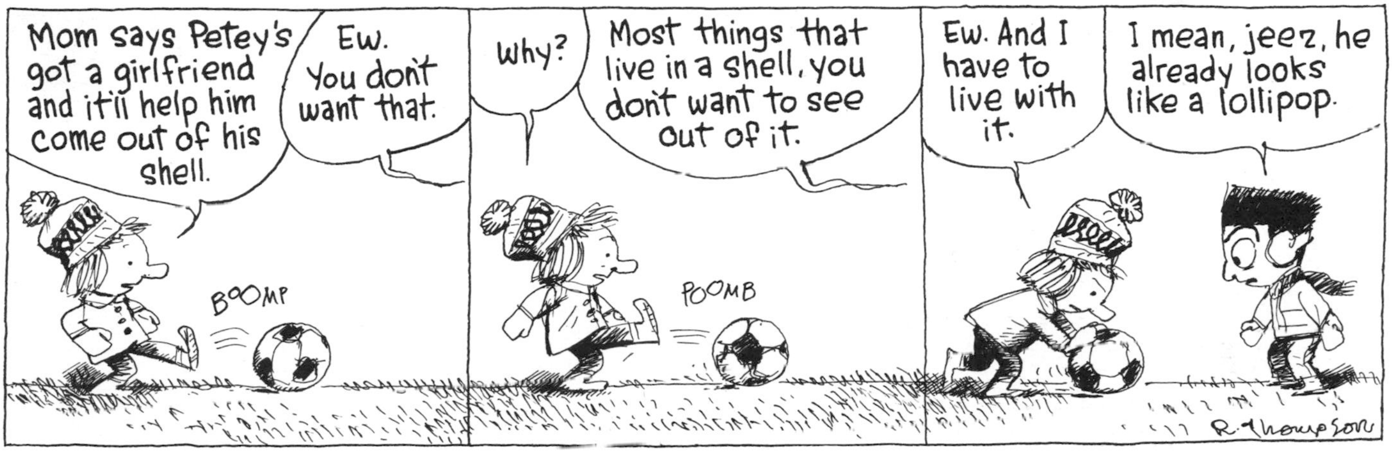
Mom says Petey's got a girlfriend and it'll help him come out of his shell.
Ew. You don't want that.
BOOMP
Why?
Most things that live in a shell, you don't want to see out of it.
POOMB
Ew. And I have to live with it.
I mean, jeez, he already looks like a lollipop.
R. Thompson

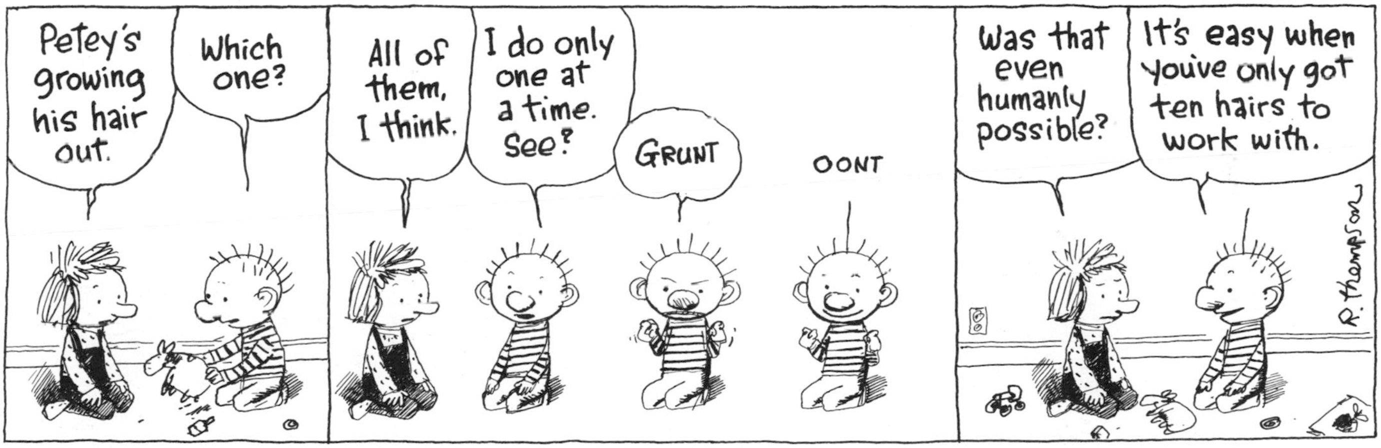
Petey's growing his hair out.
Which one?
All of them, I think.
I do only one at a time. See?
GRUNT
OONT
Was that even humanly possible?
It's easy when you've only got ten hairs to work with.
R. Thompson

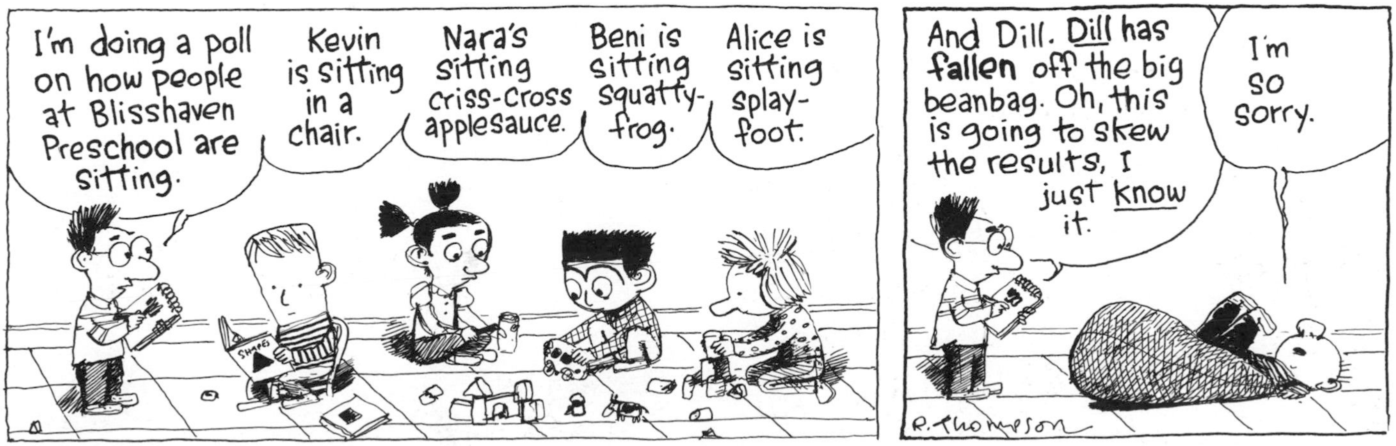
I'm doing a poll on how people at Blisshaven Preschool are sitting.
Kevin is sitting in a chair.
Nara's sitting criss-cross applesauce.
Beni is sitting squatty-frog.
Alice is sitting splay-foot.
SHAPES
And Dill. Dill has **fallen** off the big beanbag. Oh, this is going to skew the results, I just know it.
I'm so sorry.
R. Thompson

Why're you always dancing around on that manhole cover?
It's like a stage!
You can get on it and show off what you're good at. C'mon, try it!
But-
I feel silly.
You know what drives me crazy? When people say, "Be in the moment." I hate being in the moment.
I always wish it was last week, or last Saturday, or the day before Christmas. I'm never happy when it's now.
I wish I could be happy whenever it's now.
That's, um-
That's all.
So what you're good at is fretting.
Is he through? I'd like to show off how good I've gotten at blowing spit bubbles.
R. thompson

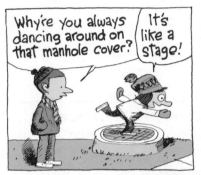

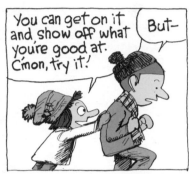

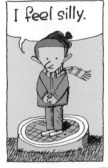

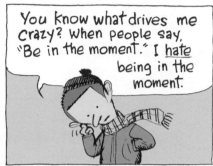

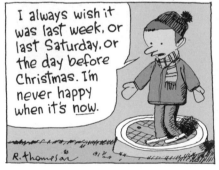

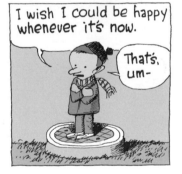

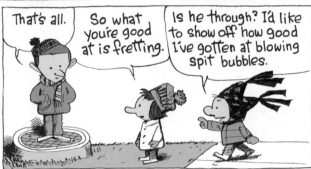

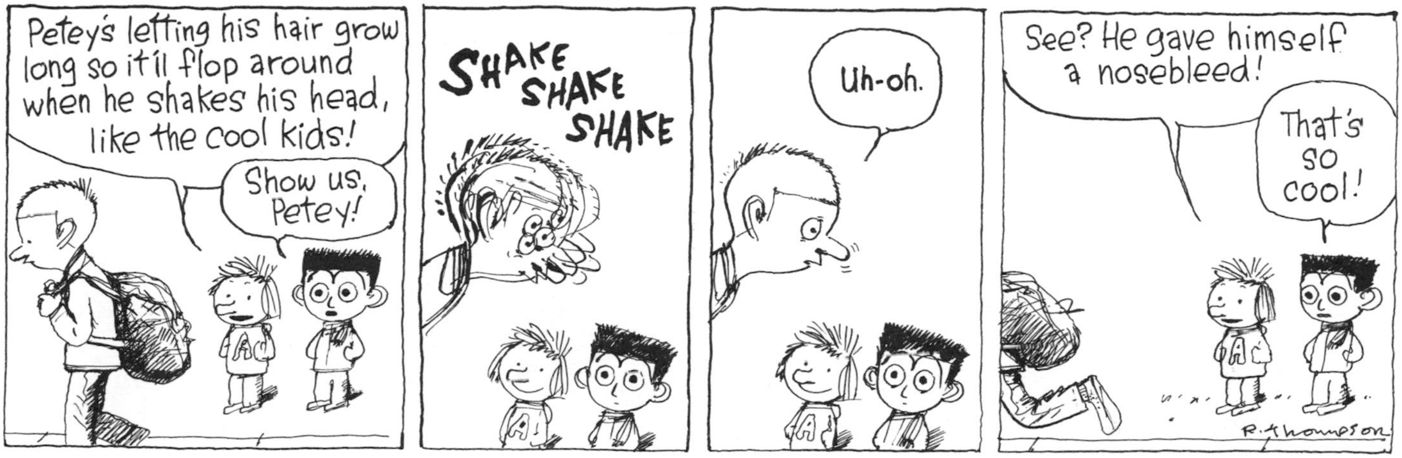
Petey's letting his hair grow long so it'll flop around when he shakes his head, like the cool kids!
Show us, Petey!
SHAKE SHAKE SHAKE
Uh-oh.
See? He gave himself a nosebleed!
That's so cool!
R. Thompson

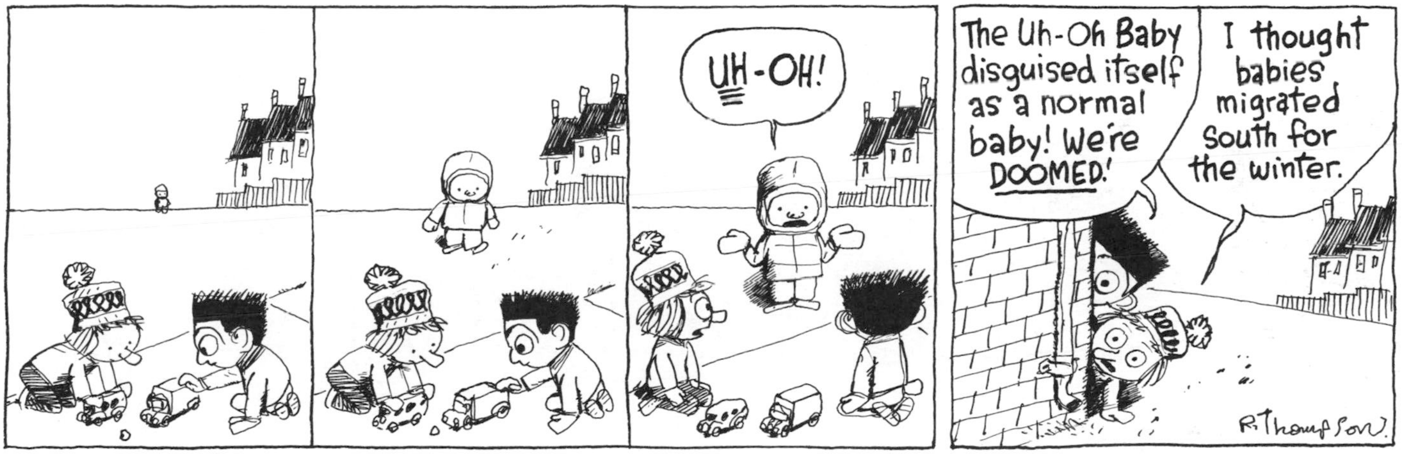
UH-OH!
The Uh-Oh Baby disguised itself as a normal baby! We're DOOMED!
I thought babies migrated South for the winter.
R. Thompson

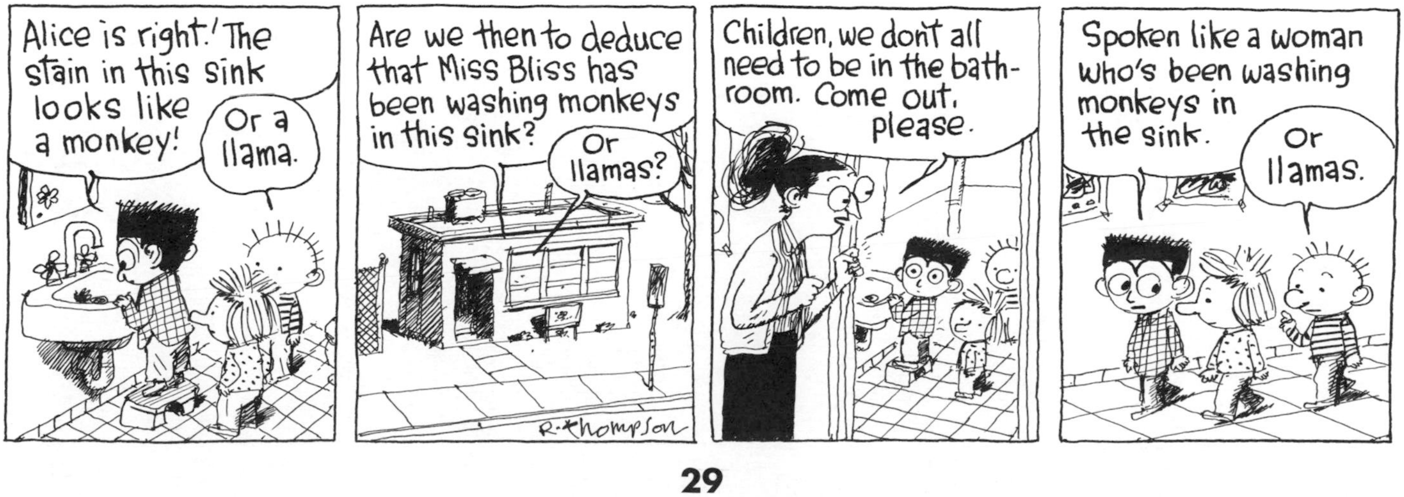
Alice is right! The stain in this sink looks like a monkey!
Or a llama.
Are we then to deduce that Miss Bliss has been washing monkeys in this sink?
Or llamas?
R. Thompson
Children, we don't all need to be in the bathroom. Come out, please.
Spoken like a woman who's been washing monkeys in the sink.
Or llamas.

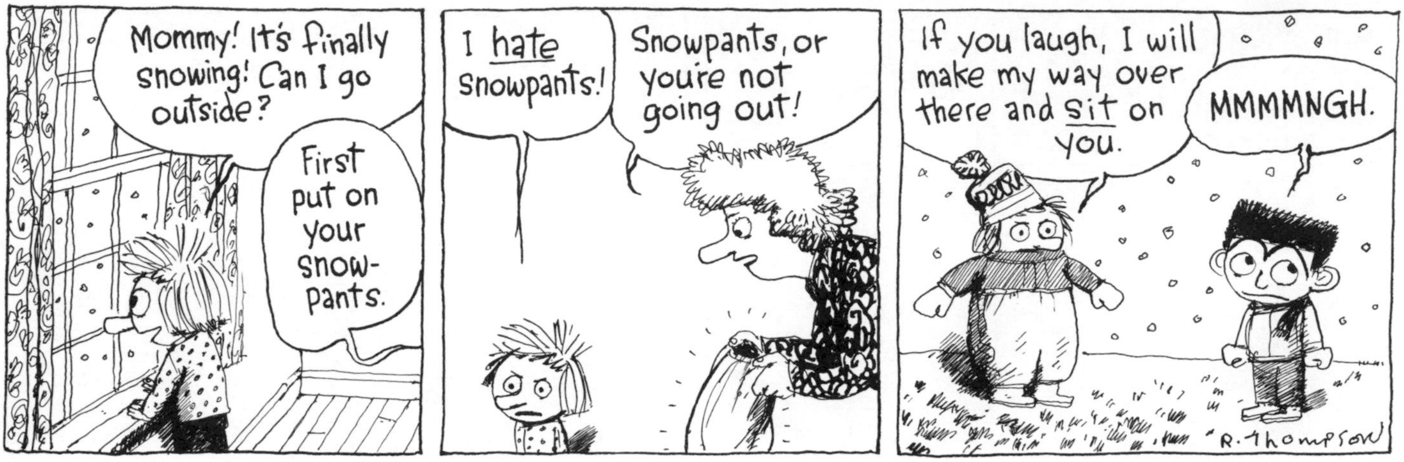
Mommy! It's finally snowing! Can I go outside?
First put on your snow-pants.
I hate snowpants!
Snowpants, or you're not going out!
If you laugh, I will make my way over there and sit on you.
MMMMNGH.
R. Thompson

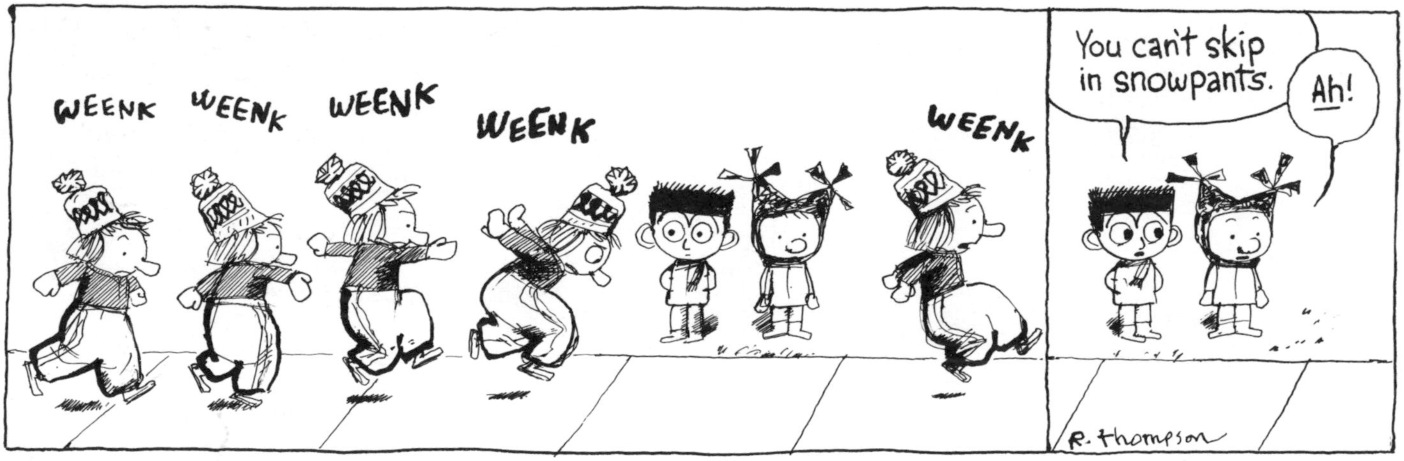
WEENK
WEENK
WEENK
WEENK
WEENK
You can't skip in snowpants.
Ah!
R. Thompson

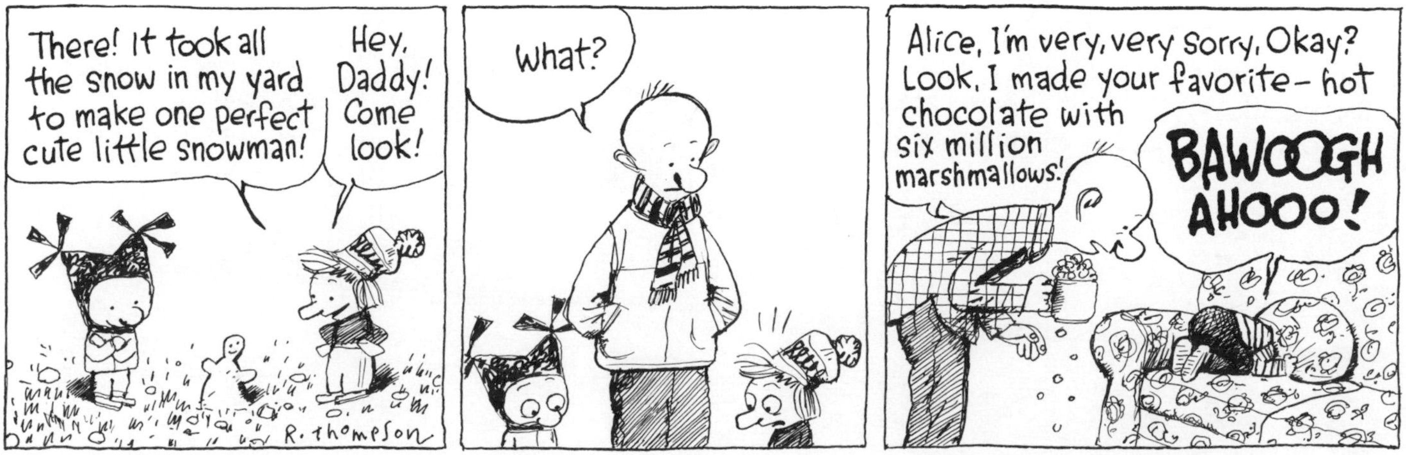
There! It took all the snow in my yard to make one perfect cute little snowman!
Hey, Daddy! Come look!
R. Thompson
What?
Alice, I'm very, very sorry, Okay? Look, I made your favorite- hot chocolate with six million marshmallows!
BAWOOGH AHOOO!

I thought up the best scary movie of all time!

What is it?

R. Thompson

So you go to the theater and the movie starts-

You're waiting for it to be scary but nothing scary happens.

You're so tense, your stomach hurts!

But nothing scary happens during the whole movie!

Then it's over! And you're so relieved it wasn't scary!

But as you leave the theater, an usher jumps out from behind a trash can-

PUSH

And he says,

BOO!

That was so scary, my stomach hurts.

If he jumps out and tells you a joke, would it be a comedy?

Not if it made your stomach hurt.

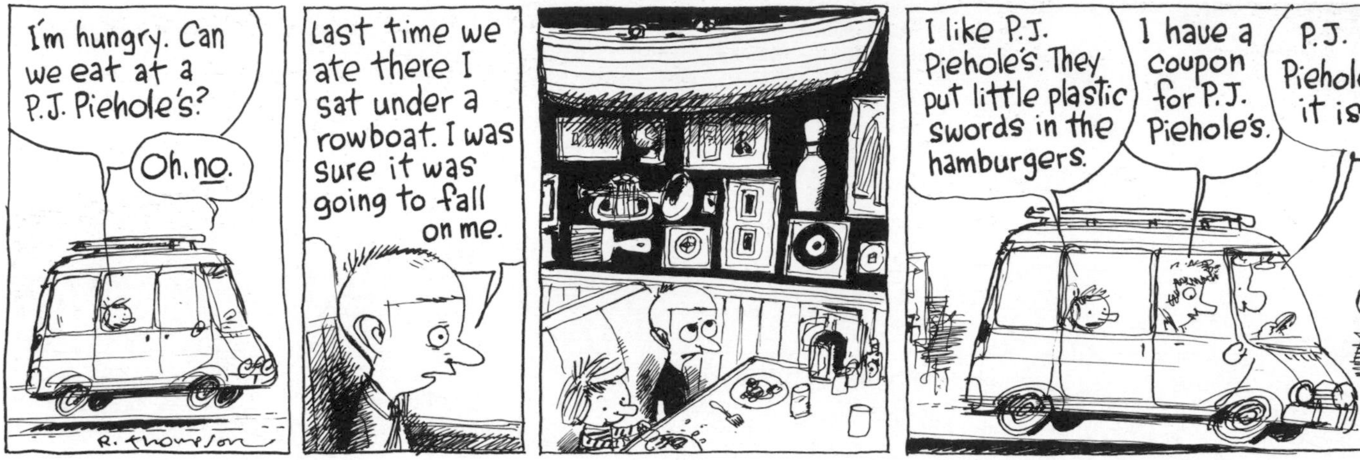
I'm hungry. Can we eat at a P.J. Piehole's?
Oh, no.
R. Thompson
Last time we ate there I sat under a rowboat. I was sure it was going to fall on me.
I like P.J. Piehole's. They put little plastic swords in the hamburgers.
I have a coupon for P.J. Piehole's.
P.J. Piehole's it is!

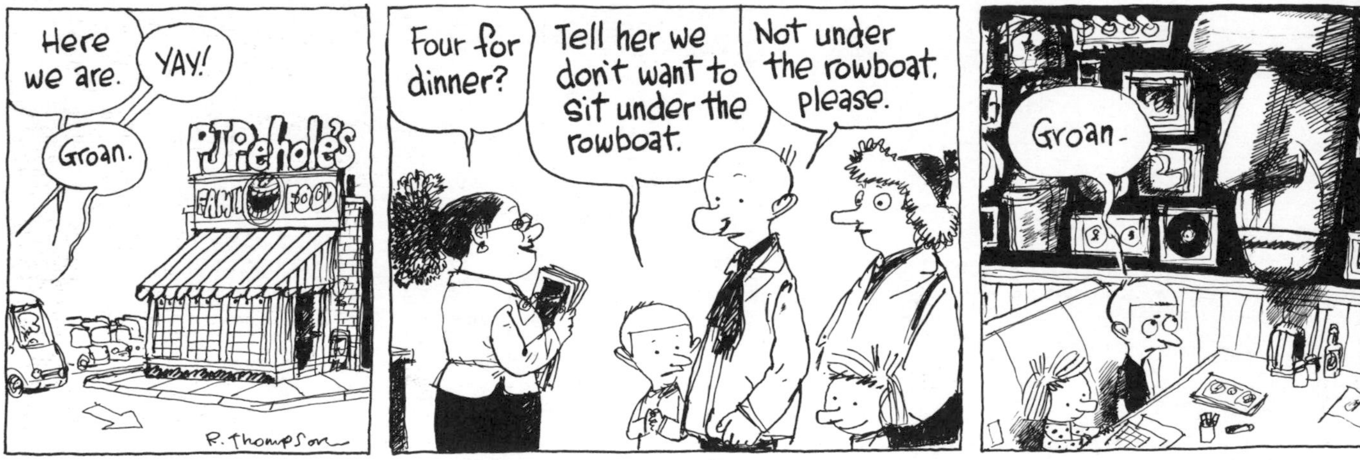
Here we are.
YAY!
Groan.
P.J. Piehole's
R. Thompson
Four for dinner?
Tell her we don't want to sit under the rowboat.
Not under the rowboat, please.
Groan.

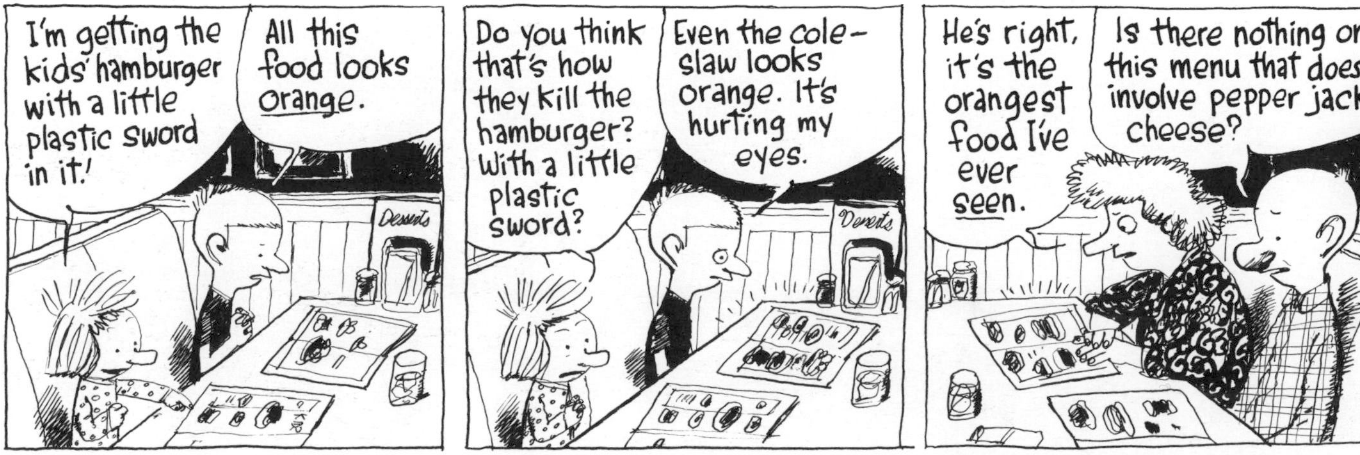
I'm getting the kids' hamburger with a little plastic sword in it!
All this food looks orange.
Desserts
Do you think that's how they kill the hamburger? With a little plastic sword?
Even the cole-slaw looks orange. It's hurting my eyes.
Desserts
He's right, it's the orangest food I've ever seen.
Is there nothing on this menu that doesn't involve pepper jack cheese?
R. Thompson

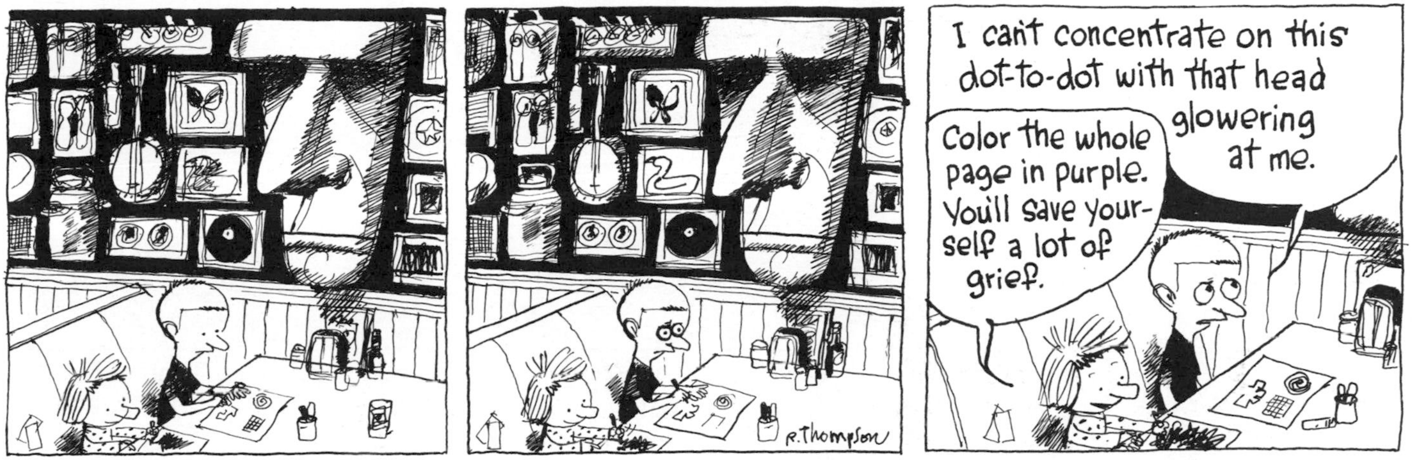
I can't concentrate on this dot-to-dot with that head glowering at me.
Color the whole page in purple. You'll save yourself a lot of grief.

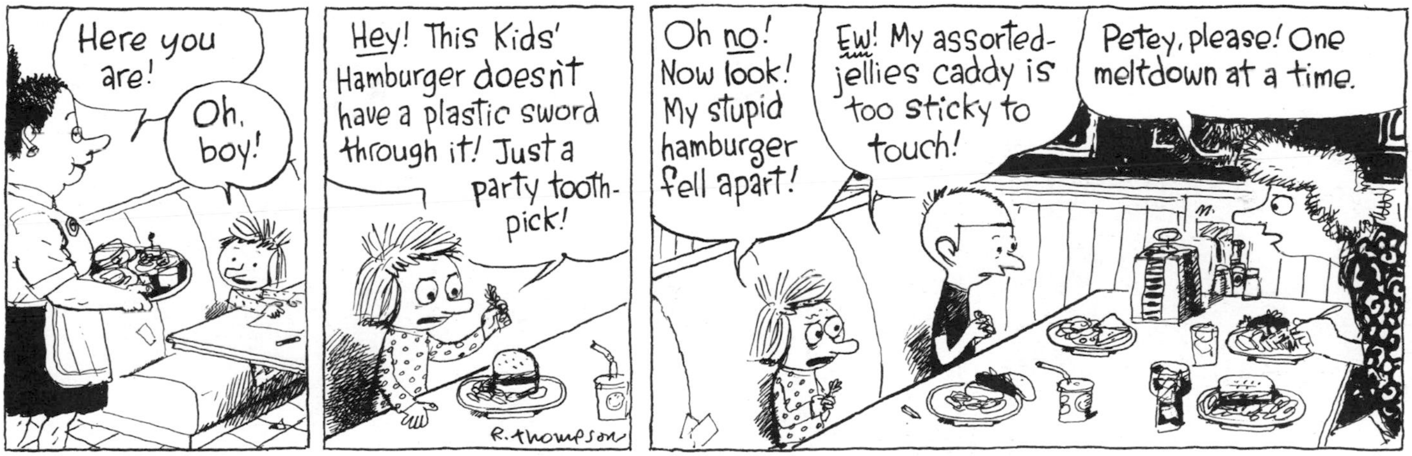
Here you are!
Oh, boy!
Hey! This Kids' Hamburger doesn't have a plastic sword through it! Just a party toothpick!
Oh no! Now look! My stupid hamburger fell apart!
Ew! My assorted-jellies caddy is too sticky to touch!
Petey, please! One meltdown at a time.

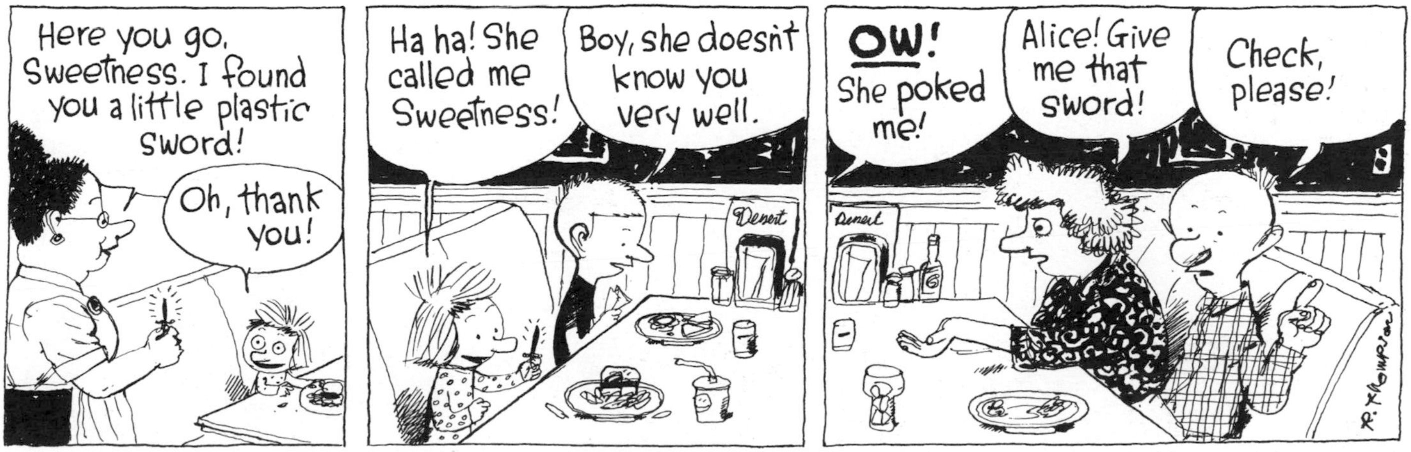
Here you go, Sweetness. I found you a little plastic sword!
Oh, thank you!
Ha ha! She called me Sweetness!
Boy, she doesn't know you very well.
OW! She poked me!
Alice! Give me that sword!
Check, please!

Hey!
That's a baby toy!
This is a preschool.
It's not a baby day-care center!
There shouldn't be any baby toys here!
You did it wrong.
Huh?
The big doughnut goes on the bottom.
Oh, no!
If you can't handle a simple baby toy, they'll make you repeat babyhood.
Diapers, teething, the whole deal.
I miss teething. Now, if I chew on the furniture, I get yelled at.
R. Thompson

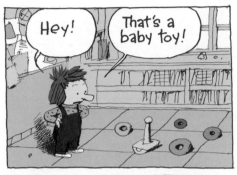

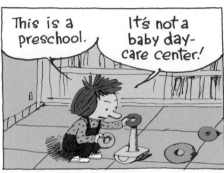

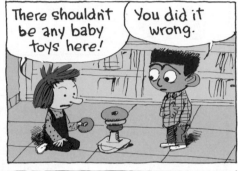

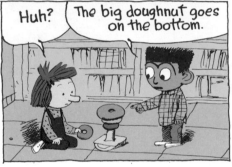

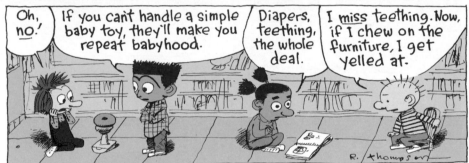

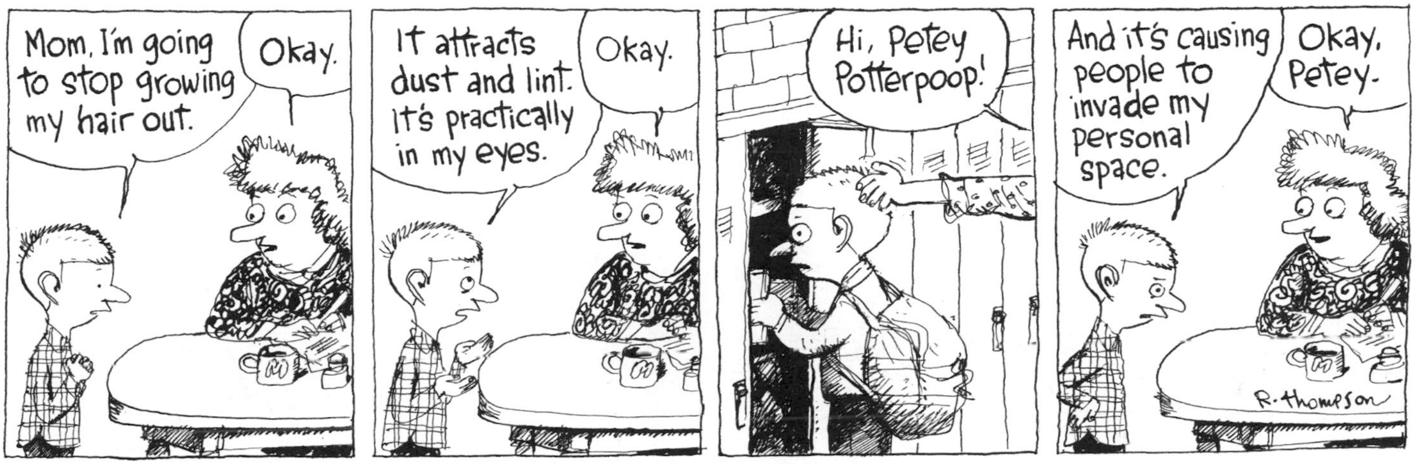
Mom, I'm going to stop growing my hair out.
Okay.
It attracts dust and lint. It's practically in my eyes.
Okay.
Hi, Petey Potterpoop!
And it's causing people to invade my personal space.
Okay, Petey.
R. Thompson

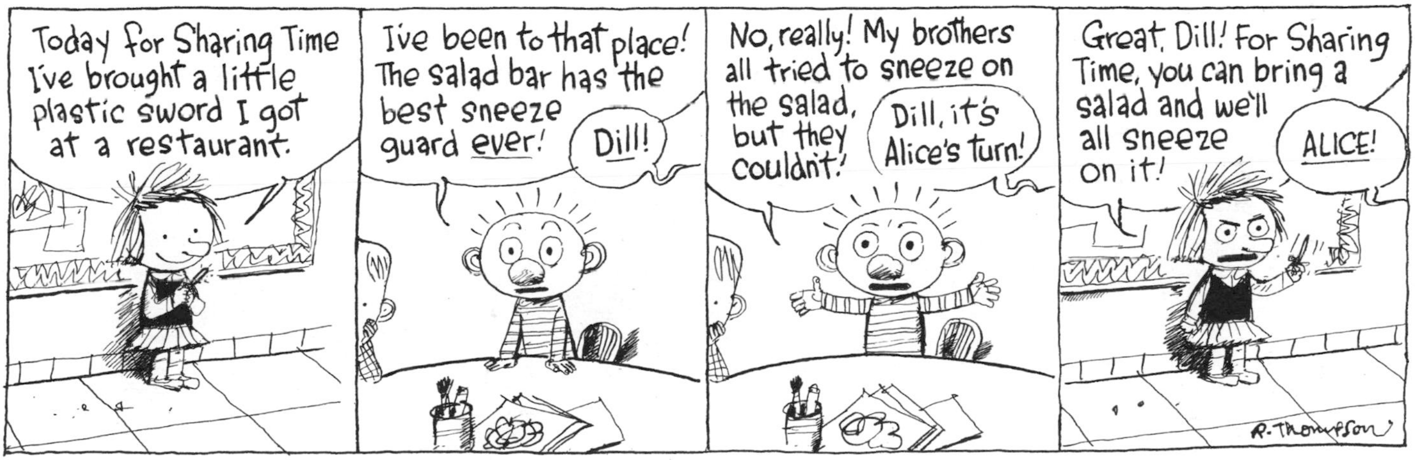
Today for Sharing Time I've brought a little plastic sword I got at a restaurant.
I've been to that place! The salad bar has the best sneeze guard ever!
Dill!
No, really! My brothers all tried to sneeze on the salad, but they couldn't!
Dill, it's Alice's turn!
Great, Dill! For Sharing Time, you can bring a salad and we'll all sneeze on it!
ALICE!
R. Thompson

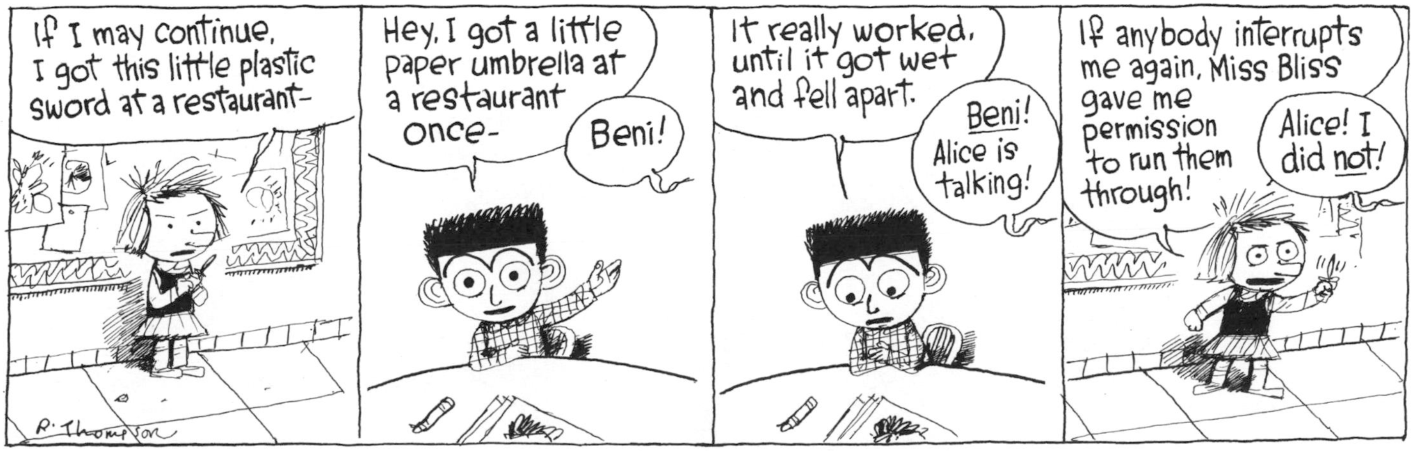
If I may continue, I got this little plastic sword at a restaurant-
Hey, I got a little paper umbrella at a restaurant once-
Beni!
It really worked, until it got wet and fell apart.
Beni! Alice is talking!
If anybody interrupts me again, Miss Bliss gave me permission to run them through!
Alice! I did not!
R. Thompson

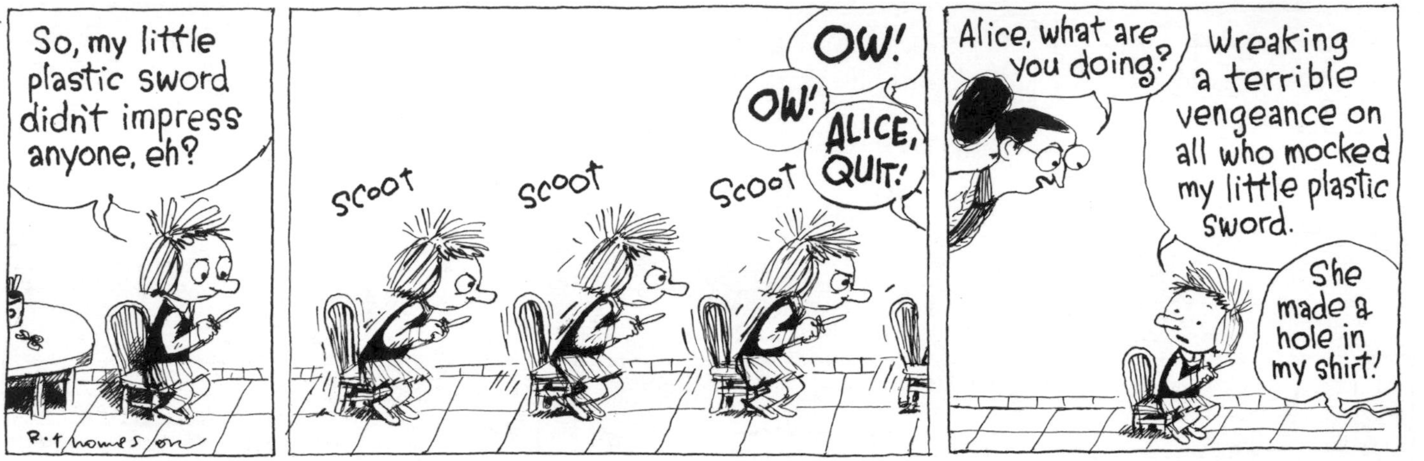
So, my little plastic sword didn't impress anyone, eh?
Scoot
Scoot
Scoot
OW!
OW!
ALICE, QUIT!
Alice, what are you doing?
Wreaking a terrible vengeance on all who mocked my little plastic sword.
She made a hole in my shirt!

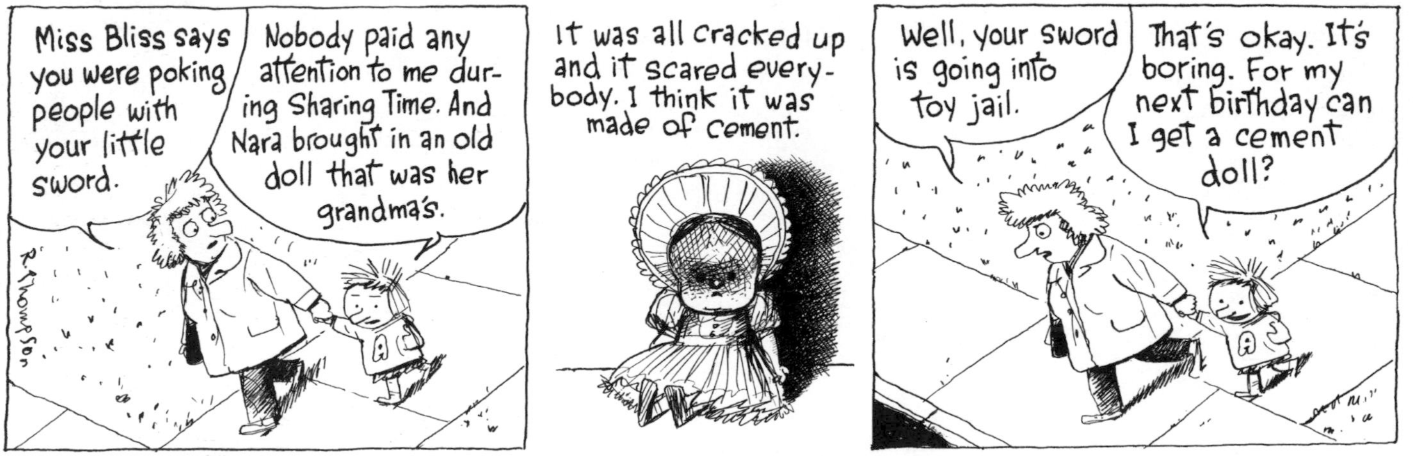
Miss Bliss says you were poking people with your little sword.
Nobody paid any attention to me during Sharing Time. And Nara brought in an old doll that was her grandma's.
It was all cracked up and it scared everybody. I think it was made of cement.
Well, your sword is going into toy jail.
That's okay. It's boring. For my next birthday can I get a cement doll?

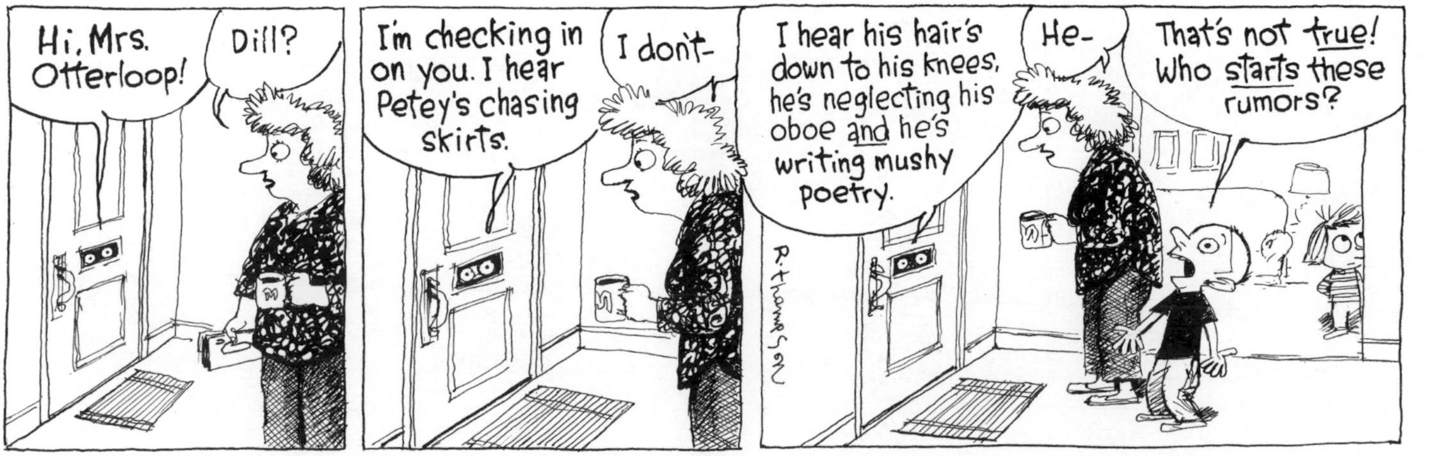
Hi, Mrs. Otterloop!
Dill?
I'm checking in on you. I hear Petey's chasing skirts.
I don't-
I hear his hair's down to his knees, he's neglecting his oboe and he's writing mushy poetry.
He-
That's not true! Who starts these rumors?

I know what that letter is! It's A, like in Alice!
Know how I know?
It's got two legs and a belt, just like me!
That's right! Two legs and a belt, and a pointy little head, just like you!
Yeah! Two legs and a belt and a pointy little head!
R. Thompson
TWO LEGS AND A BELT, AND A POINTY LITTLE HEAD!
TWO LEGS AND A BELT, AND A POINTY LITTLE HEAD!
You know, in a few minutes it'll hit her, and she'll come after you.
Maybe I'd better squat down under the sink in the utility room till this blows over.

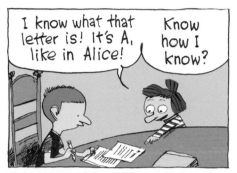

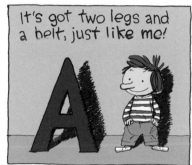

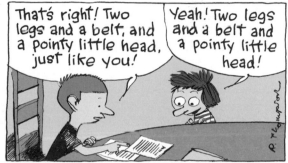

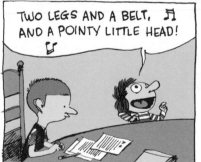

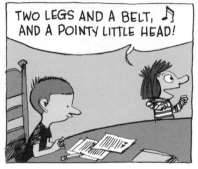

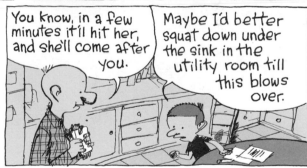

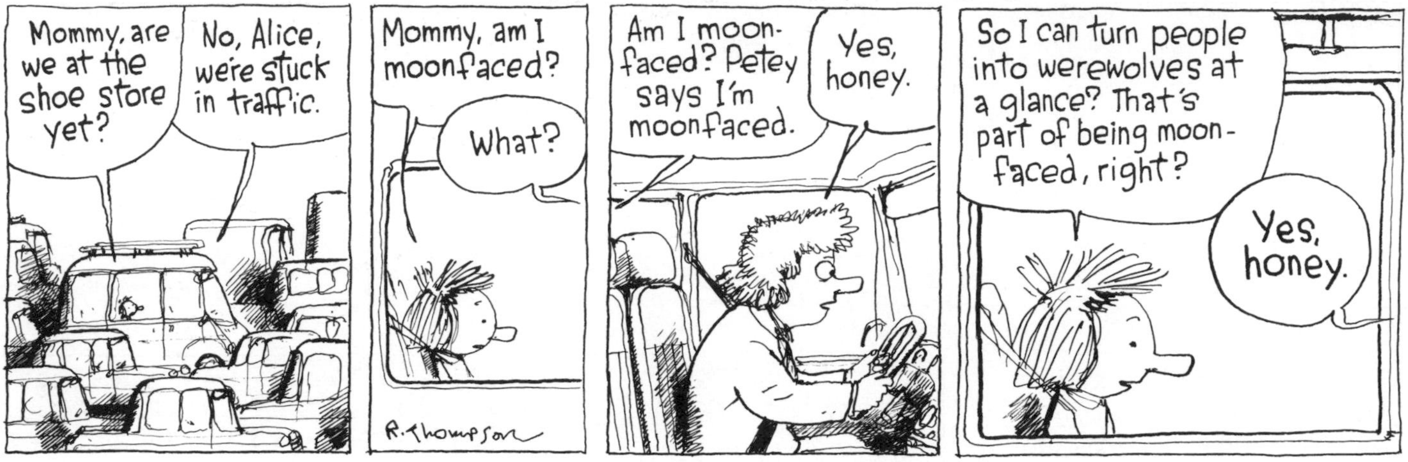
Mommy, are we at the shoe store yet?
No, Alice, we're stuck in traffic.
Mommy, am I moonfaced?
What?
R. Thompson
Am I moon-faced? Petey says I'm moonfaced.
Yes, honey.
So I can turn people into werewolves at a glance? That's part of being moon-faced, right?
Yes, honey.

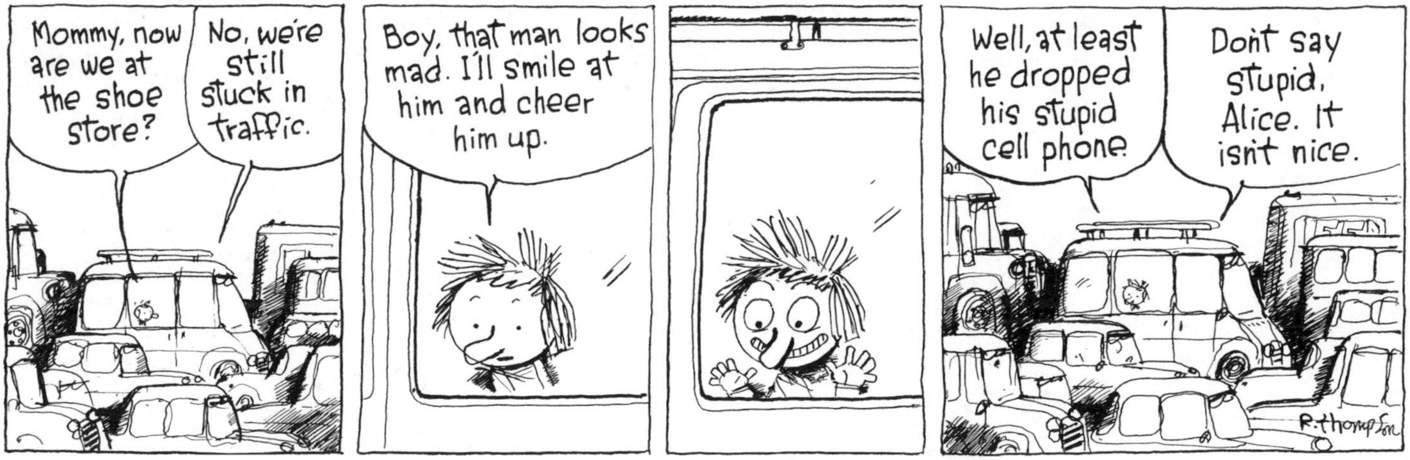
Mommy, now are we at the shoe store?
No, we're still stuck in traffic.
Boy, that man looks mad. I'll smile at him and cheer him up.
Well, at least he dropped his stupid cell phone.
Don't say stupid, Alice. It isn't nice.
R. Thompson

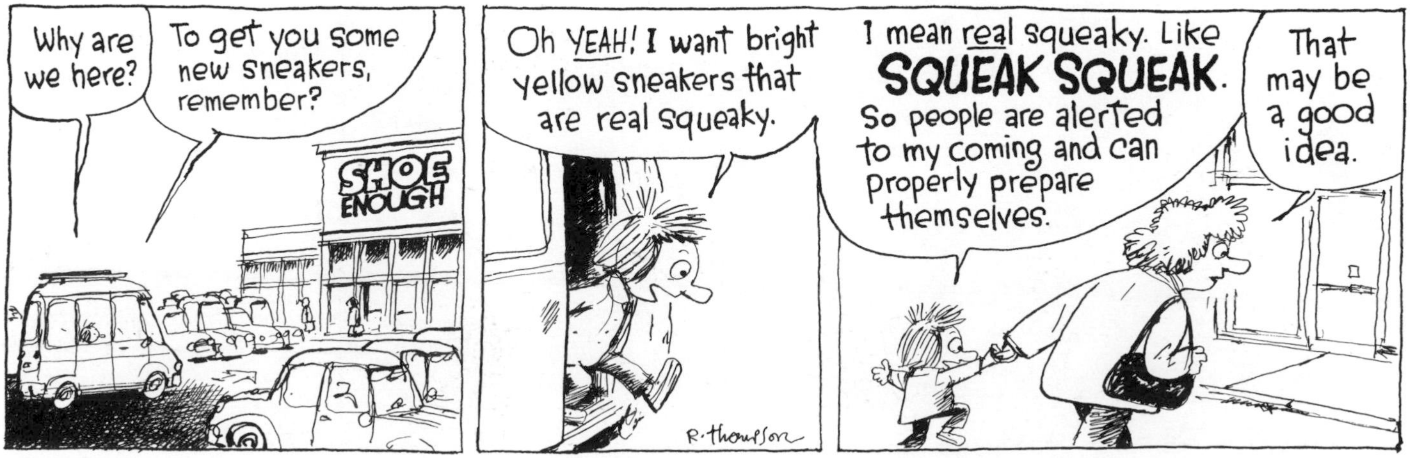
Why are we here?
To get you some new sneakers, remember?
SHOE ENOUGH
Oh YEAH! I want bright yellow sneakers that are real squeaky.
R. Thompson
I mean real squeaky. Like SQUEAK SQUEAK. So people are alerted to my coming and can properly prepare themselves.
That may be a good idea.

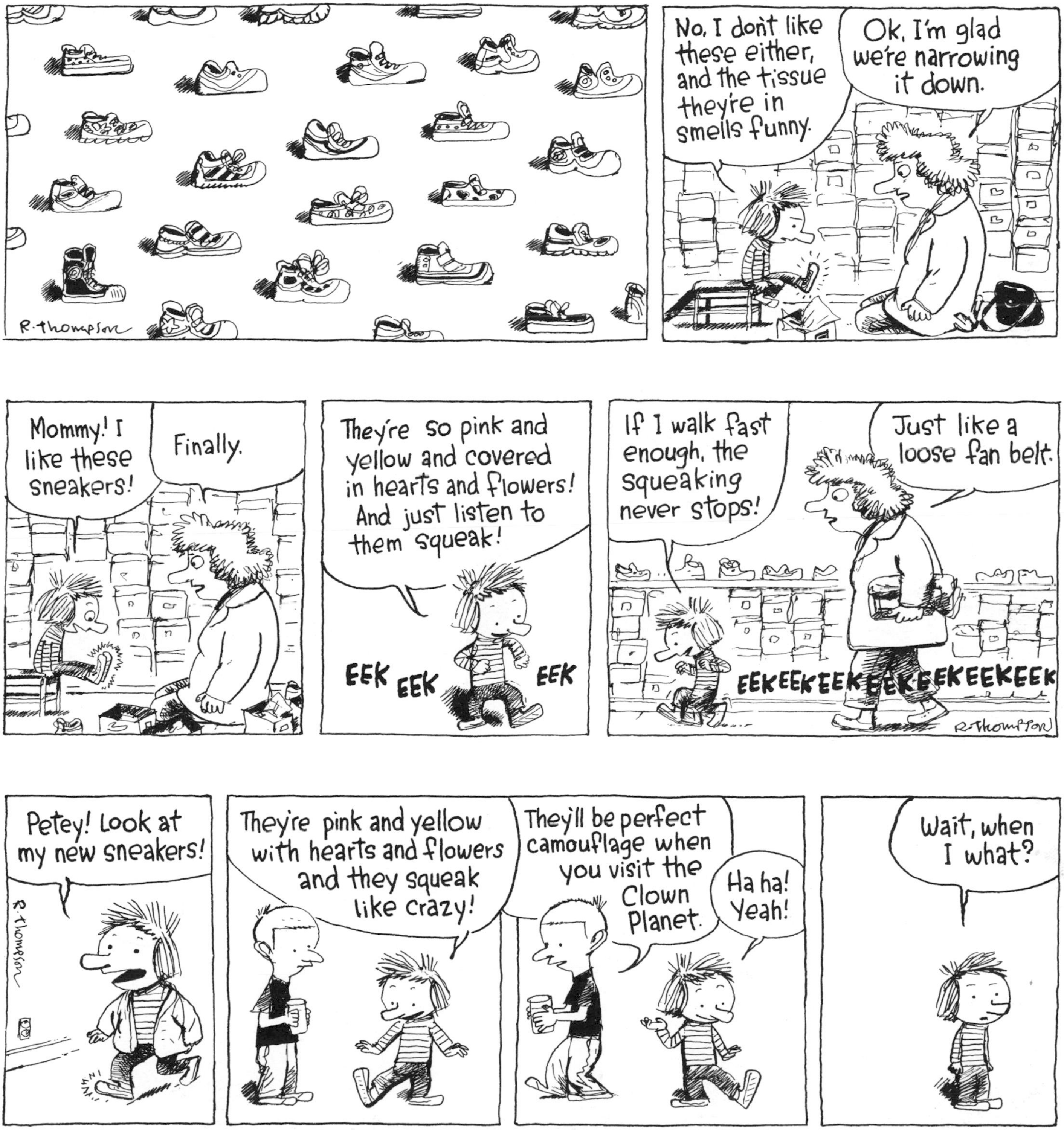
R. Thompson
No, I don't like these either, and the tissue they're in smells funny.
Ok, I'm glad we're narrowing it down.
Mommy! I like these sneakers!
Finally.
They're so pink and yellow and covered in hearts and flowers! And just listen to them squeak!
EEK EEK EEK
If I walk fast enough, the squeaking never stops!
Just like a loose fan belt.
EEKEEKEEKEEKEEKEEKEEK
R. Thompson
Petey! Look at my new sneakers!
R. Thompson
They're pink and yellow with hearts and flowers and they squeak like crazy!
They'll be perfect camouflage when you visit the Clown Planet.
Ha ha! Yeah!
Wait, when I what?

Let's see what Alice has painted!
I call this "No More Stupid Naps."
It's very pretty, Alice! Thank you for brightening our classroom with your art!
I'm exploring issues of dominance, ageism and unchecked adult supervisory fascism through post-expressionistic imagery of power, innocence and repression.
R. Thompson
I think it flew right over her head.
So did my performance piece "No More Stupid Baby Carrots", especially the part where I pretended to regurgitate the orange crayon.

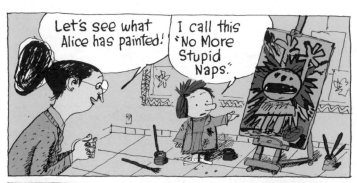

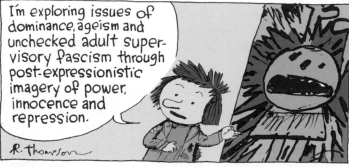

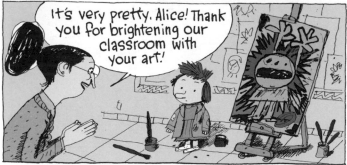

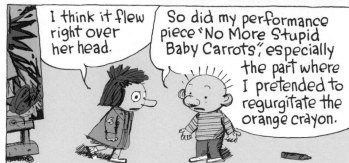

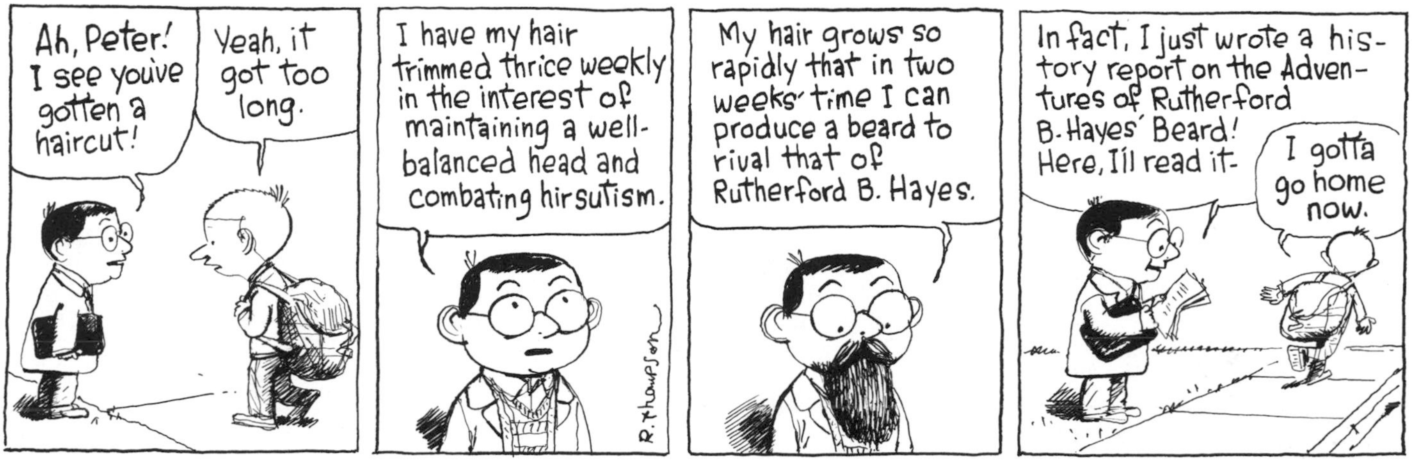
Ah, Peter! I see you've gotten a haircut!
Yeah, it got too long.
I have my hair trimmed thrice weekly in the interest of maintaining a well-balanced head and combating hirsutism.
My hair grows so rapidly that in two weeks' time I can produce a beard to rival that of Rutherford B. Hayes.
In fact, I just wrote a history report on the Adventures of Rutherford B. Hayes' Beard! Here, I'll read it-
I gotta go home now.

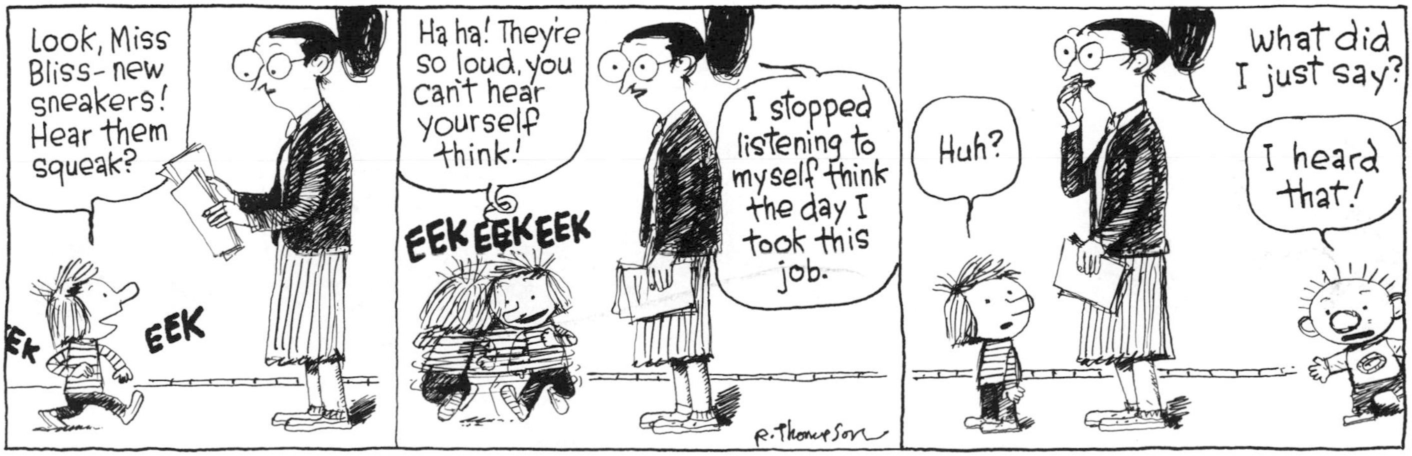
Look, Miss Bliss- new sneakers! Hear them squeak?
EEK
EEK
Ha ha! They're so loud, you can't hear yourself think!
EEK EEK EEK
I stopped listening to myself think the day I took this job.
Huh?
What did I just say?
I heard that!

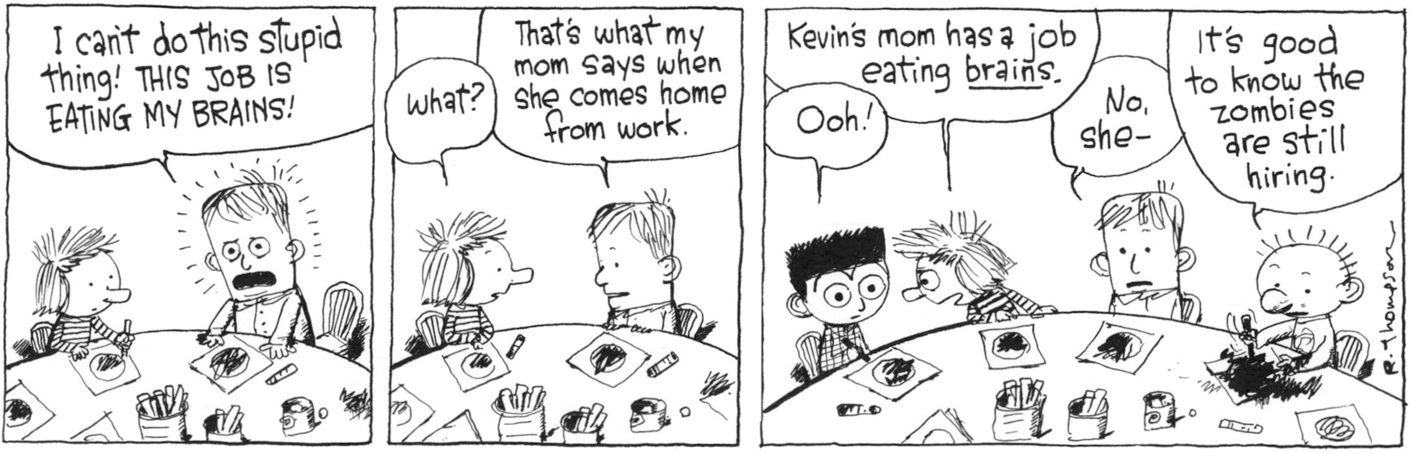
I can't do this stupid thing! THIS JOB IS EATING MY BRAINS!
What?
That's what my mom says when she comes home from work.
Kevin's mom has a job eating brains.
Ooh!
No, she-
It's good to know the zombies are still hiring.

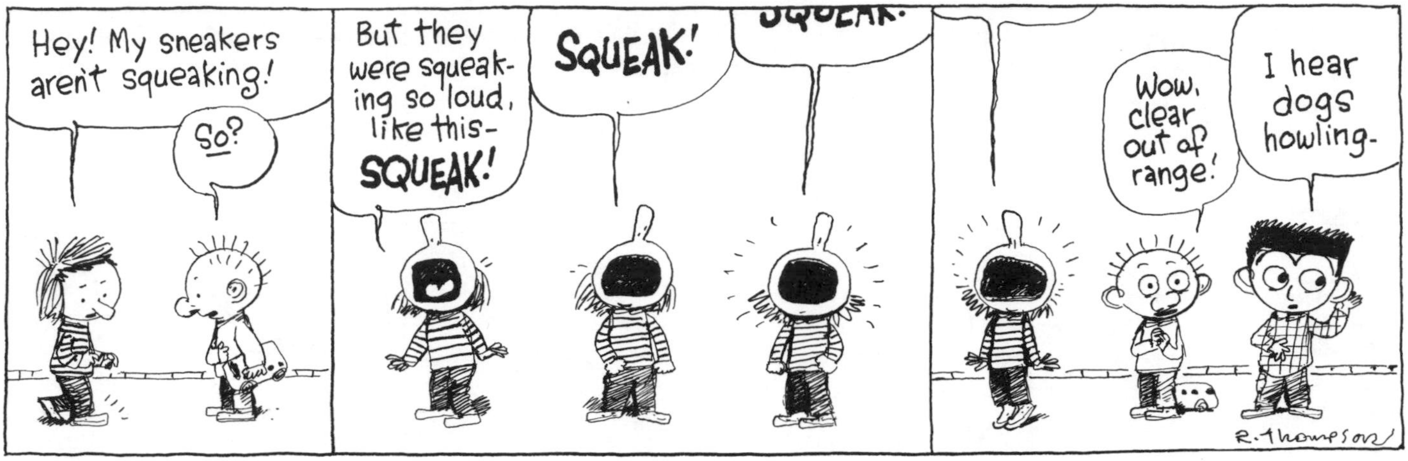
Hey! My sneakers aren't squeaking!
So?
But they were squeaking so loud, like this- SQUEAK!
SQUEAK!
Wow, clear out of range!
I hear dogs howling.
R. Thompson

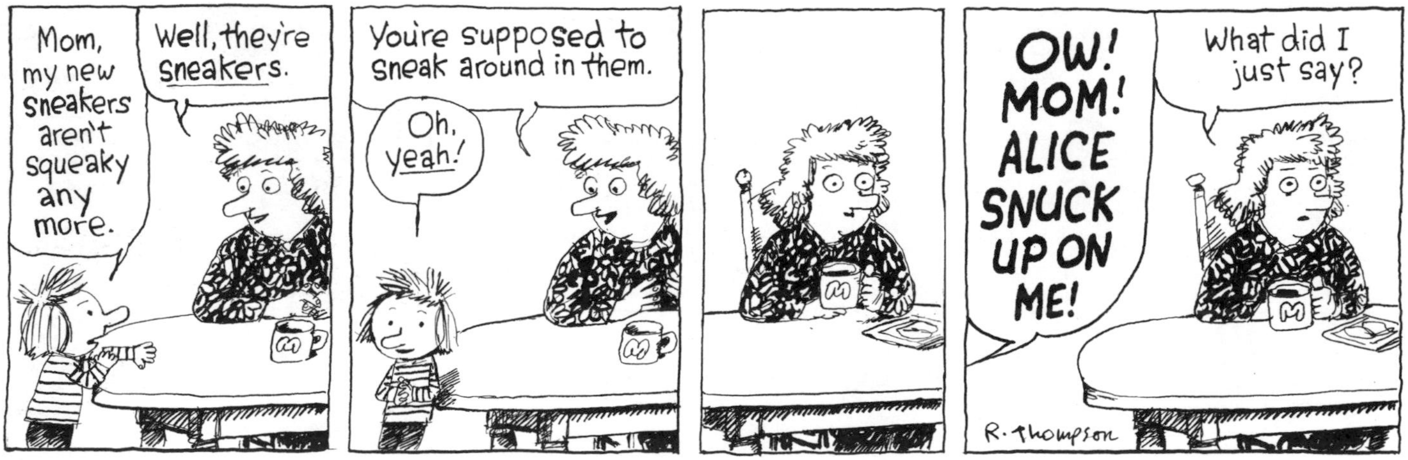
Mom, my new sneakers aren't squeaky any more.
Well, they're sneakers.
You're supposed to sneak around in them.
Oh, yeah!
OW! MOM! ALICE SNUCK UP ON ME!
What did I just say?
R. Thompson

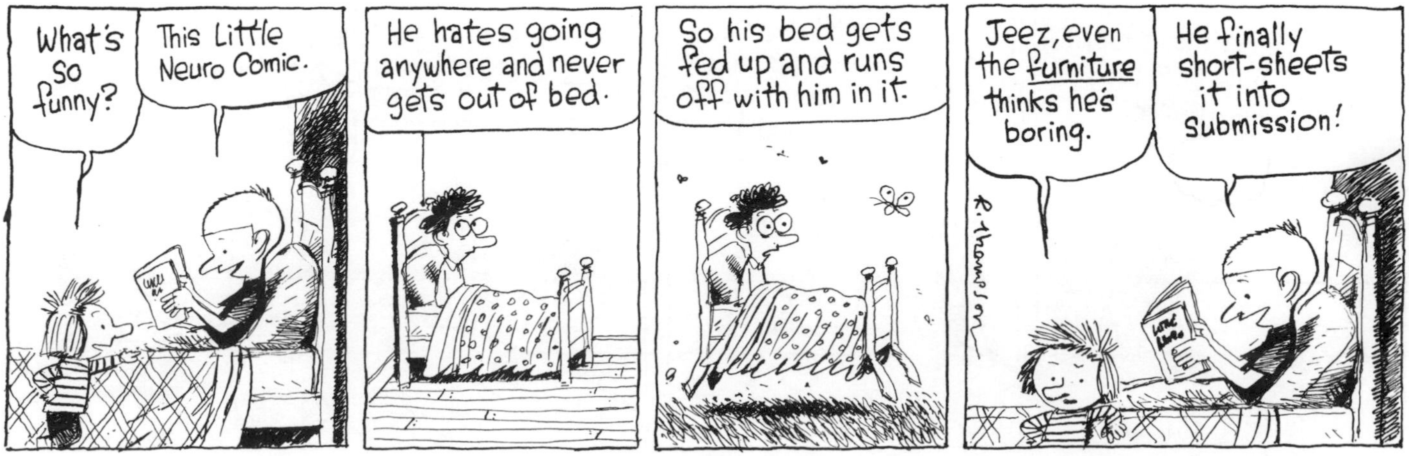
What's so funny?
This Little Neuro Comic.
He hates going anywhere and never gets out of bed.
So his bed gets fed up and runs off with him in it.
Jeez, even the furniture thinks he's boring.
He finally short-sheets it into submission!
R. Thompson

Mommy and Daddy were talking, and Daddy said something disturbing.
What?
He called Mommy "Madeline," like it's her name.
It is her name
WHAT? Since when?
"Mommy" is her position, or possibly it's an honorific.
I don't think I like this business of people having secret lives with names of their own. It's thoughtless and sneaky and just plain rude.
Daddy's name is Peter.
HAMAHAMA HAMA I CAN'T HEEEEEEEAR YOU HAMA HAMAHAMA!
Mom's maiden name is URQUHART.

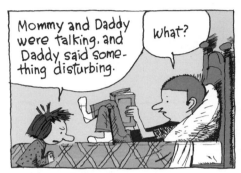

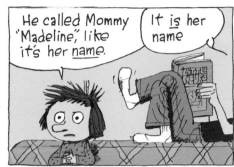

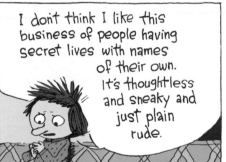

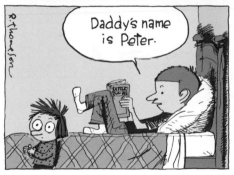

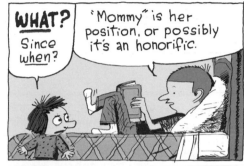

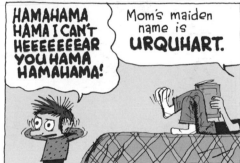

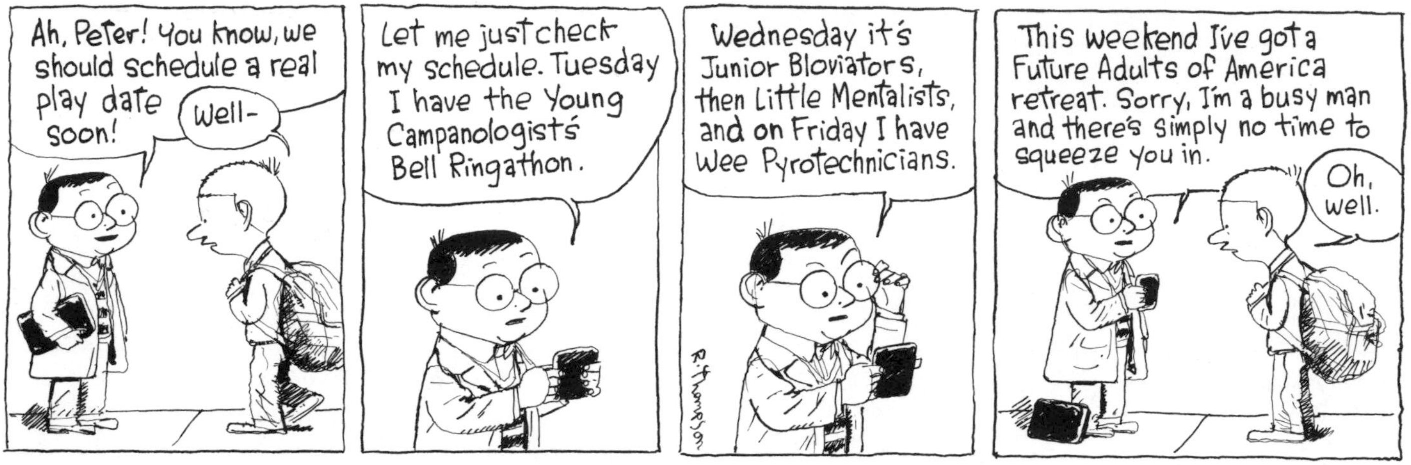
Ah, Peter! You know, we should schedule a real play date soon!
Well-
Let me just check my schedule. Tuesday I have the Young Campanologists' Bell Ringathon.
Wednesday it's Junior Bloviators, then Little Mentalists, and on Friday I have Wee Pyrotechnicians.
This weekend I've got a Future Adults of America retreat. Sorry, I'm a busy man and there's simply no time to squeeze you in.
Oh, well.

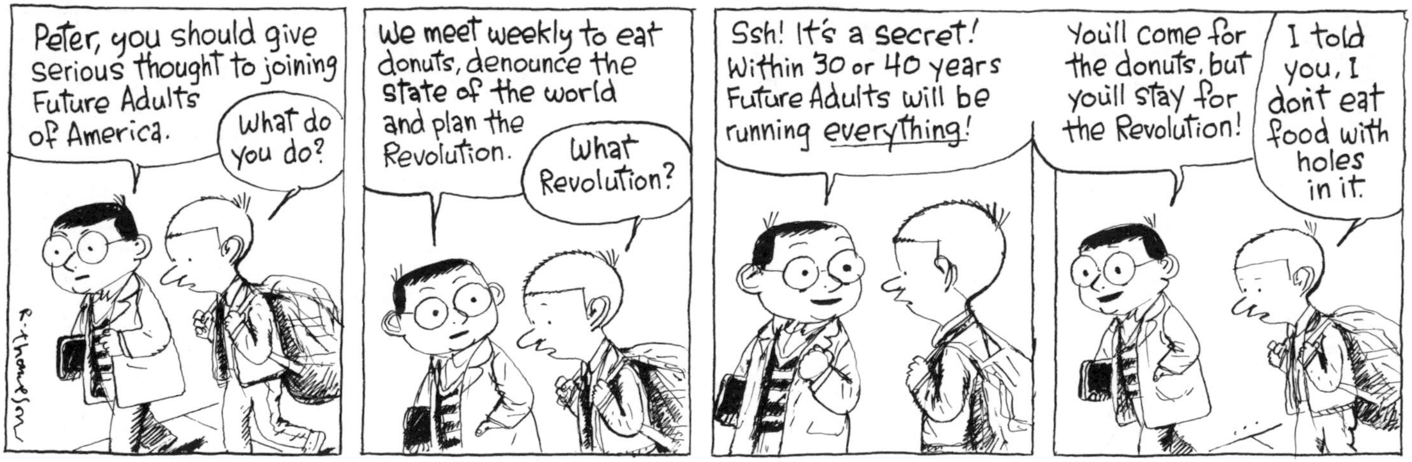
Peter, you should give serious thought to joining Future Adults of America.
What do you do?
We meet weekly to eat donuts, denounce the state of the world and plan the Revolution.
What Revolution?
Ssh! It's a secret! Within 30 or 40 years Future Adults will be running everything!
You'll come for the donuts, but you'll stay for the Revolution!
I told you, I don't eat food with holes in it.

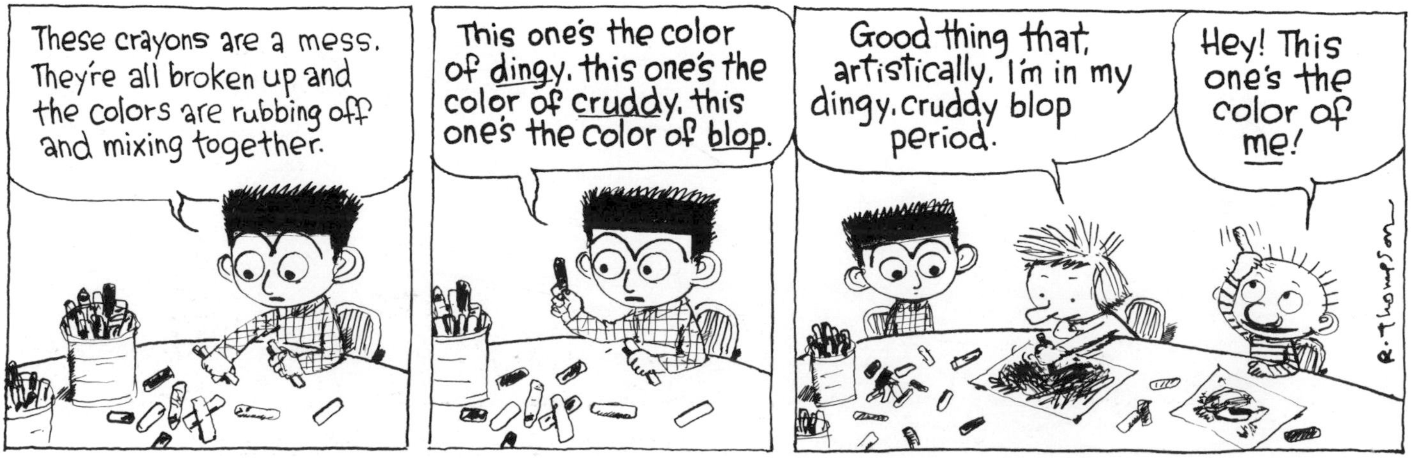
These crayons are a mess. They're all broken up and the colors are rubbing off and mixing together.
This one's the color of dingy, this one's the color of cruddy, this one's the color of blop.
Good thing that, artistically, I'm in my dingy, cruddy blop period.
Hey! This one's the color of me!

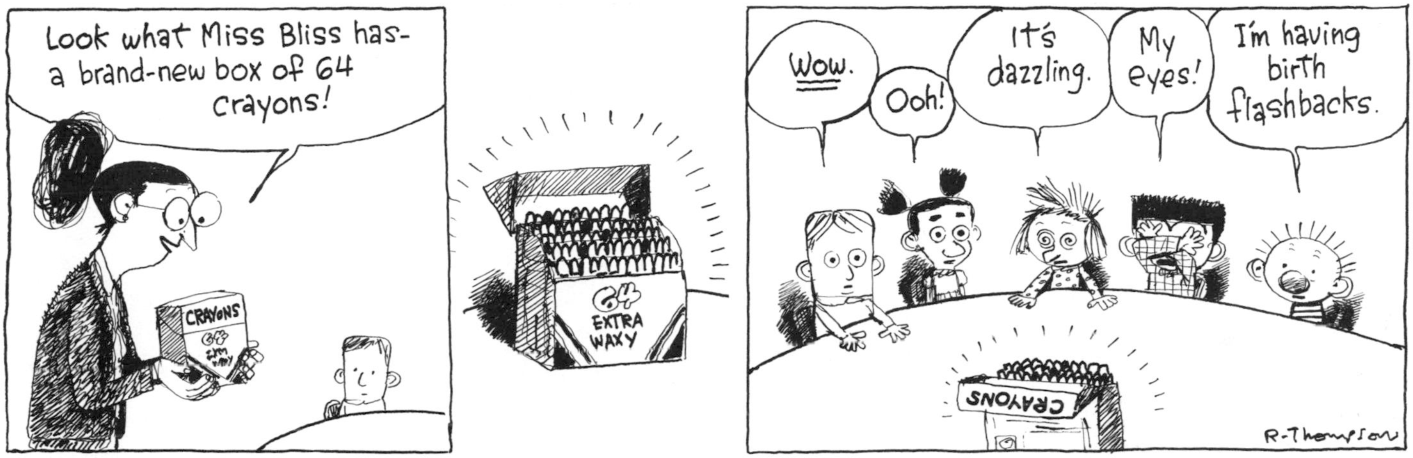
Look what Miss Bliss has- a brand-new box of 64 crayons!
CRAYONS
64
EXTRA WAXY
Wow.
Ooh!
It's dazzling.
My eyes!
I'm having birth flashbacks.
CRAYONS
R. Thompson

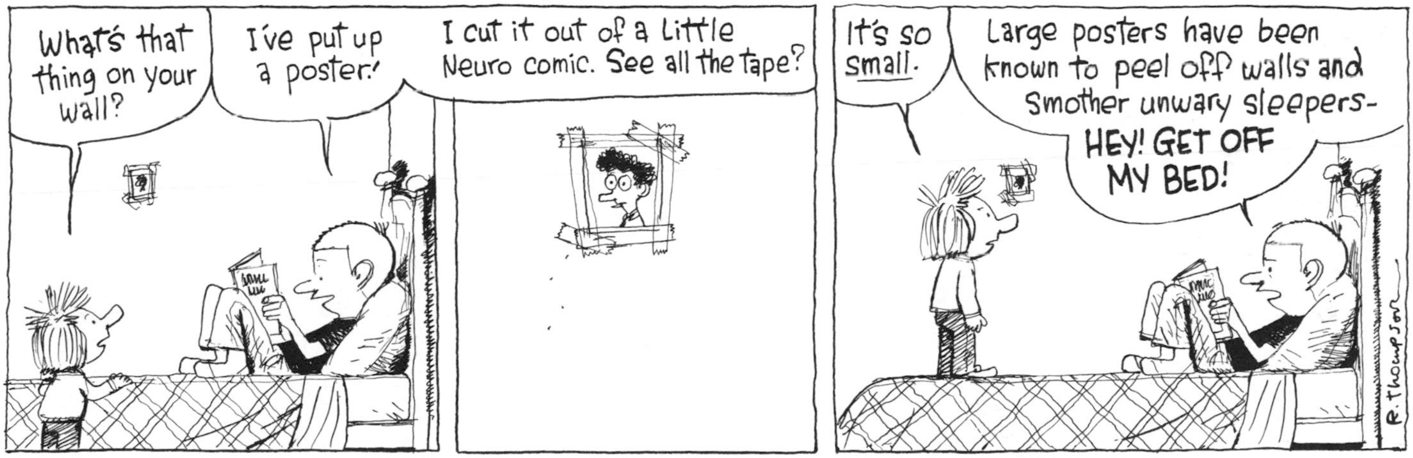
What's that thing on your wall?
I've put up a poster!
I cut it out of a Little Neuro comic. See all the tape?
It's so small.
Large posters have been known to peel off walls and smother unwary sleepers-
HEY! GET OFF MY BED!
R. Thompson

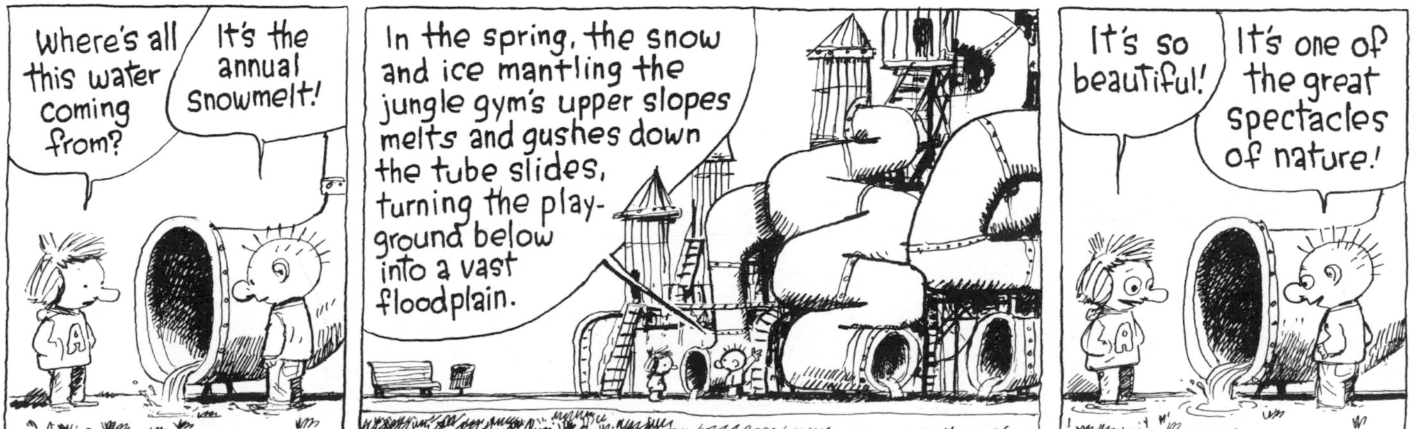
Where's all this water coming from?
It's the annual snowmelt!
In the spring, the snow and ice mantling the jungle gym's upper slopes melts and gushes down the tube slides, turning the playground below into a vast floodplain.
It's so beautiful!
It's one of the great spectacles of nature!
R. Thompson

I'M ALICE!
I know. Stop yelling.
It's a windy day.
Yeah. So?
I'M ALICE!
If you yell on a windy day, the wind will pick up your words and blow them around the world.
R. Thompson
I'M ALICE!
And if you go outside the next day and listen, you'll hear what you said!
Really?
It's a well-known fact.
I'M BENI!
I'M ALICE!
Tell me again. I always get you two mixed up.

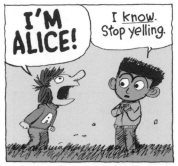

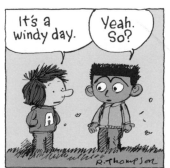

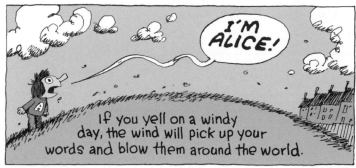

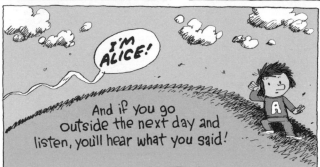

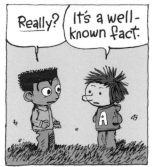

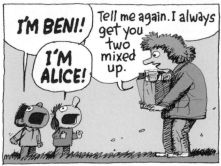

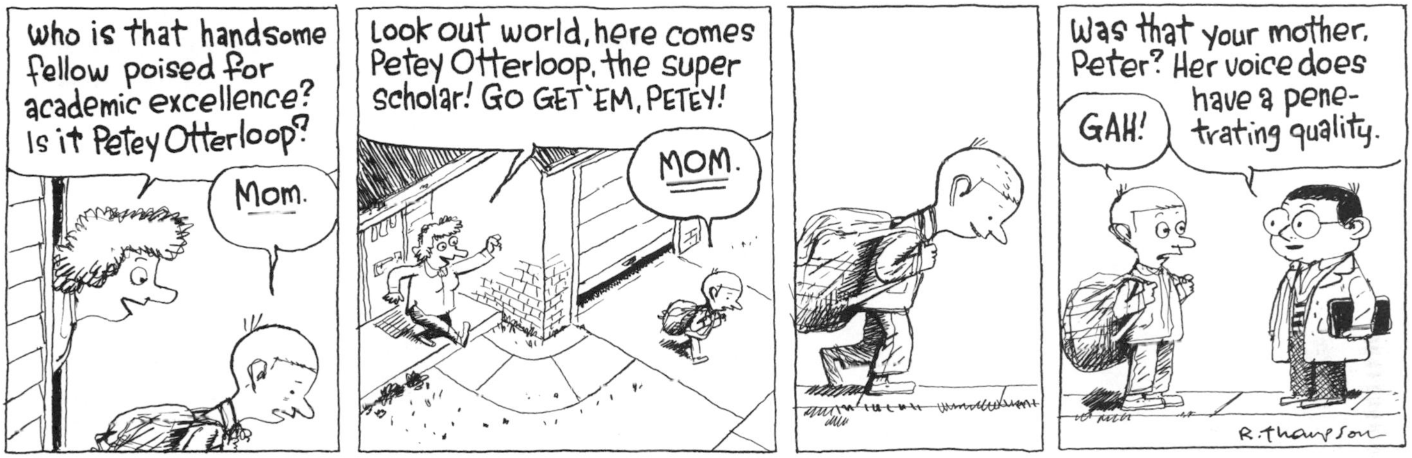
Who is that handsome fellow poised for academic excellence? Is it Petey Otterloop?
Mom.
Look out world, here comes Petey Otterloop, the super scholar! GO GET 'EM, PETEY!
MOM.
GAH!
Was that your mother, Peter? Her voice does have a pene-trating quality.
R. Thompson

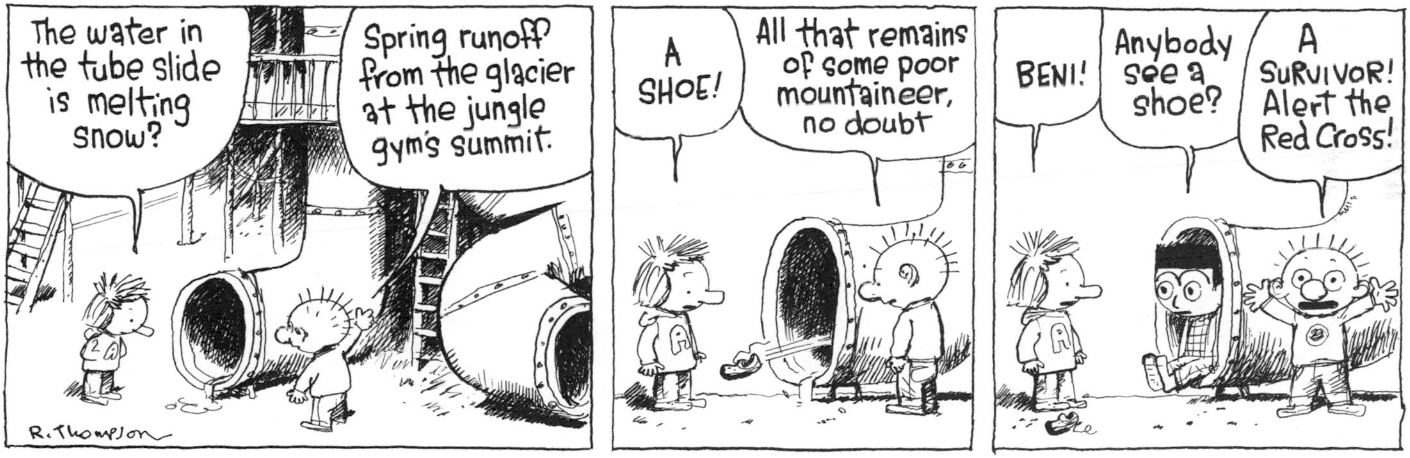
The water in the tube slide is melting snow?
Spring runoff from the glacier at the jungle gym's summit.
R. Thompson
A SHOE!
All that remains of some poor mountaineer, no doubt
BENI!
Anybody see a shoe?
A SURVIVOR! Alert the Red Cross!

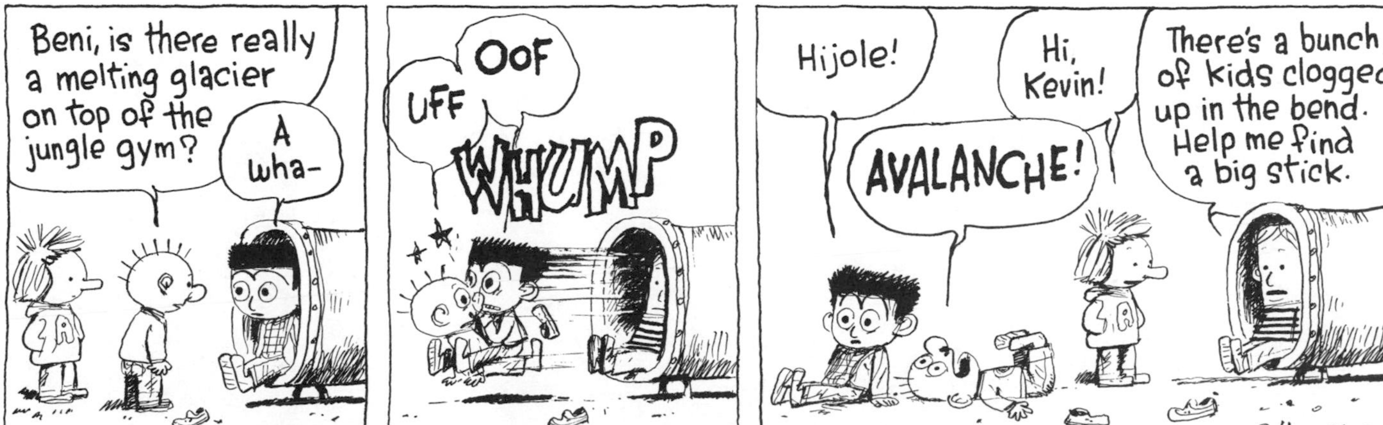
Beni, is there really a melting glacier on top of the jungle gym?
A wha-
UFF
OOF
WHUMP
Hijole!
Hi, Kevin!
AVALANCHE!
There's a bunch of kids clogged up in the bend. Help me find a big stick.
R. Thompson

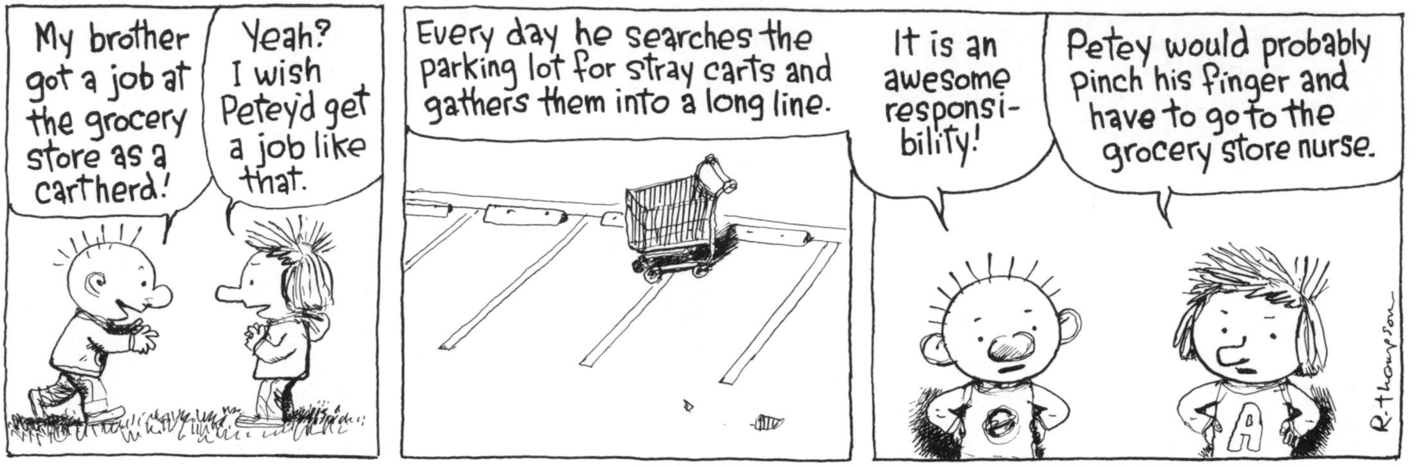
My brother got a job at the grocery store as a carTherd!
Yeah? I wish Peteyd get a job like that.
Every day he searches the parking lot for stray carts and gathers them into a long line.
It is an awesome responsi-bility!
Petey would probably pinch his finger and have to go to the grocery store nurse.
R. Thompson

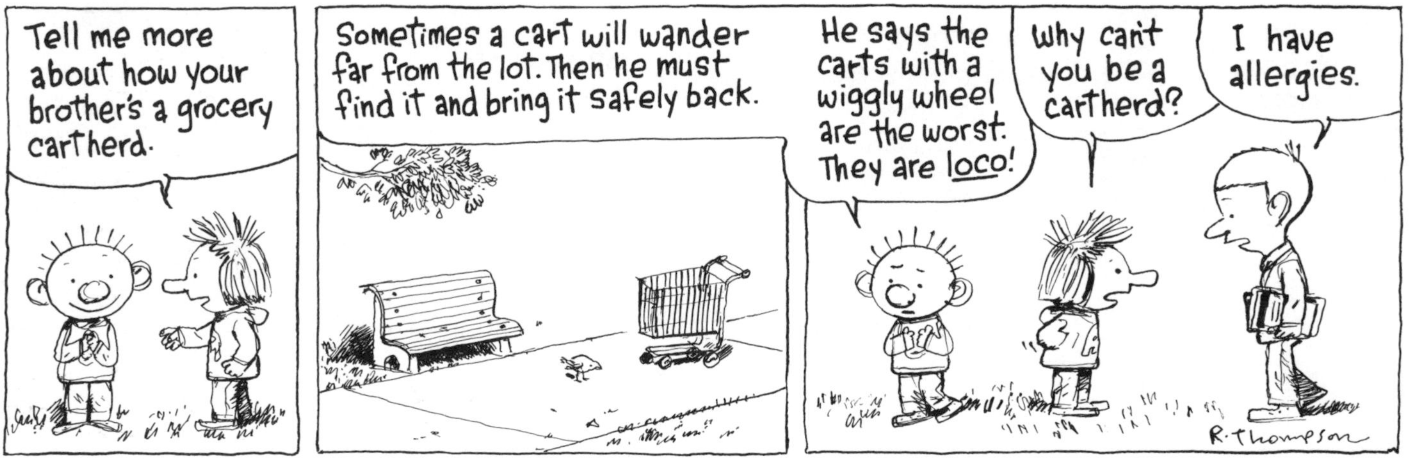
Tell me more about how your brother's a grocery carTherd.
Sometimes a cart will wander far from the lot. Then he must find it and bring it safely back.
He says the carts with a wiggly wheel are the worst. They are loco!
Why can't you be a carTherd?
I have allergies.
R. Thompson

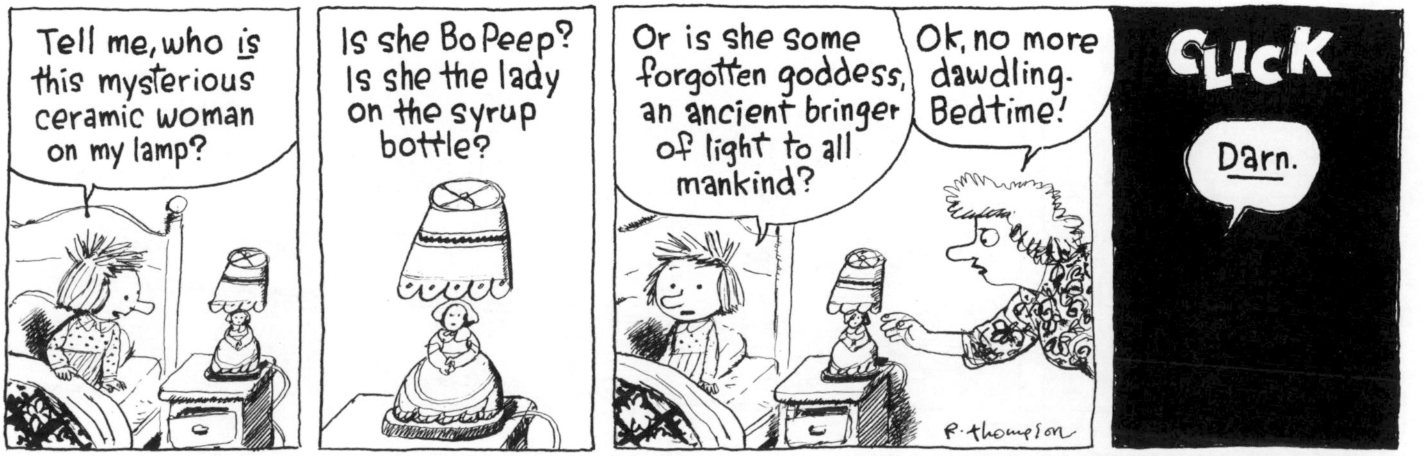
Tell me, who is this mysterious ceramic woman on my lamp?
Is she Bo Peep? Is she the lady on the syrup bottle?
Or is she some forgotten goddess, an ancient bringer of light to all mankind?
Ok, no more dawdling. Bedtime!
R. Thompson
CLICK
Darn.

Alice! Get out of the way!
I want to ride in the car now.
But I just got in it! I'm playing like I'm on a trip!
You can play something else.
I'll play like I'm on a hike.
Stick out your thumb and you can play like you're a disappointed hitchhiker.
R. Thompson

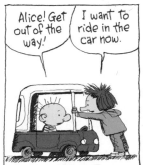

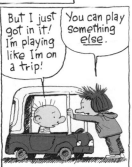

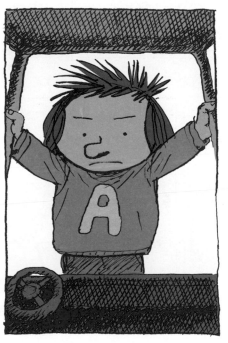

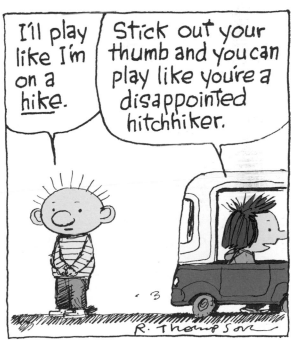

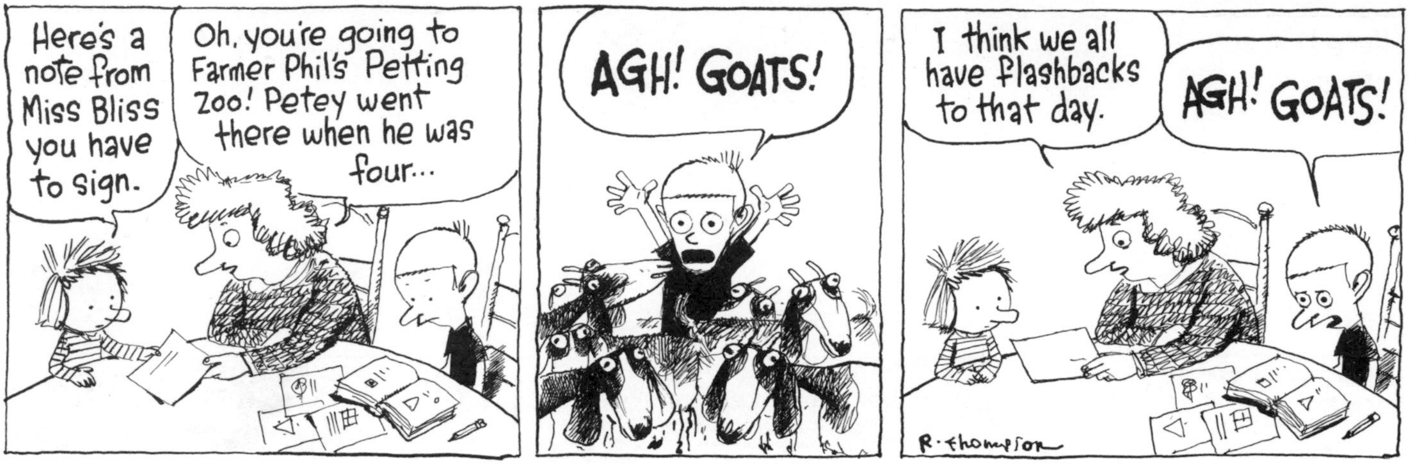
Here's a note from Miss Bliss you have to sign.
Oh, you're going to Farmer Phil's Petting Zoo! Petey went there when he was four...
AGH! GOATS!
I think we all have flashbacks to that day.
AGH! GOATS!
R. Thompson

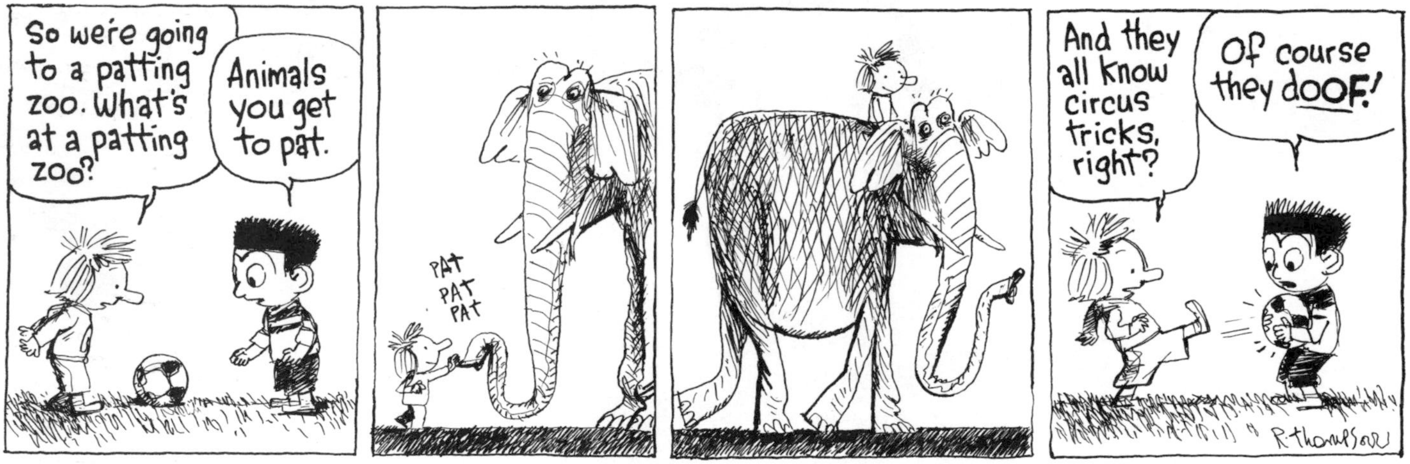
So we're going to a patting zoo. What's at a patting zoo?
Animals you get to pat.
PAT
PAT
PAT
And they all know circus tricks, right?
Of course they dOOF!
R. Thompson

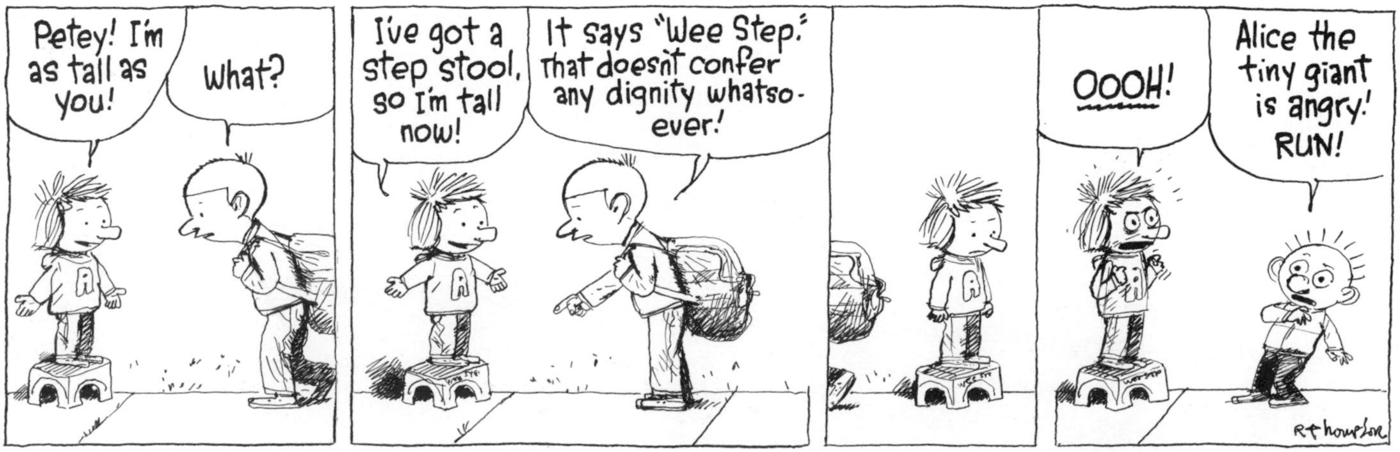
Petey! I'm as tall as you!
What?
I've got a step stool, so I'm tall now!
It says "Wee Step." That doesn't confer any dignity whatsoever!
OOOH!
Alice the tiny giant is angry! RUN!
R. Thompson

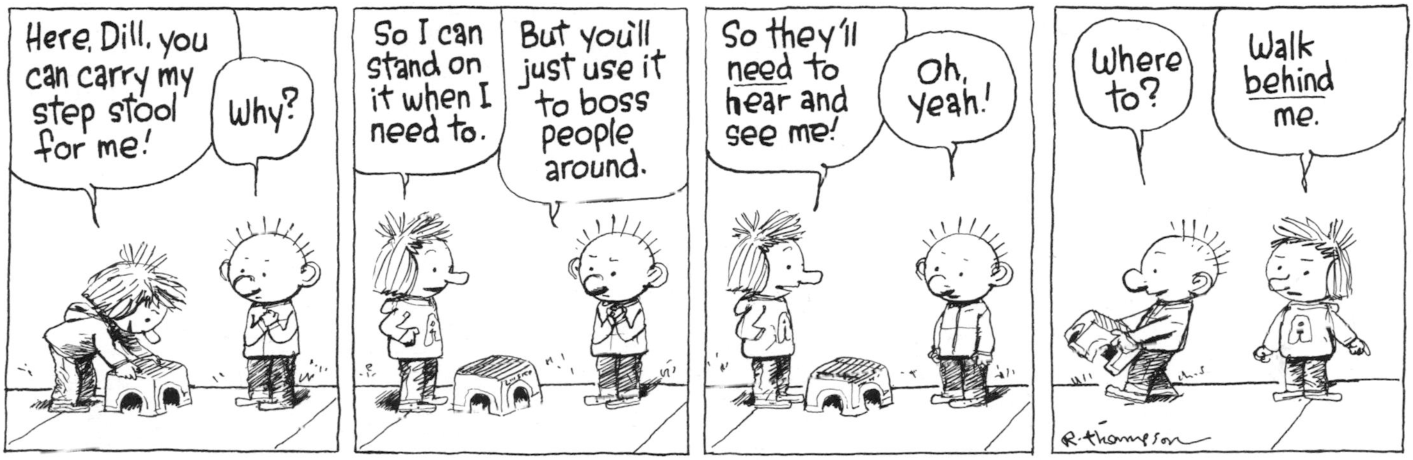
Here, Dill, you can carry my step stool for me!
Why?
So I can stand on it when I need to.
But you'll just use it to boss people around.
So they'll need to hear and see me!
Oh, yeah!
Where to?
Walk behind me.

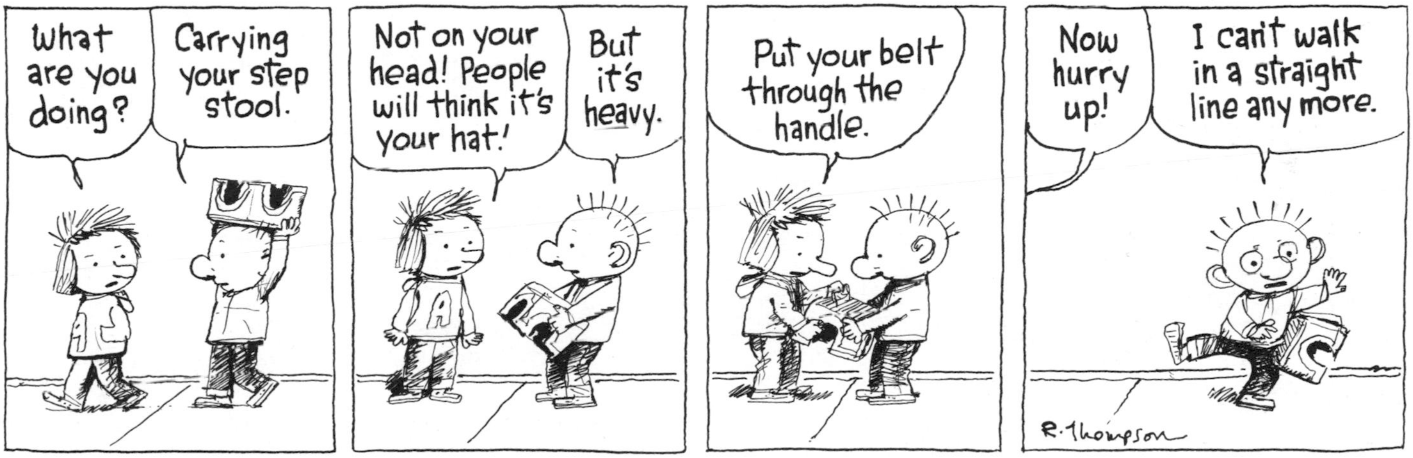
What are you doing?
Carrying your step stool.
Not on your head! People will think it's your hat!
But it's heavy.
Put your belt through the handle.
Now hurry up!
I can't walk in a straight line any more.

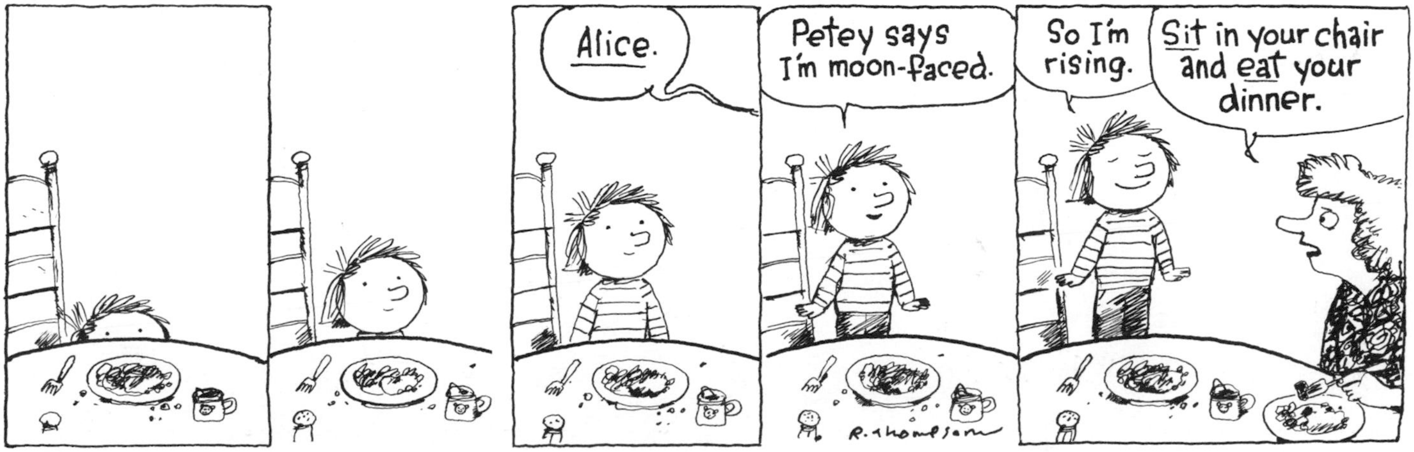
Alice.
Petey says I'm moon-faced.
So I'm rising.
Sit in your chair and eat your dinner.

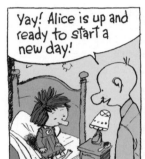

Yay! Alice is up and ready to start a new day!
Oh, she's eating breakfast! Look how colorful her cereal is!
Now we're in the car and on the way!
Look at all the cars! Everybody has somewhere to go!
Here we go down the big long hill! Wheeeee!
Uh-oh! Railroad crossing! Ding ding ding!
RAIL CROSSING ROAD
Three more blocks and we'll be at Blisshaven Preschool!
Here we are! All of Alice's friends are waiting for her!
I thought my Dad was going to narrate my whole day.
Adults do that in an attempt to understand a big scary world.
HA! Good luck with that.
R. T. Thompson

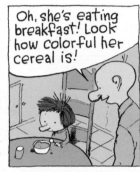

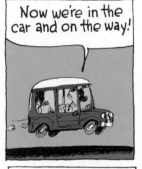

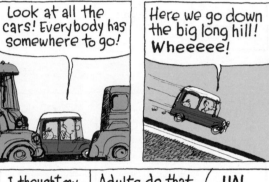

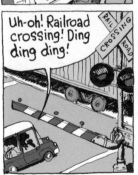

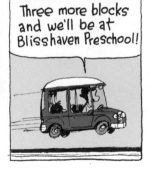

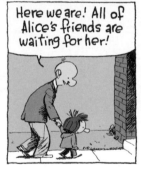

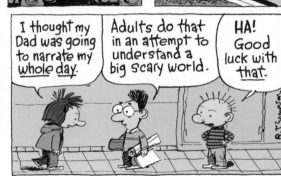

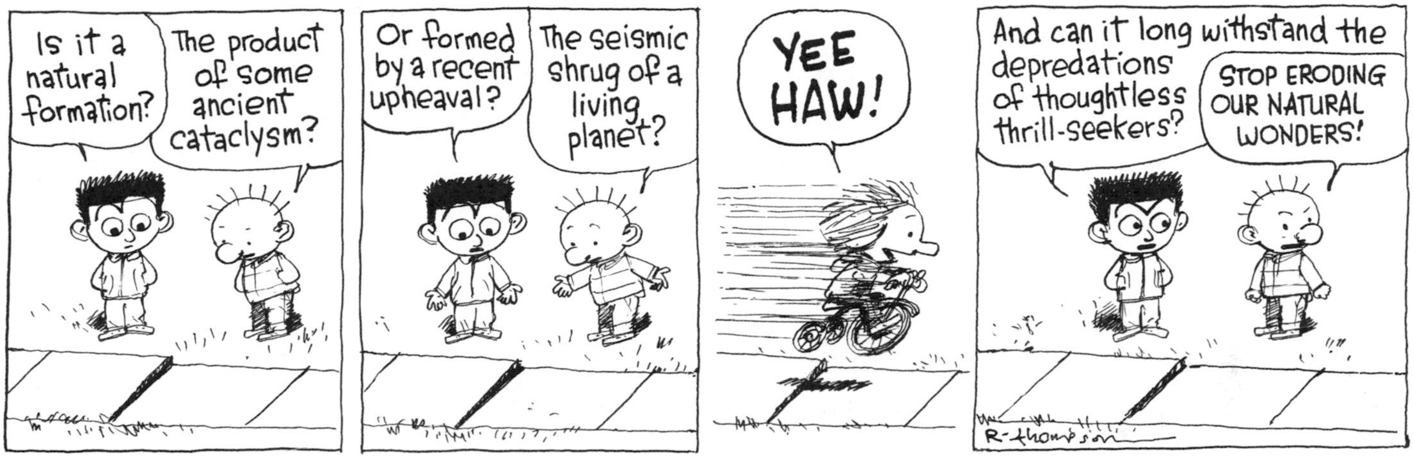
Is it a natural formation?
The product of some ancient cataclysm?
Or formed by a recent upheaval?
The seismic shrug of a living planet?
YEE HAW!
And can it long withstand the depredations of thoughtless thrill-seekers?
STOP ERODING OUR NATURAL WONDERS!

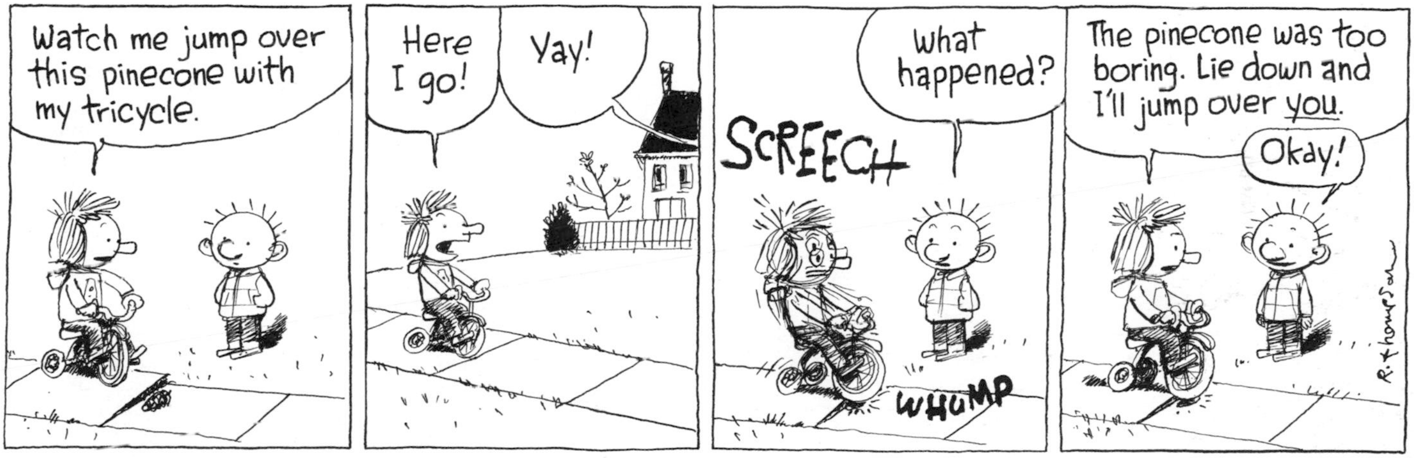
Watch me jump over this pinecone with my tricycle.
Here I go!
Yay!
SCREECH
What happened?
WHUMP
The pinecone was too boring. Lie down and I'll jump over you.
Okay!

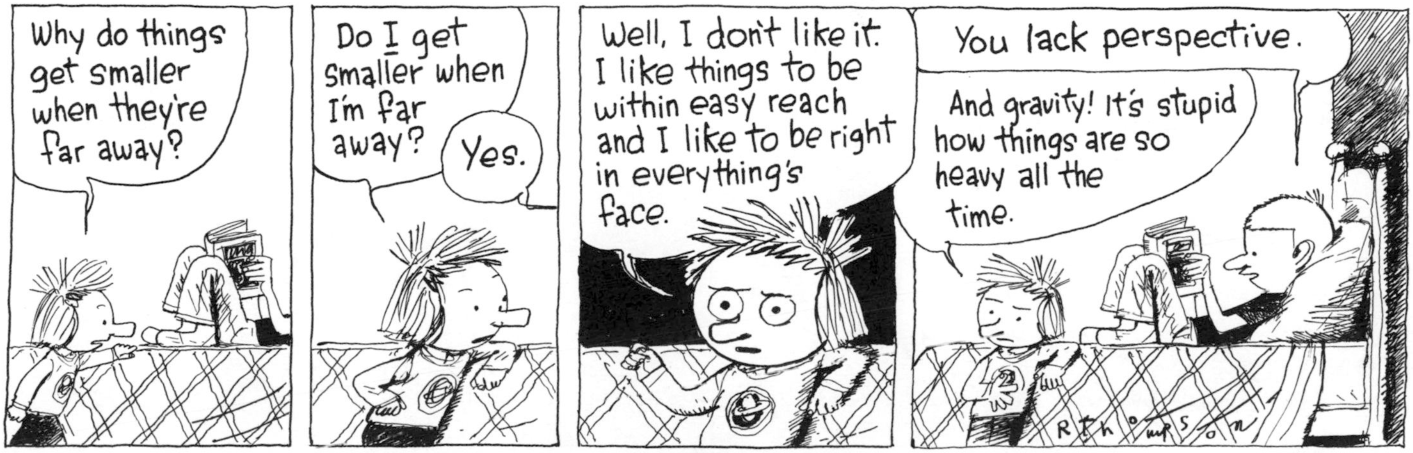
Why do things get smaller when they're far away?
Do I get smaller when I'm far away?
Yes.
Well, I don't like it. I like things to be within easy reach and I like to be right in everything's face.
You lack perspective.
And gravity! It's stupid how things are so heavy all the time.

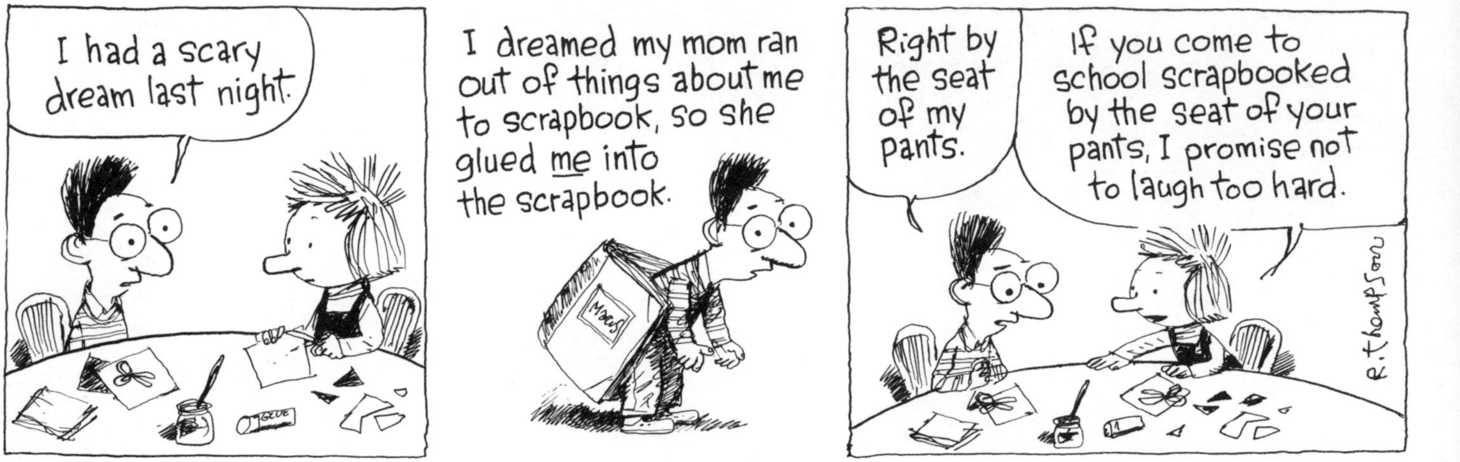
I had a scary dream last night.
I dreamed my mom ran out of things about me to scrapbook, so she glued me into the scrapbook.
Right by the seat of my pants.
If you come to school scrapbooked by the seat of your pants, I promise not to laugh too hard.

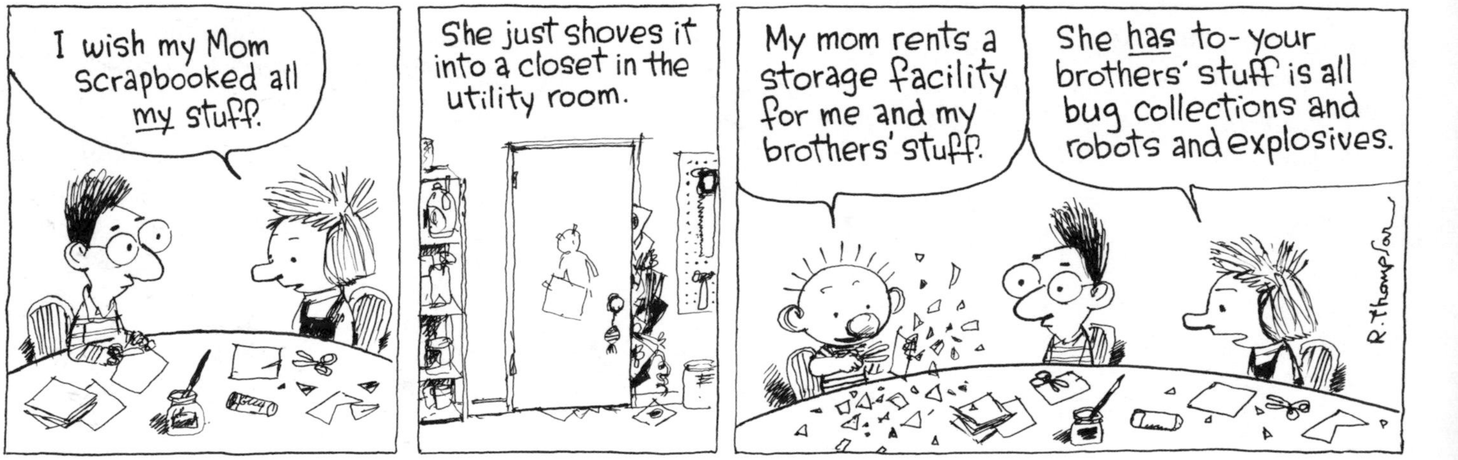
I wish my Mom scrapbooked all my stuff.
She just shoves it into a closet in the utility room.
My mom rents a storage facility for me and my brothers' stuff.
She has to- your brothers' stuff is all bug collections and robots and explosives.

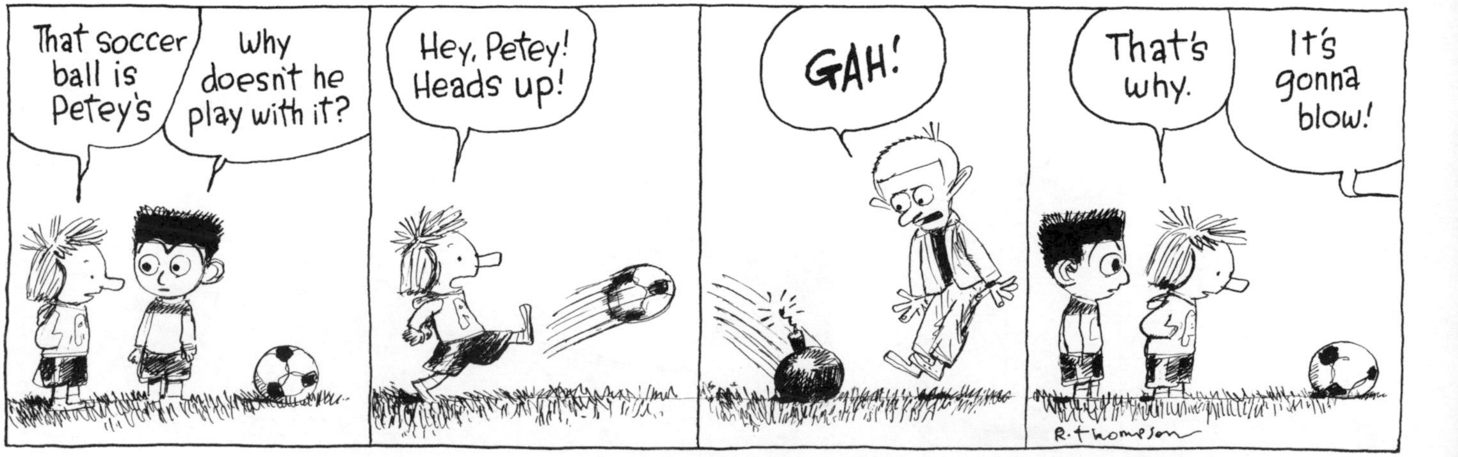
That soccer ball is Petey's
Why doesn't he play with it?
Hey, Petey! Heads up!
GAH!
That's why.
It's gonna blow!

Petey, look how fast youre growing!
You're going to be all arms and legs!
Ha ha!
SHARING TIME
ALICE
How soon?
How soon what?
Make Alice quit staring at me.
R. Thompson

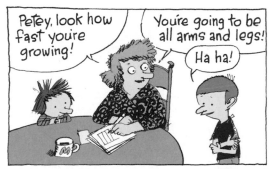

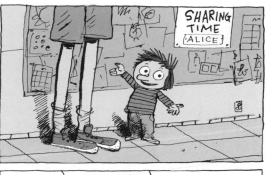

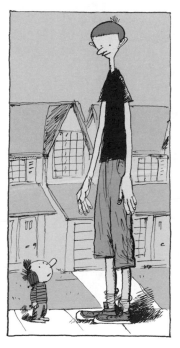

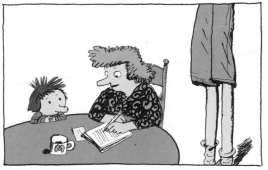

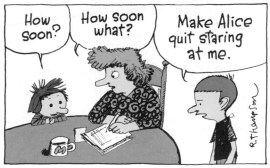

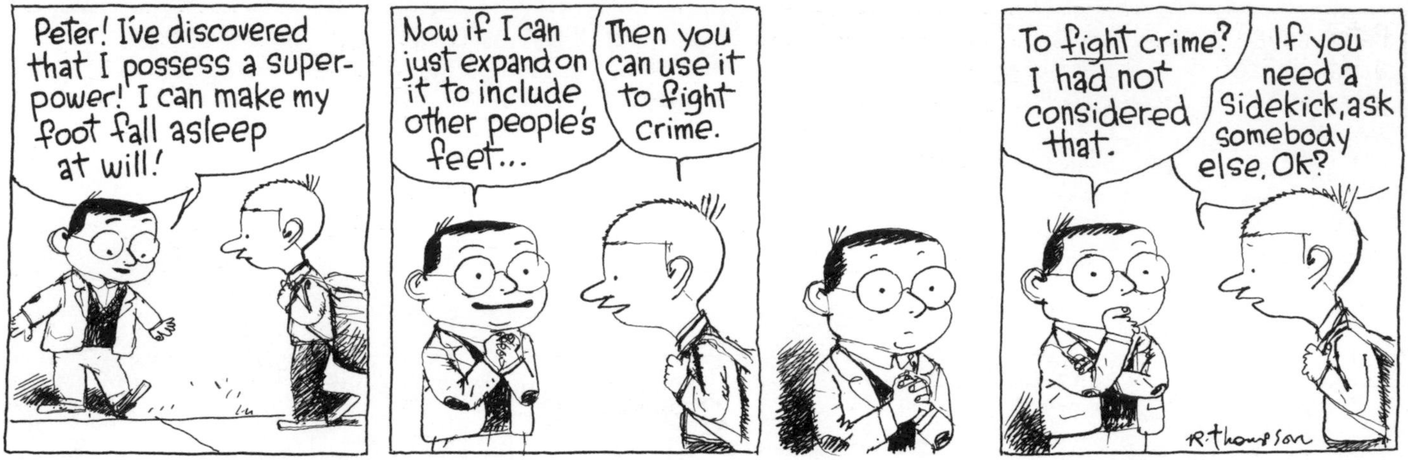
Peter! I've discovered that I possess a superpower! I can make my foot fall asleep at will!
Now if I can just expand on it to include other people's feet...
Then you can use it to fight crime.
To fight crime? I had not considered that.
If you need a sidekick, ask somebody else, OK?
R. Thompson

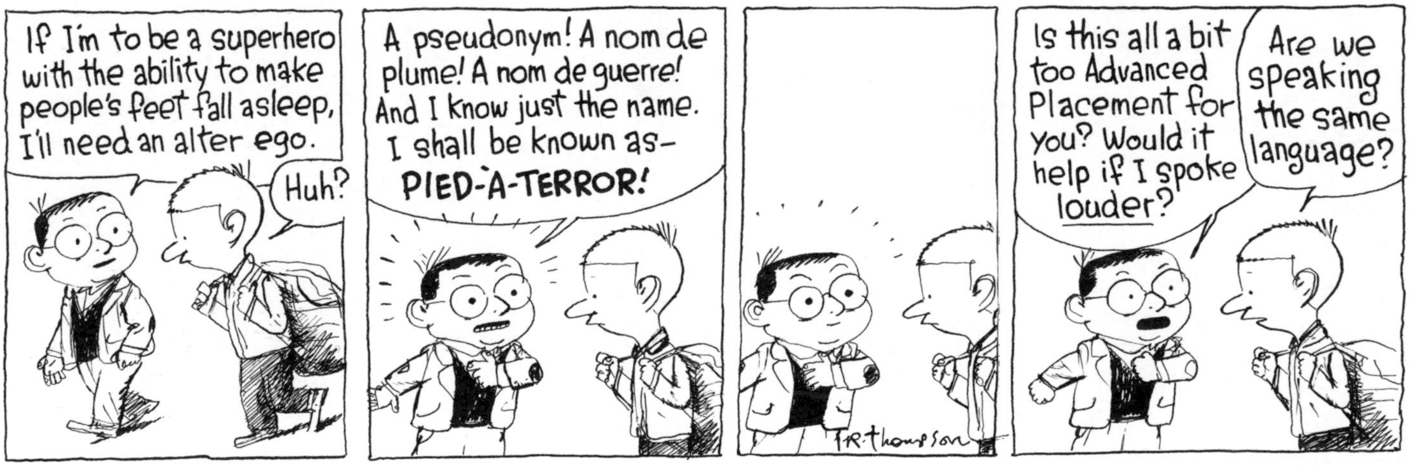
If I'm to be a superhero with the ability to make people's feet fall asleep, I'll need an alter ego.
Huh?
A pseudonym! A nom de plume! A nom de guerre! And I know just the name. I shall be known as—
PIED-À-TERROR!
R. Thompson
Is this all a bit too Advanced Placement for you? Would it help if I spoke louder?
Are we speaking the same language?

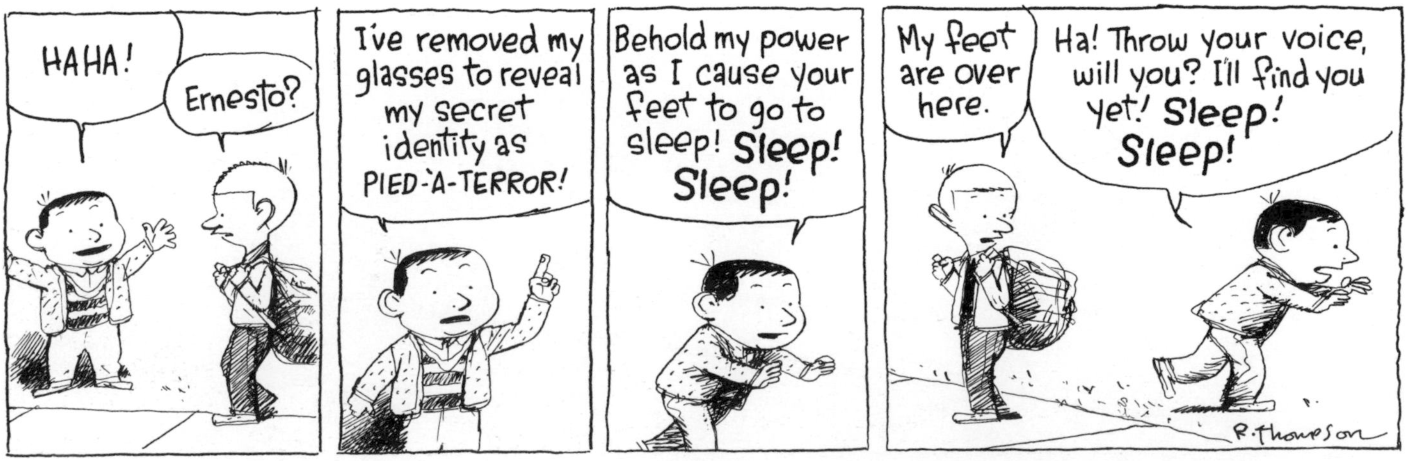
HAHA!
Ernesto?
I've removed my glasses to reveal my secret identity as PIED-À-TERROR!
Behold my power as I cause your feet to go to sleep! Sleep! Sleep!
My feet are over here.
Ha! Throw your voice, will you? I'll find you yet! Sleep! Sleep!
R. Thompson

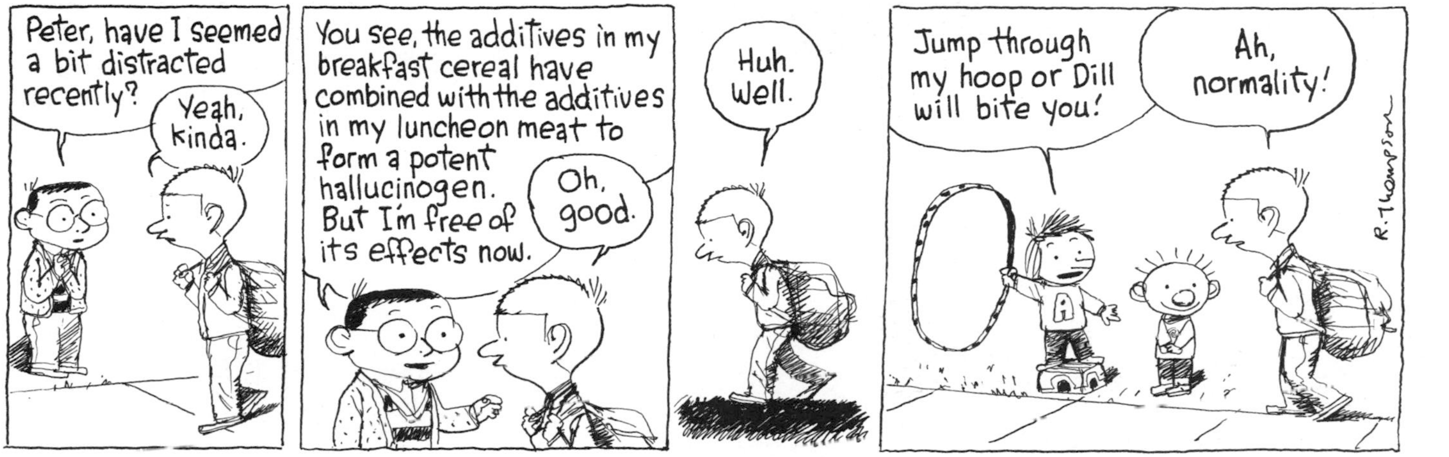
Peter, have I seemed a bit distracted recently?
Yeah, kinda.
You see, the additives in my breakfast cereal have combined with the additives in my luncheon meat to form a potent hallucinogen. But I'm free of its effects now.
Oh, good.
Huh. Well.
Jump through my hoop or Dill will bite you!
Ah, normality!

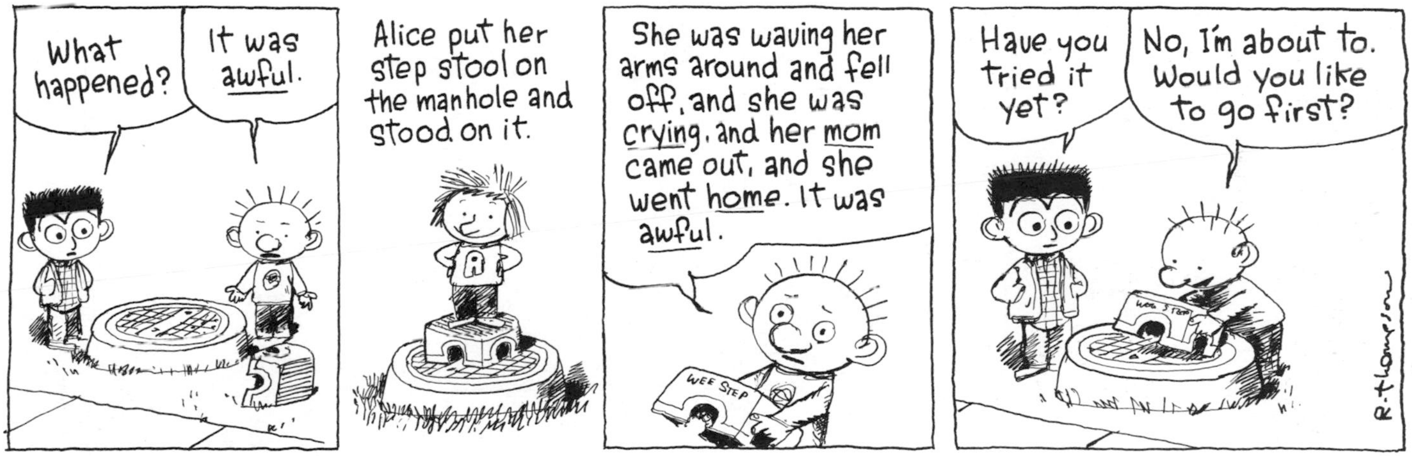
What happened?
It was awful.
Alice put her step stool on the manhole and stood on it.
She was waving her arms around and fell off, and she was crying, and her mom came out, and she went home. It was awful.
WEE STEP
Have you tried it yet?
No, I'm about to. Would you like to go first?

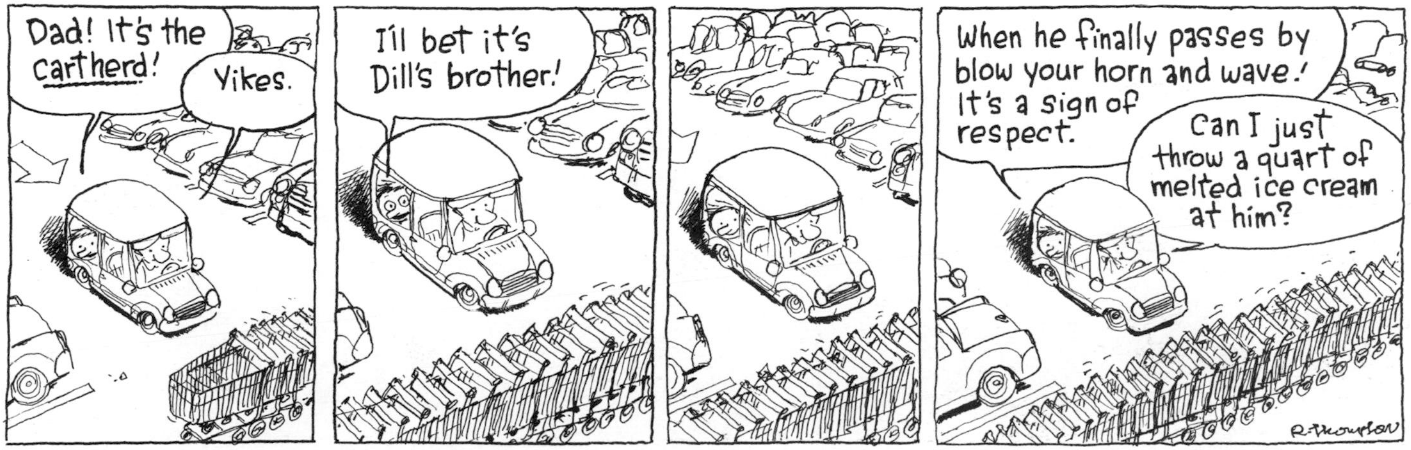
Dad! It's the cartherd!
Yikes.
I'll bet it's Dill's brother!
When he finally passes by blow your horn and wave! It's a sign of respect.
Can I just throw a quart of melted ice cream at him?

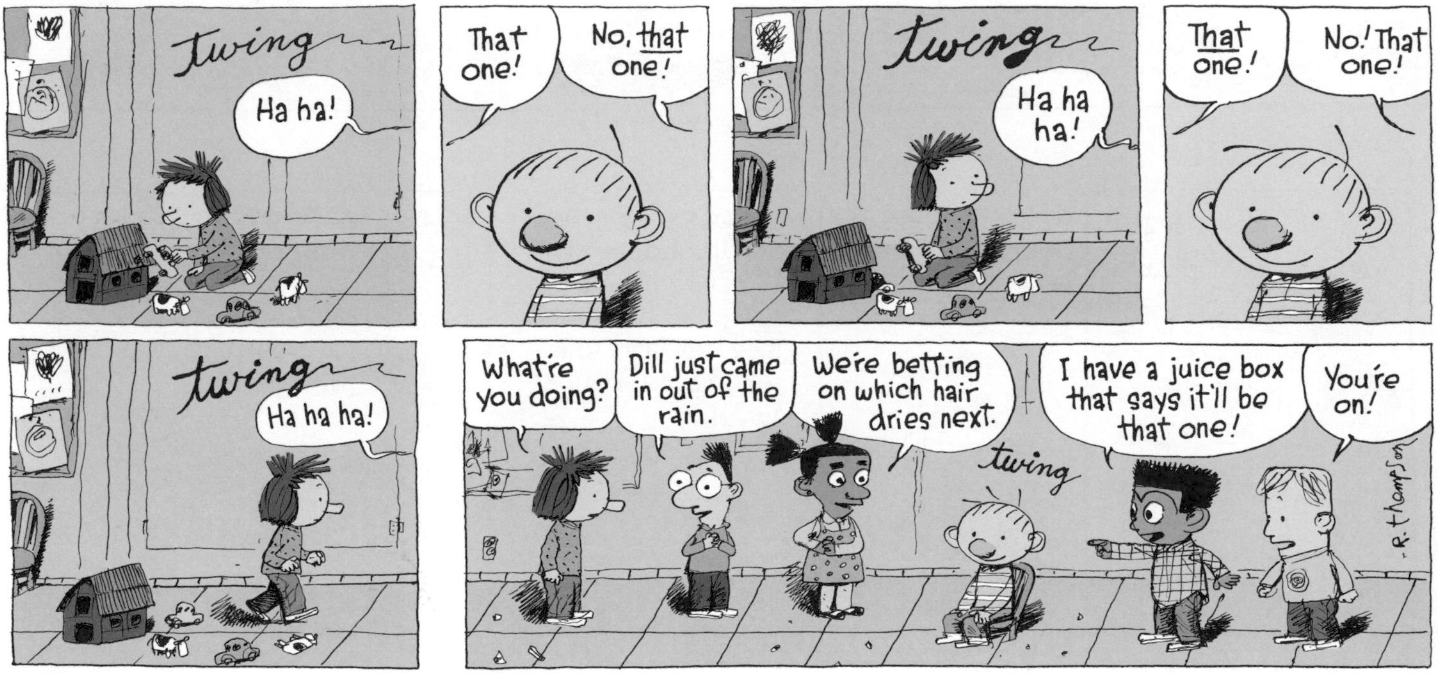
twing
Ha ha!
That one!
No, that one!
twing
Ha ha ha!
That one!
No! That one!
twing
Ha ha ha!
What're you doing?
Dill just came in out of the rain.
We're betting on which hair dries next.
twing
I have a juice box that says it'll be that one!
You're on!
R. thompson

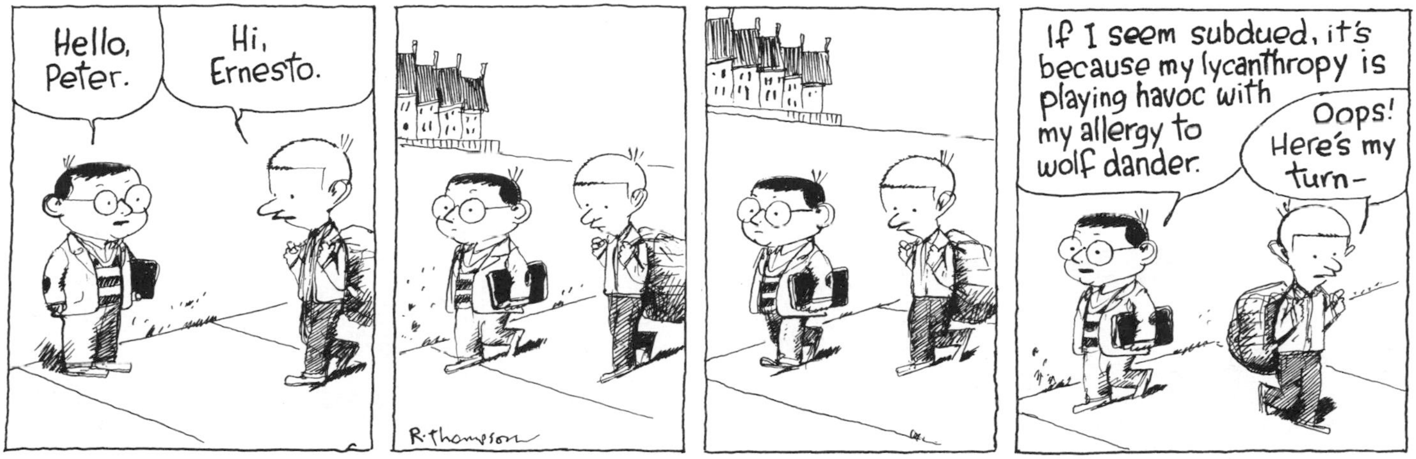
Hello, Peter.
Hi, Ernesto.
R·thompson
If I seem subdued, it's because my lycanthropy is playing havoc with my allergy to wolf dander.
Oops! Here's my turn-

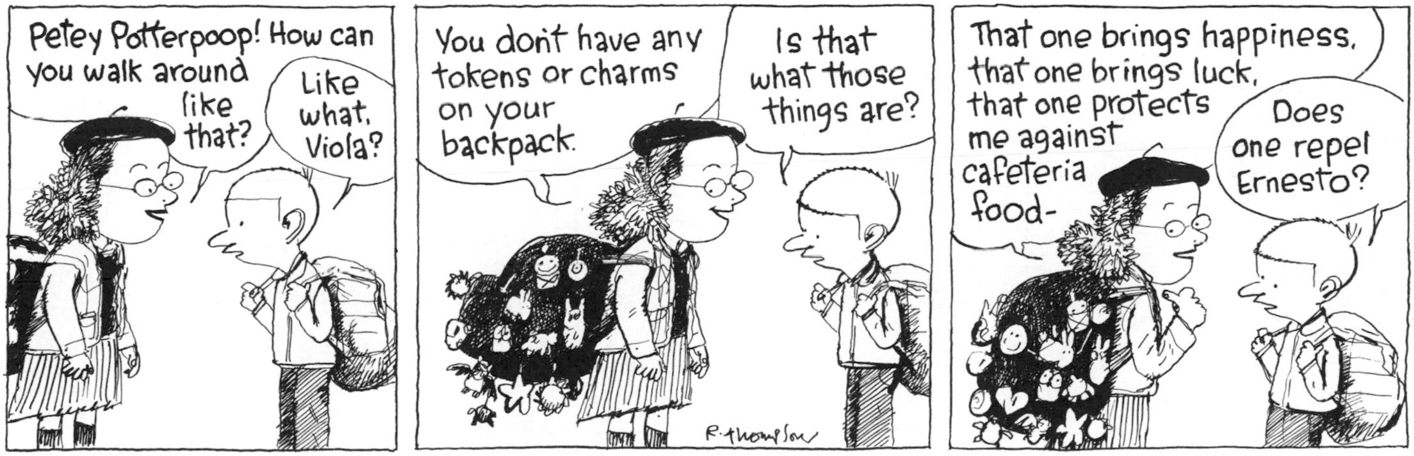
Petey Potterpoop! How can you walk around like that?
Like what, Viola?
You don't have any tokens or charms on your backpack.
Is that what those things are?
R·thompson
That one brings happiness, that one brings luck, that one protects me against cafeteria food-
Does one repel Ernesto?

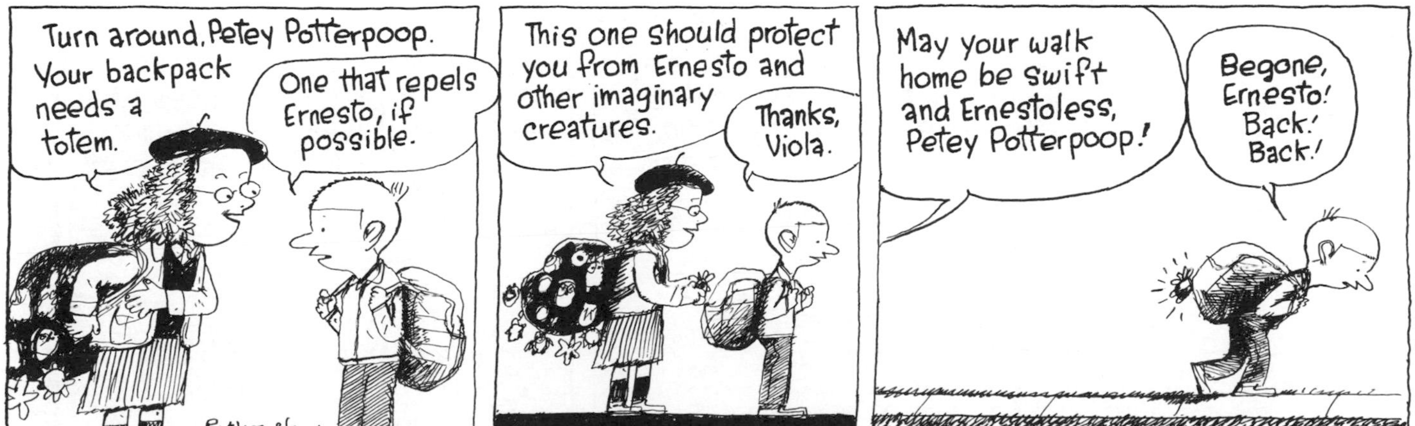
Turn around, Petey Potterpoop. Your backpack needs a totem.
One that repels Ernesto, if possible.
R·thompson
This one should protect you from Ernesto and other imaginary creatures.
Thanks, Viola.
May your walk home be swift and Ernestoless, Petey Potterpoop!
Begone, Ernesto! Back! Back!

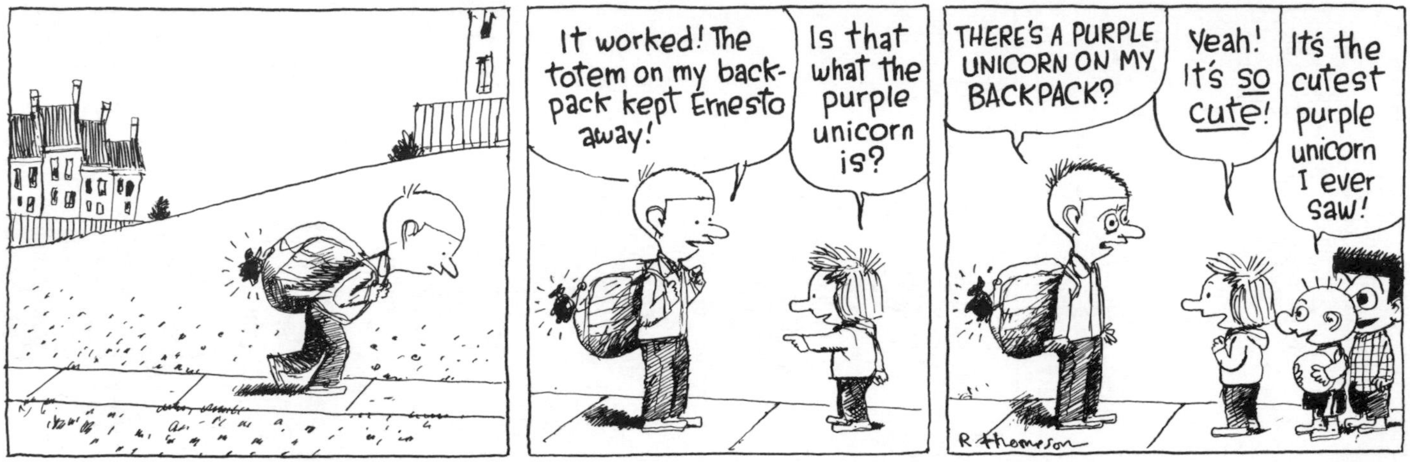
It worked! The totem on my back-pack kept Ernesto away!
Is that what the purple unicorn is?
THERE'S A PURPLE UNICORN ON MY BACKPACK?
Yeah! It's so cute!
It's the cutest purple unicorn I ever saw!
R. thompson

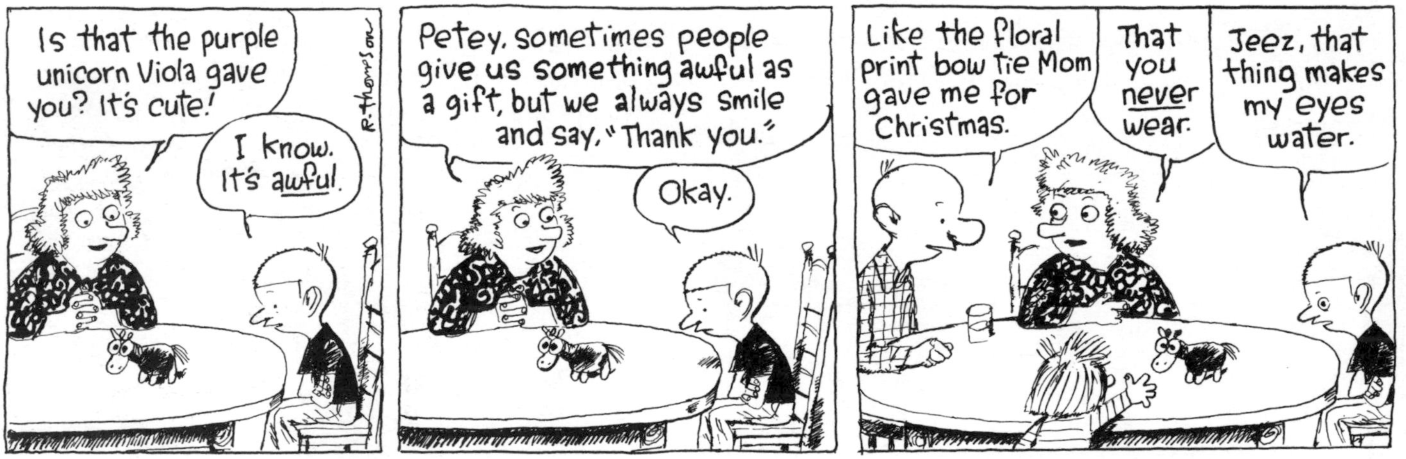
Is that the purple unicorn Viola gave you? It's cute!
I know. It's awful.
R. thompson
Petey, sometimes people give us something awful as a gift, but we always smile and say, "Thank you."
Okay.
Like the floral print bow tie Mom gave me for Christmas.
That you never wear.
Jeez, that thing makes my eyes water.

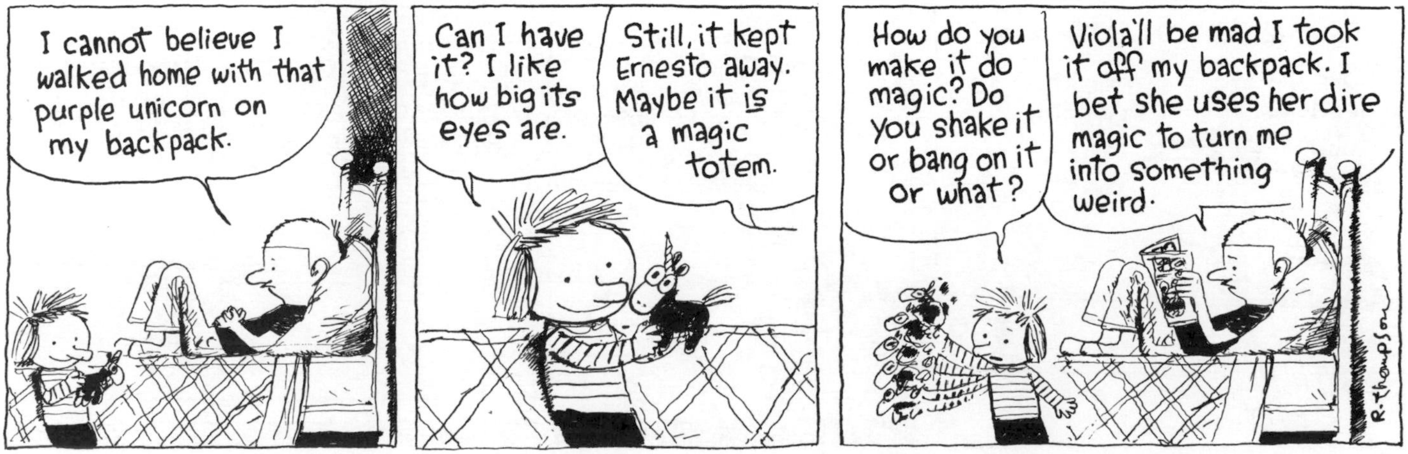
I cannot believe I walked home with that purple unicorn on my backpack.
Can I have it? I like how big its eyes are.
Still, it kept Ernesto away. Maybe it is a magic totem.
How do you make it do magic? Do you shake it or bang on it or what?
Viola'll be mad I took it off my backpack. I bet she uses her dire magic to turn me into something weird.
R. thompson

Hi, Petey! Hee hee hee!
Hi, Petey! Ha ha ha!
Hee hee hee!
La la la la la la!
La la la la la la la la!
Hi, Petey!
Alice, will you and your friends get outta my room?
Dill!
Good one, Dill. You blew our cover.
Yeah, Dill.
I forgot which hand I had the puppet on.
thompson

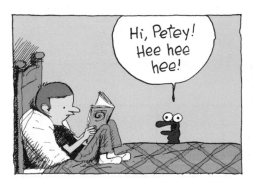

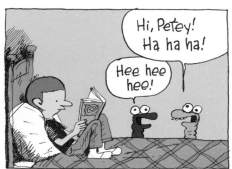

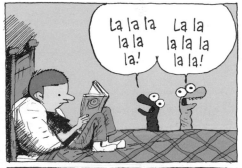

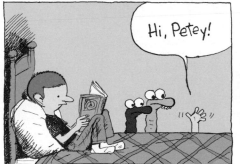

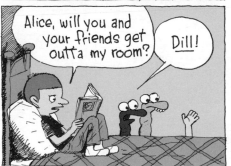

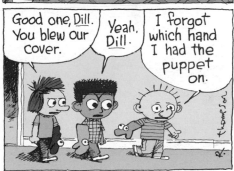

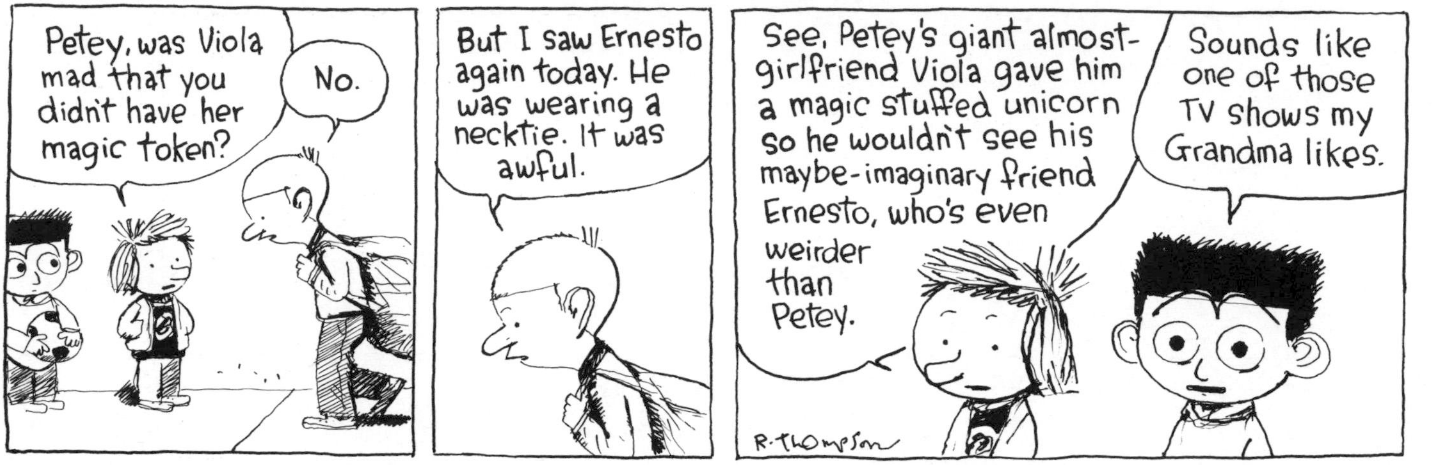
Petey, was Viola mad that you didn't have her magic token?
No.
But I saw Ernesto again today. He was wearing a necktie. It was awful.
See, Petey's giant almost-girlfriend Viola gave him a magic stuffed unicorn so he wouldn't see his maybe-imaginary friend Ernesto, who's even weirder than Petey.
Sounds like one of those TV shows my Grandma likes.
R. Thompson

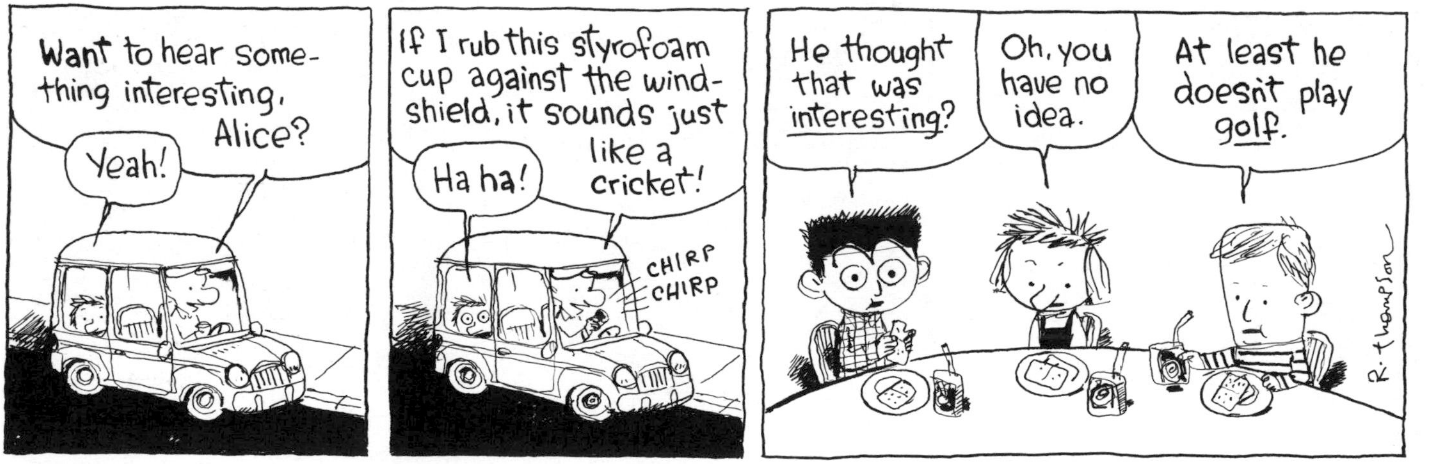
Want to hear some-thing interesting, Alice?
Yeah!
If I rub this styrofoam cup against the wind-shield, it sounds just like a cricket!
Ha ha!
CHIRP CHIRP
He thought that was interesting?
Oh, you have no idea.
At least he doesn't play golf.
R. Thompson

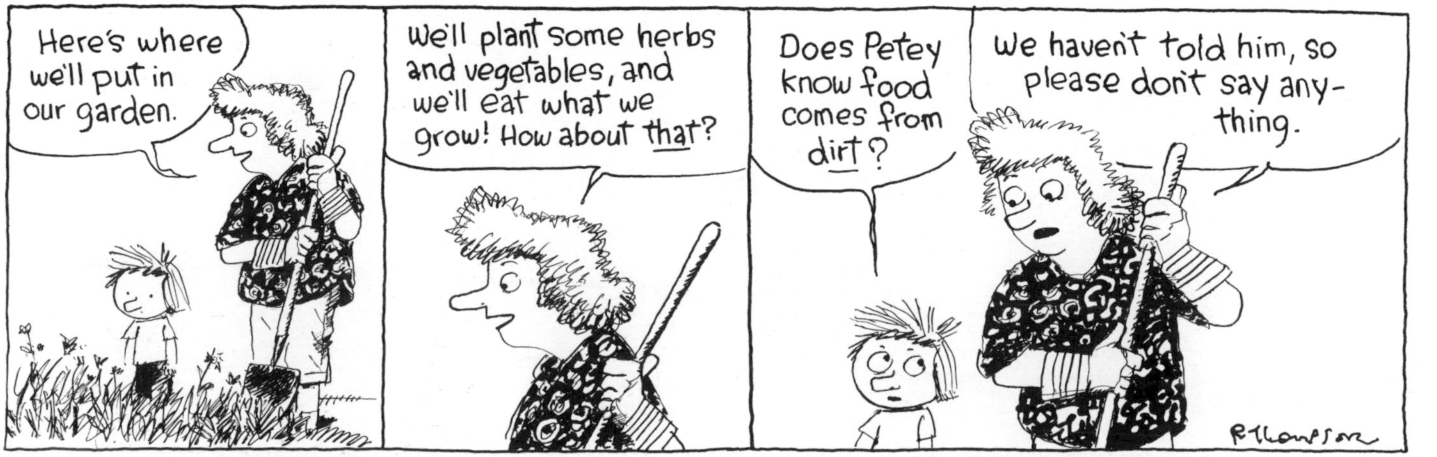
Here's where we'll put in our garden.
We'll plant some herbs and vegetables, and we'll eat what we grow! How about that?
Does Petey know food comes from dirt?
We haven't told him, so please don't say any-thing.
R. Thompson

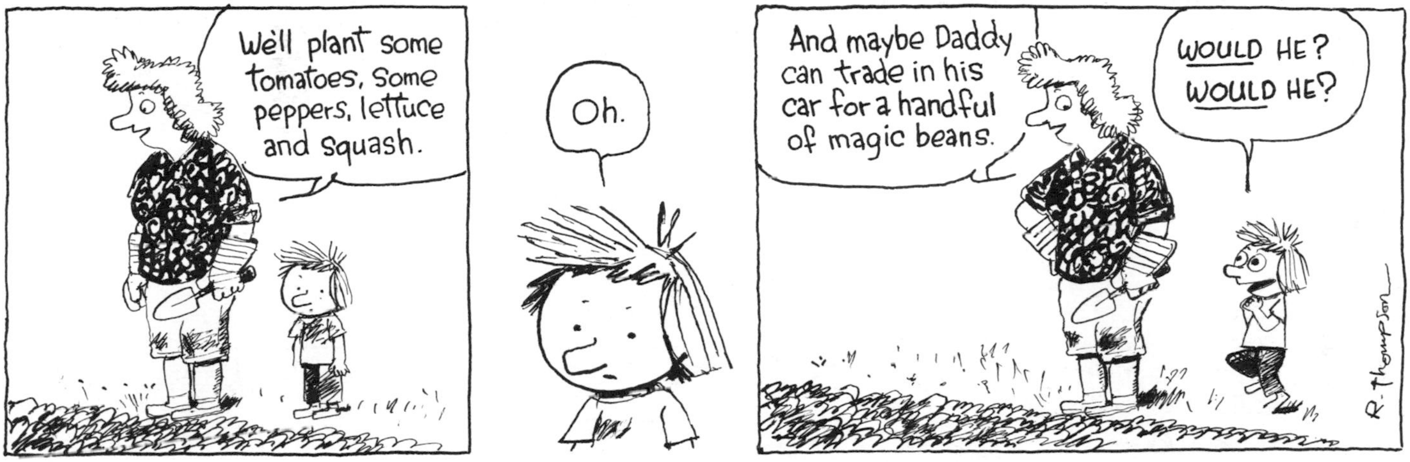
We'll plant some tomatoes, some peppers, lettuce and squash.
Oh.
And maybe Daddy can trade in his car for a handful of magic beans.
WOULD HE? WOULD HE?
R. thompson

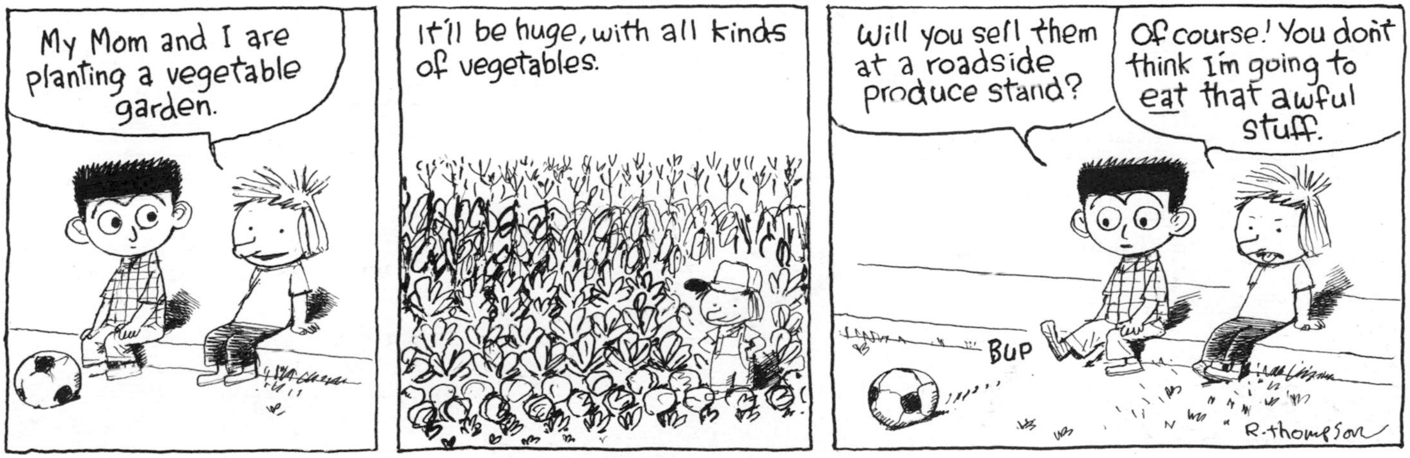
My Mom and I are planting a vegetable garden.
It'll be huge, with all kinds of vegetables.
Will you sell them at a roadside produce stand?
Of course! You don't think I'm going to eat that awful stuff.
BUP
R. thompson

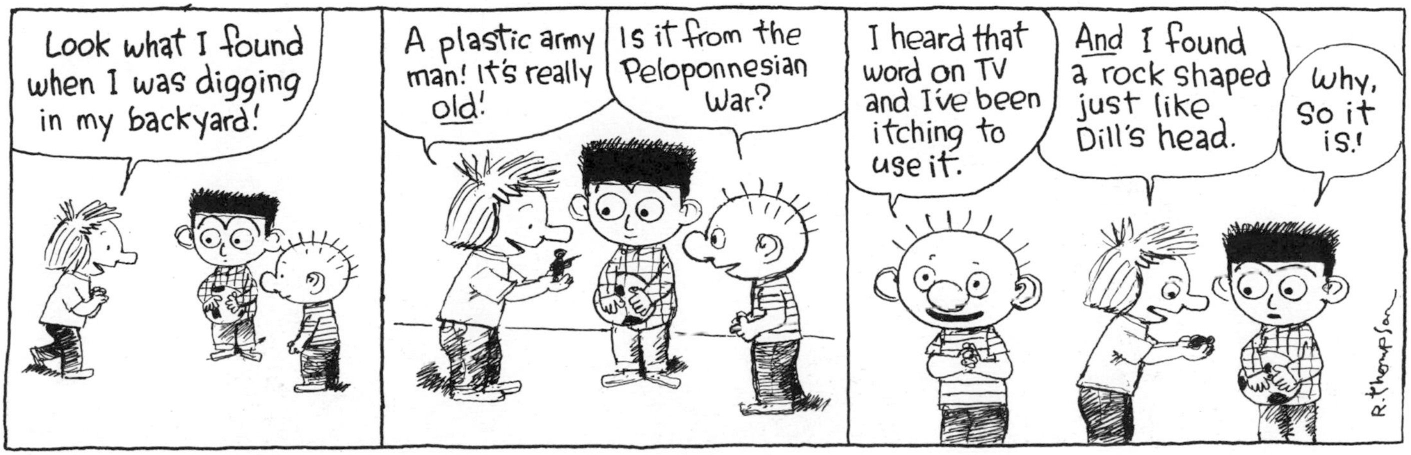
Look what I found when I was digging in my backyard!
A plastic army man! It's really old!
Is it from the Peloponnesian War?
I heard that word on TV and I've been itching to use it.
And I found a rock shaped just like Dill's head.
Why, so it is!
R. thompson

Today at preschool Miss Bliss told us about these old myths. They were <u>great</u>!

The best was about this giant named Alice who got to hold up the Earth and the sky!

MINE MINE MINE MINE MINE MINE MINE

His name was "Atlas."

Atlas? That's <u>silly</u>.

So I gotta rethink my career again.

Alice, you won't even hold <u>still</u> for five minutes.

64

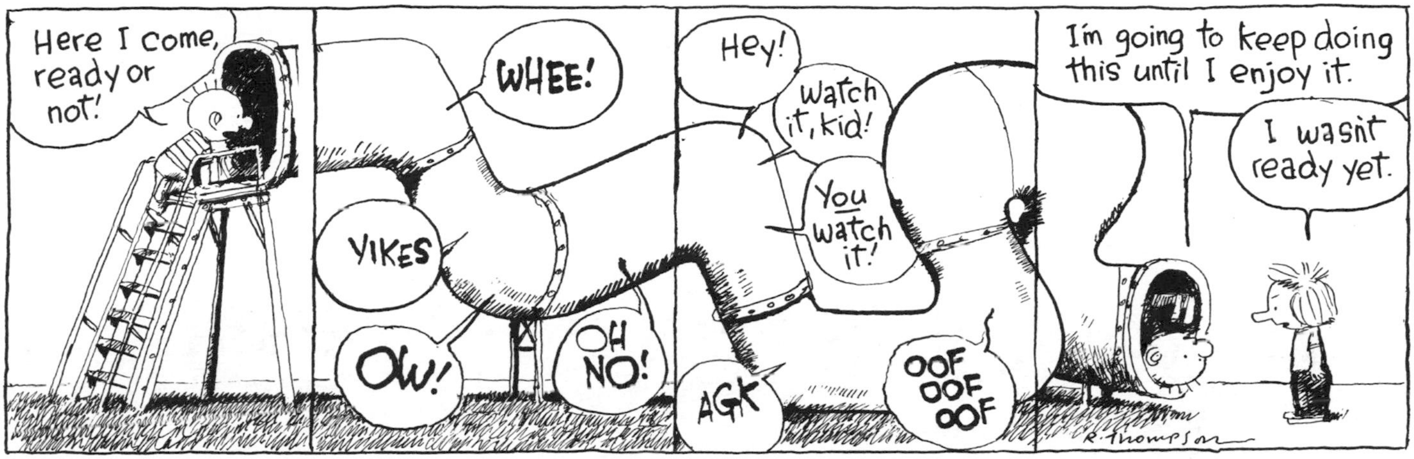
Here I come, ready or not!
WHEE!
YIKES
OW!
OH NO!
Hey!
Watch it, kid!
You watch it!
AGK
OOF OOF OOF
I'm going to keep doing this until I enjoy it.
I wasn't ready yet.

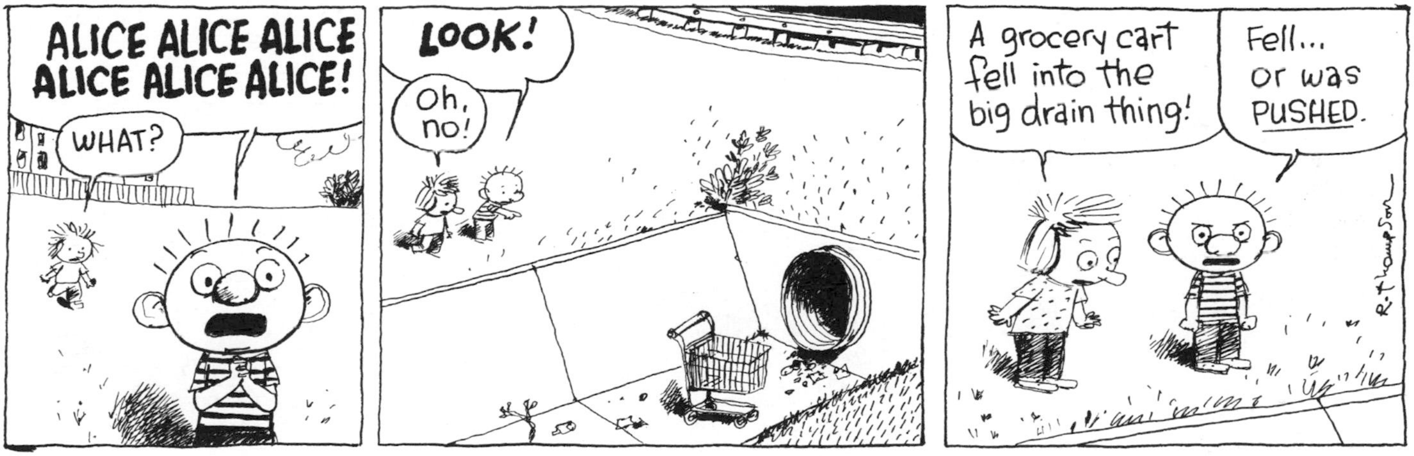
ALICE ALICE ALICE ALICE ALICE ALICE!
WHAT?
LOOK!
Oh, no!
A grocery cart fell into the big drain thing!
Fell... or was PUSHED.

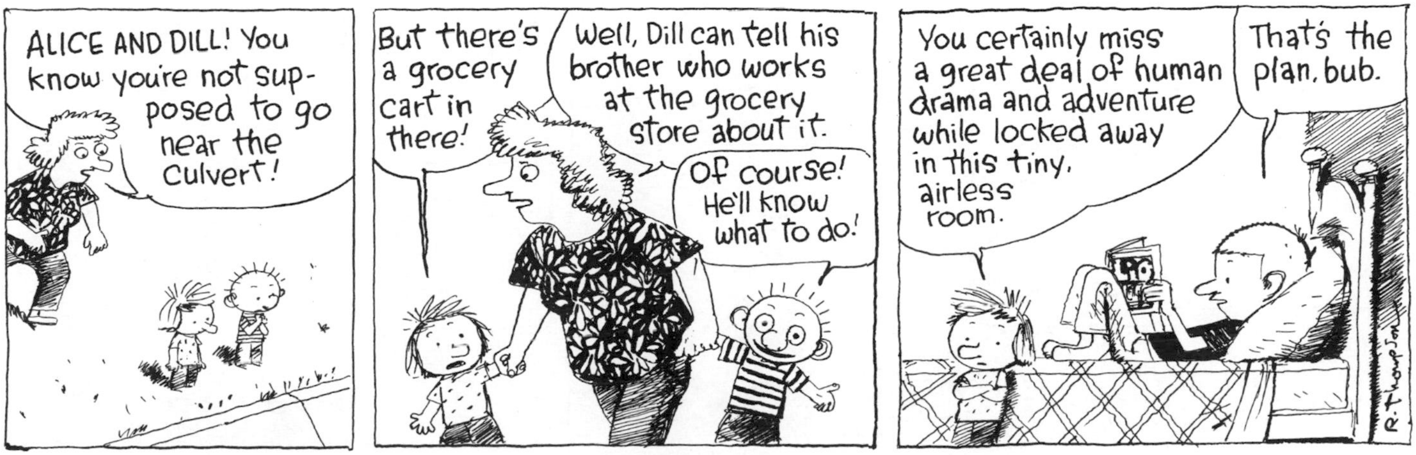
ALICE AND DILL! You know you're not supposed to go near the Culvert!
But there's a grocery cart in there!
Well, Dill can tell his brother who works at the grocery store about it.
Of course! He'll know what to do!
You certainly miss a great deal of human drama and adventure while locked away in this tiny, airless room.
That's the plan, bub.

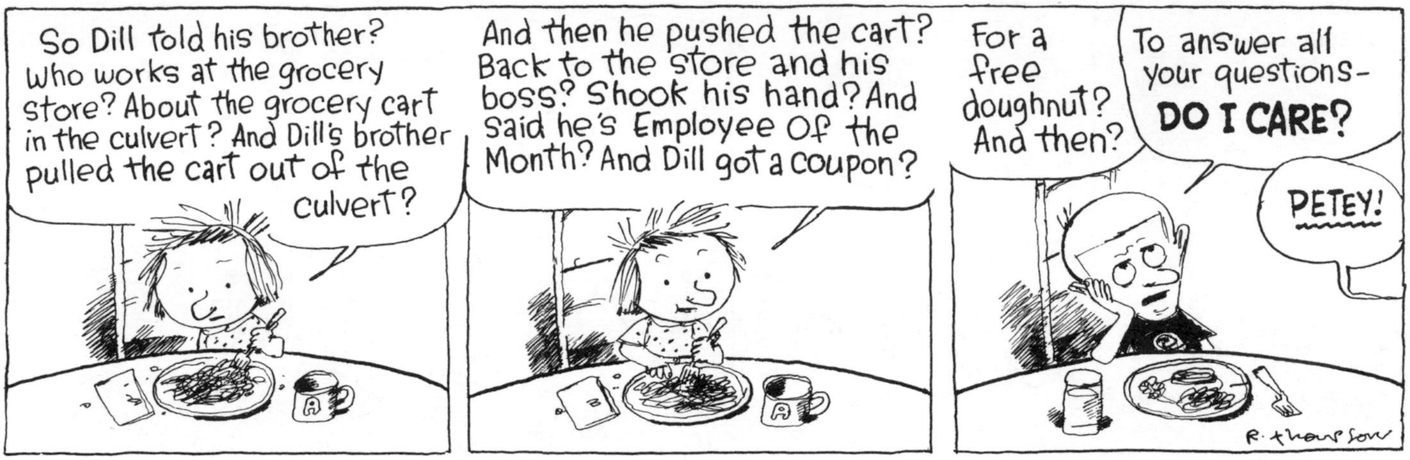
So Dill told his brother? Who works at the grocery store? About the grocery cart in the culvert? And Dill's brother pulled the cart out of the culvert?
And then he pushed the cart? Back to the store and his boss? Shook his hand? And said he's Employee Of the Month? And Dill got a coupon?
For a free doughnut? And then?
To answer all your questions- DO I CARE?
PETEY!

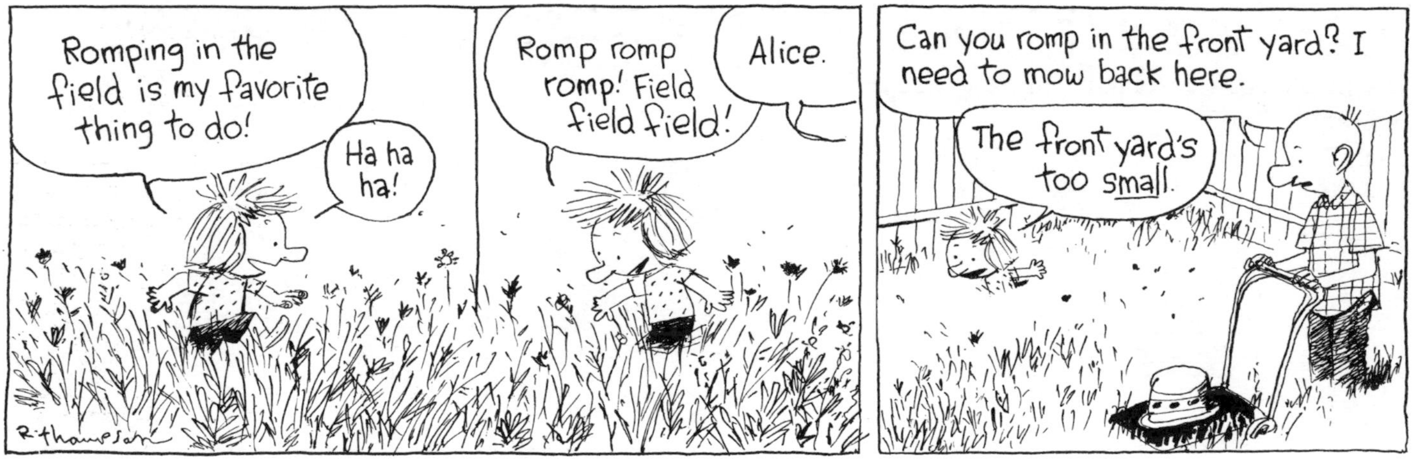
Romping in the field is my favorite thing to do!
Ha ha ha!
Romp romp romp! Field field field!
Alice.
Can you romp in the front yard? I need to mow back here.
The front yard's too small.

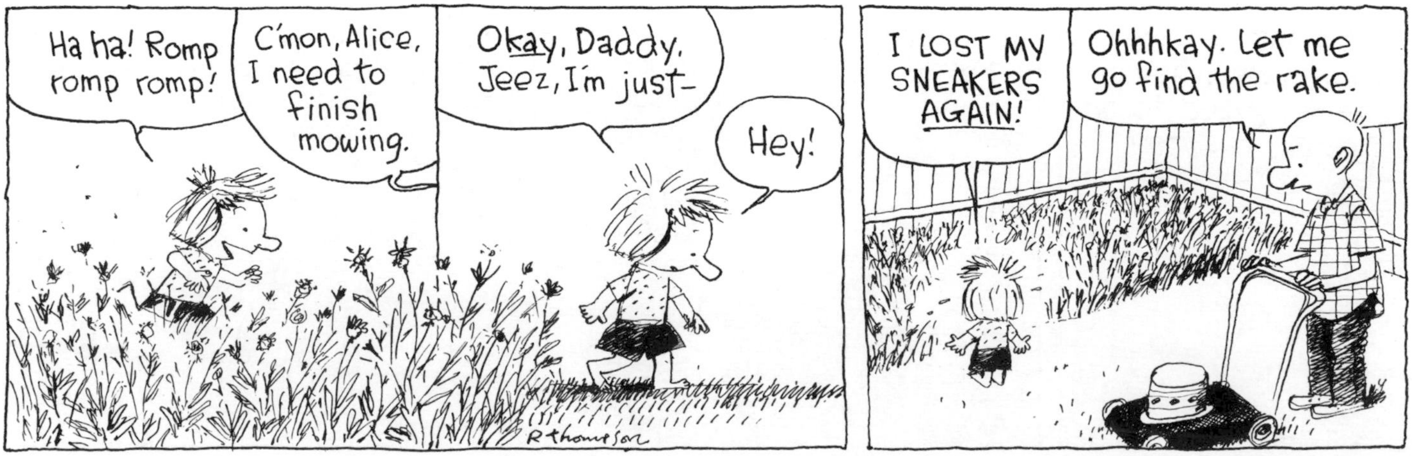
Ha ha! Romp romp romp!
C'mon, Alice, I need to finish mowing.
Okay, Daddy. Jeez, I'm just-
Hey!
I LOST MY SNEAKERS AGAIN!
Ohhhkay. Let me go find the rake.

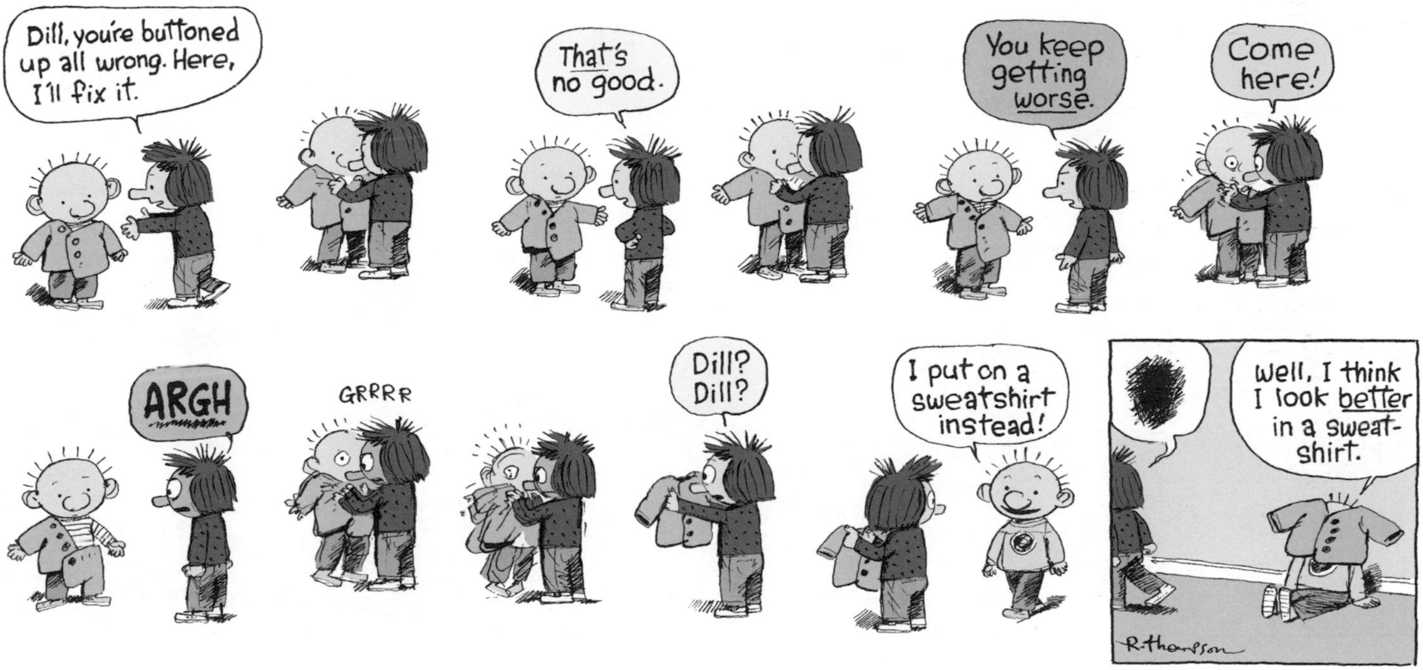
Dill, you're buttoned up all wrong. Here, I'll fix it.
That's no good.
You keep getting worse.
Come here!
ARGH
GRRRR
Dill? Dill?
I put on a sweatshirt instead!
Well, I think I look better in a sweat-shirt.
R. Thompson

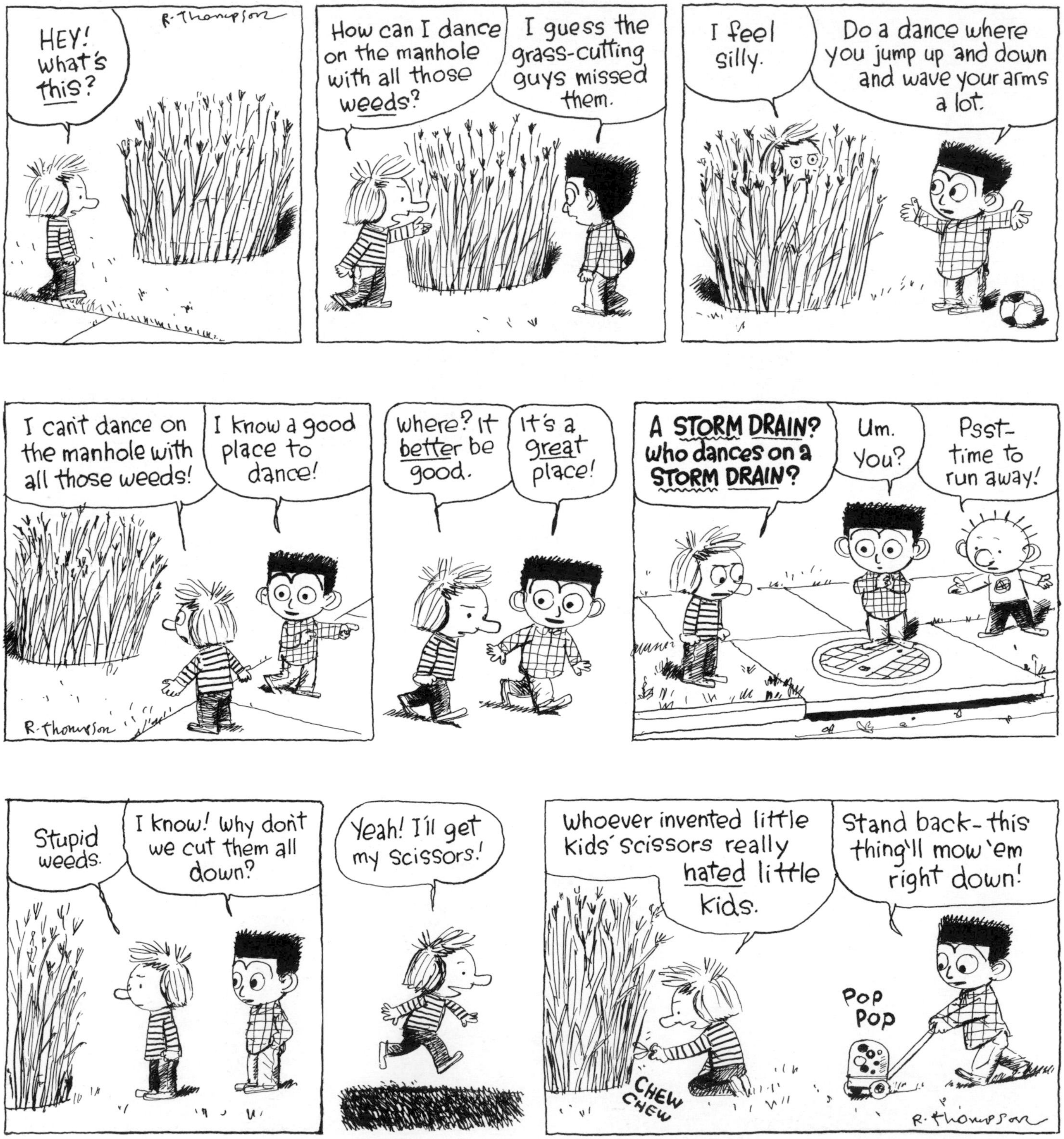
R. Thompson
HEY! what's this?
How can I dance on the manhole with all those weeds?
I guess the grass-cutting guys missed them.
I feel silly.
Do a dance where you jump up and down and wave your arms a lot.
I can't dance on the manhole with all those weeds!
I know a good place to dance!
R. Thompson
Where? It better be good.
It's a great place!
A STORM DRAIN? Who dances on a STORM DRAIN?
Um. You?
Psst- time to run away!
Stupid weeds.
I know! Why don't we cut them all down?
Yeah! I'll get my scissors!
Whoever invented little kids' scissors really hated little kids.
CHEW CHEW
Stand back- this thing'll mow 'em right down!
POP POP
R. Thompson

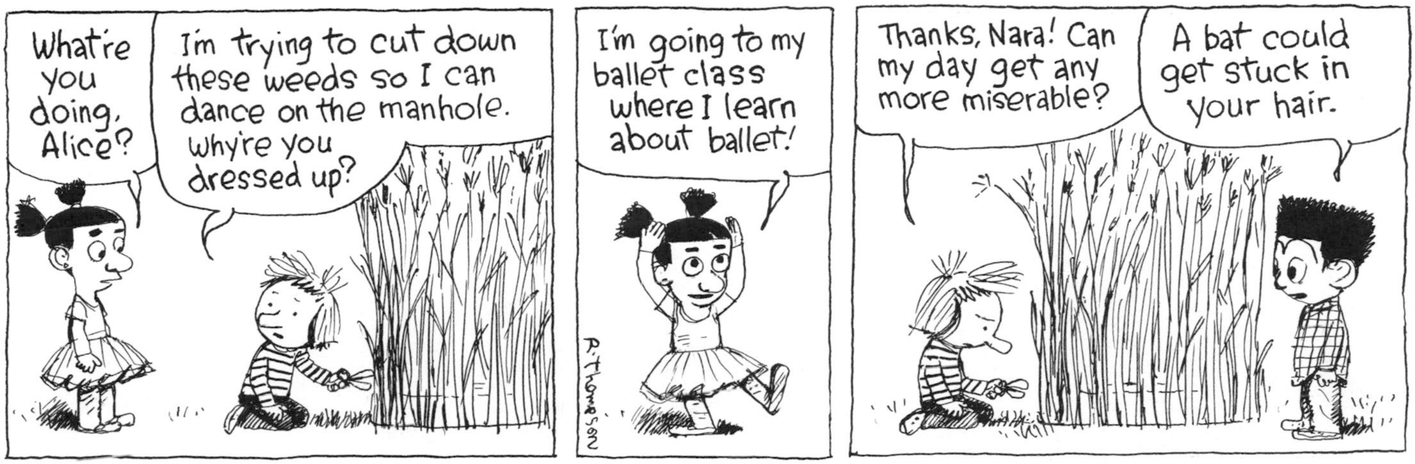

What're you doing, Alice?
I'm trying to cut down these weeds so I can dance on the manhole. Why're you dressed up?
I'm going to my ballet class where I learn about ballet!
Thanks, Nara! Can my day get any more miserable?
A bat could get stuck in your hair.
R. Thompson

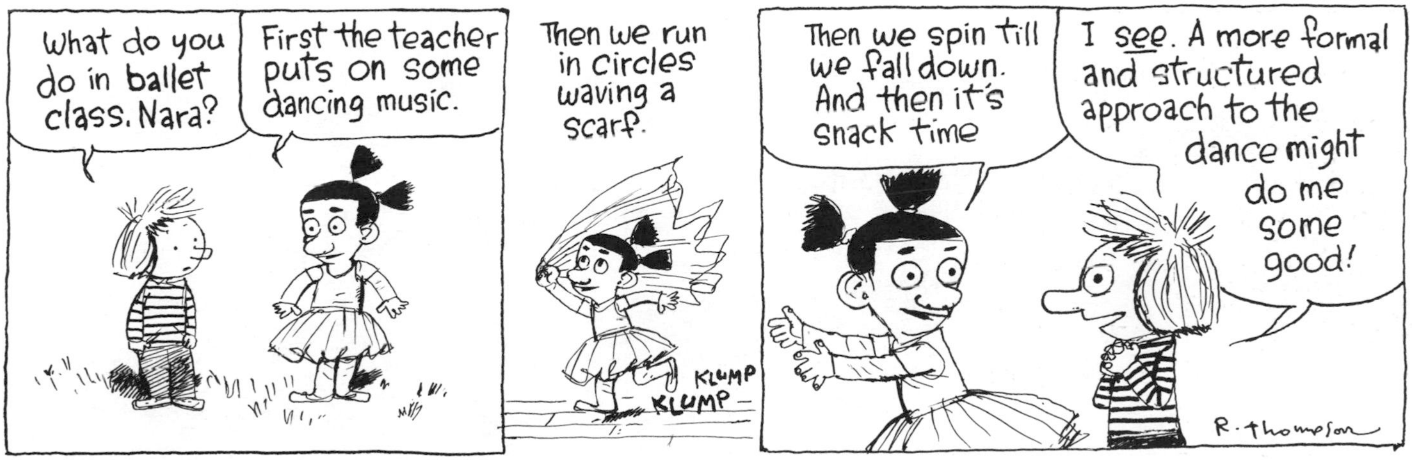

What do you do in ballet class, Nara?
First the teacher puts on some dancing music.
Then we run in circles waving a scarf.
KLUMP
KLUMP
Then we spin till we fall down. And then it's snack time
I see. A more formal and structured approach to the dance might do me some good!
R. Thompson

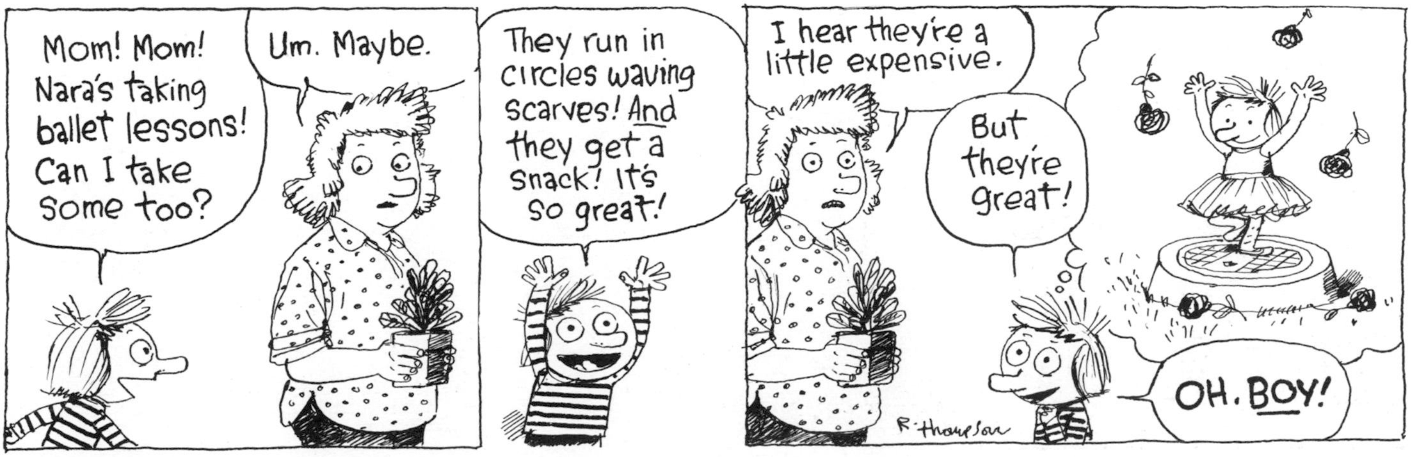

Mom! Mom! Nara's taking ballet lessons! Can I take some too?
Um. Maybe.
They run in circles waving scarves! And they get a snack! It's so great!
I hear they're a little expensive.
But they're great!
OH. BOY!
R. Thompson

Hey- what's that?
We ran out of regular napkins. That's left over from your fourth birthday party!
It's got Klanky Robot on it. You used to love him! We've got almost 500 of those left!
But now I hate Klanky Robot! I can't stand to look at him!
He's an assault on my dignity! A slap to my pride!
PETEY.
No! The very sight of Klanky Robot disgusts me profoundly!
ARRHRR RRARRH ARRGH!
Petey! Don't you dare go chewing your arm off!
You're too old for that!
Your brother chewed his foot off?
Well, he tried to.
I like Klanky Robot! He taught me everything I know!
PUBF
FBUP
R. THOMPSON

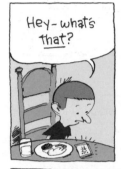

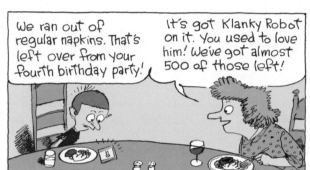

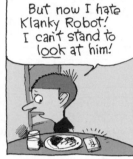

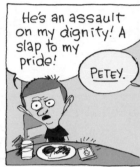

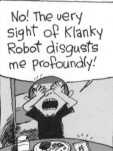

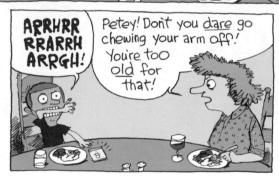

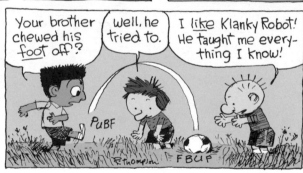

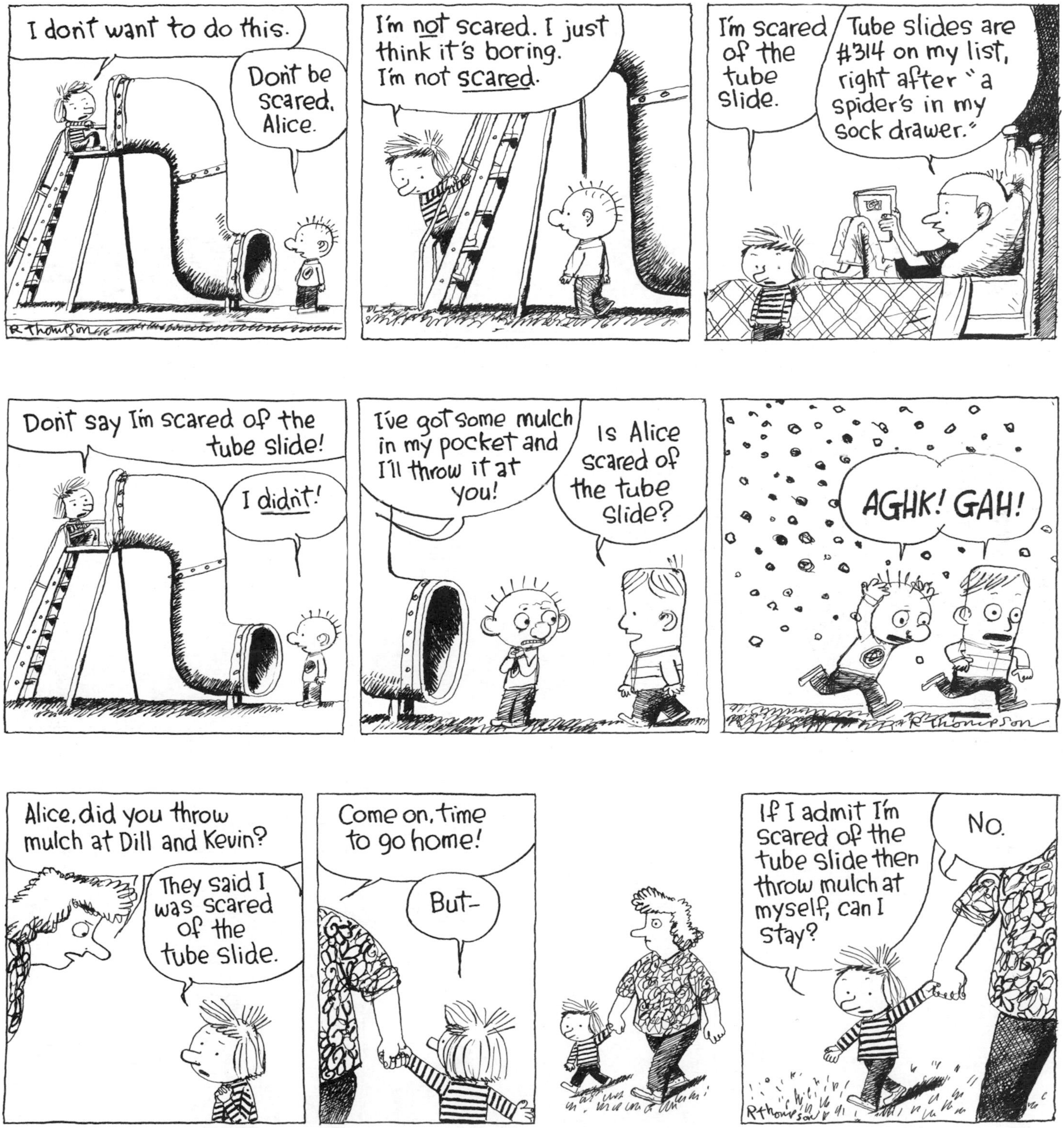
I don't want to do this.
Don't be scared, Alice.
R Thompson
I'm not scared. I just think it's boring. I'm not scared.
I'm scared of the tube slide.
Tube slides are #314 on my list, right after "a spider's in my sock drawer."
Don't say I'm scared of the tube slide!
I didn't!
I've got some mulch in my pocket and I'll throw it at you!
Is Alice scared of the tube slide?
AGHK! GAH!
R Thompson
Alice, did you throw mulch at Dill and Kevin?
They said I was scared of the tube slide.
Come on, time to go home!
But-
If I admit I'm scared of the tube slide then throw mulch at myself, can I stay?
No.
R Thompson

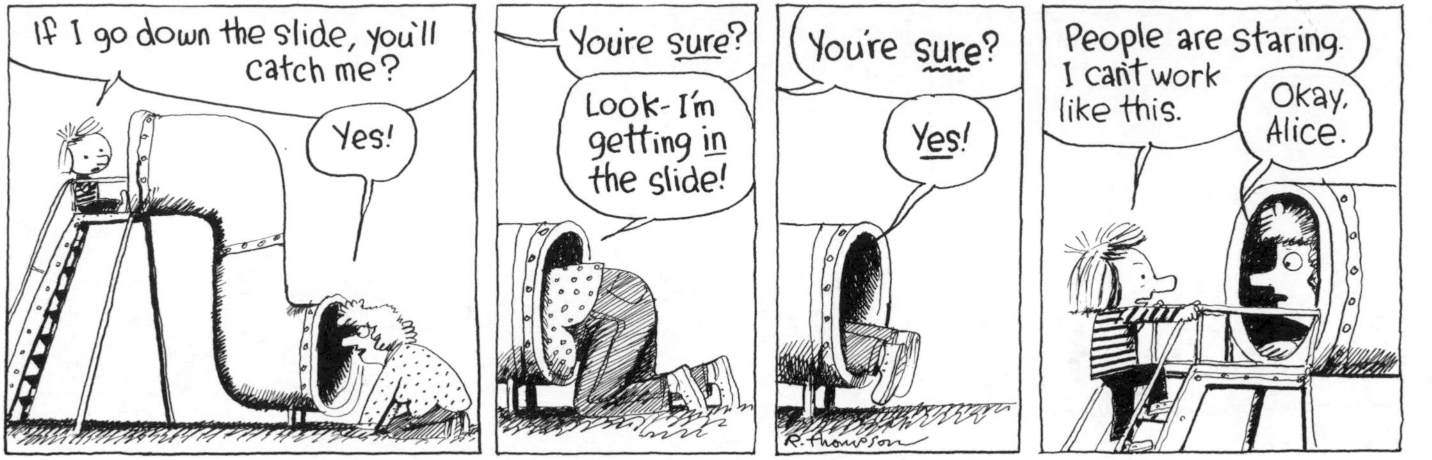
If I go down the slide, you'll catch me?
Yes!
You're sure?
Look- I'm getting in the slide!
You're sure?
Yes!
People are staring. I can't work like this.
Okay, Alice.

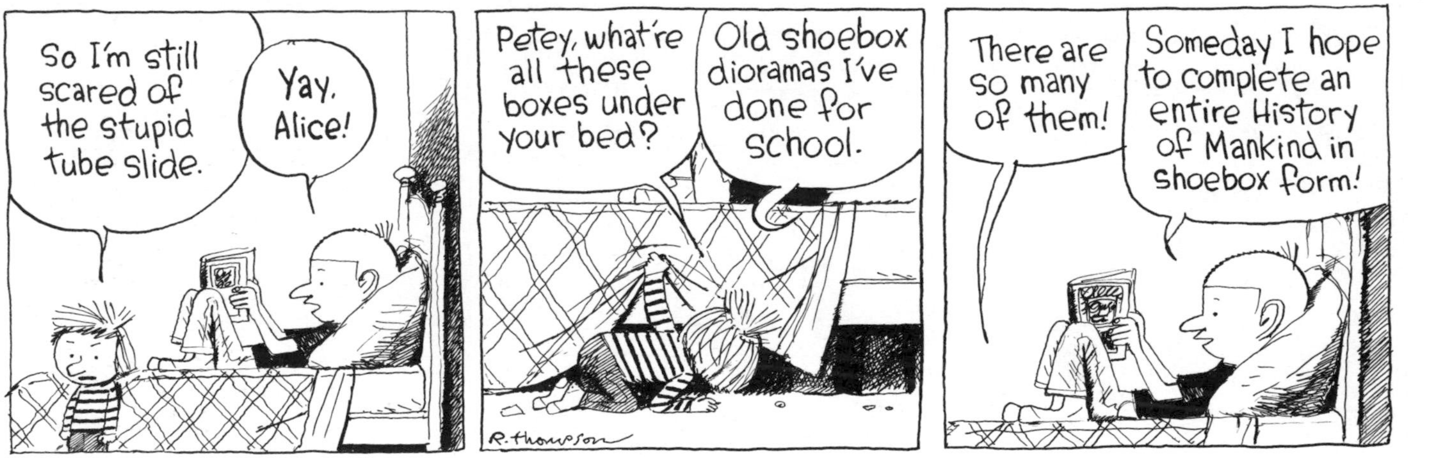
So I'm still scared of the stupid tube slide.
Yay, Alice!
Petey, what're all these boxes under your bed?
Old shoebox dioramas I've done for school.
There are so many of them!
Someday I hope to complete an entire History of Mankind in shoebox form!

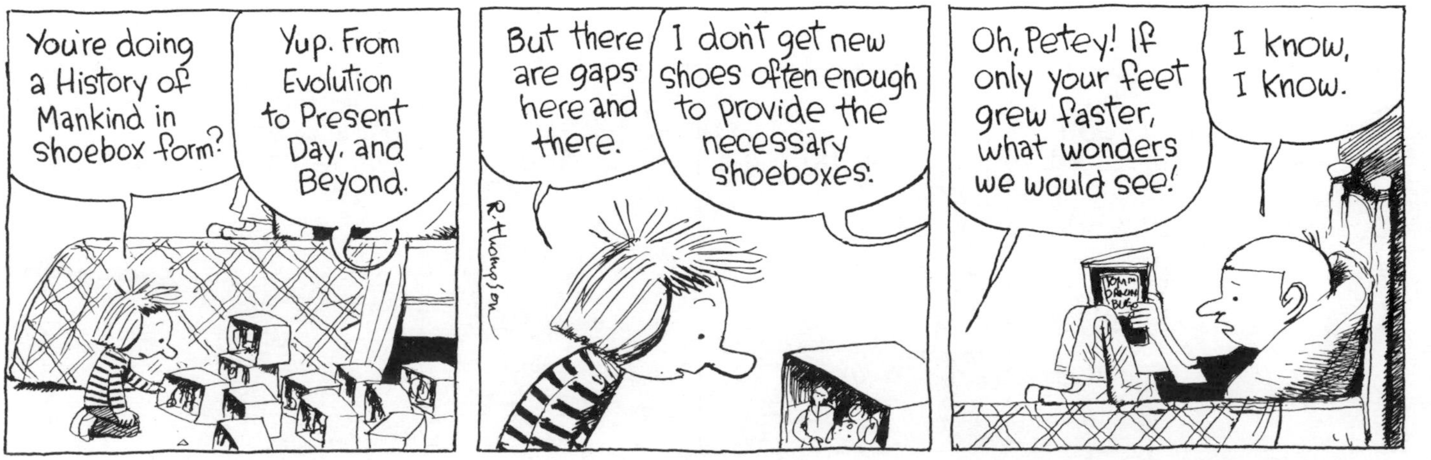
You're doing a History of Mankind in shoebox form?
Yup. From Evolution to Present Day, and Beyond.
But there are gaps here and there.
I don't get new shoes often enough to provide the necessary shoeboxes.
Oh, Petey! If only your feet grew faster, what wonders we would see!
I know, I know.

Petey, you should invite your little friend Ernesto over for a playdate!
MOM. I don't think so.
I've heard a story about a little boy who rolled his eyes so far back in his head they stuck like that.
He spent the rest of his life staring at his brains.
And I'll bet he felt pretty silly.
MOM.
I never heard of him. You'd think he'd be more famous.
Well, it's not working.
Try crossing your eyes first, just to loosen 'em up.
RThompson

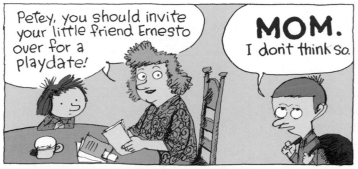

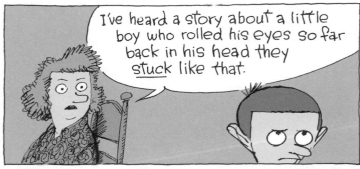

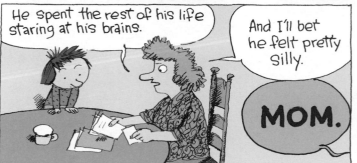

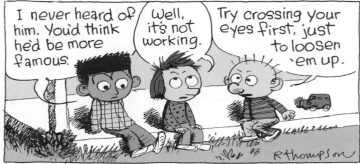

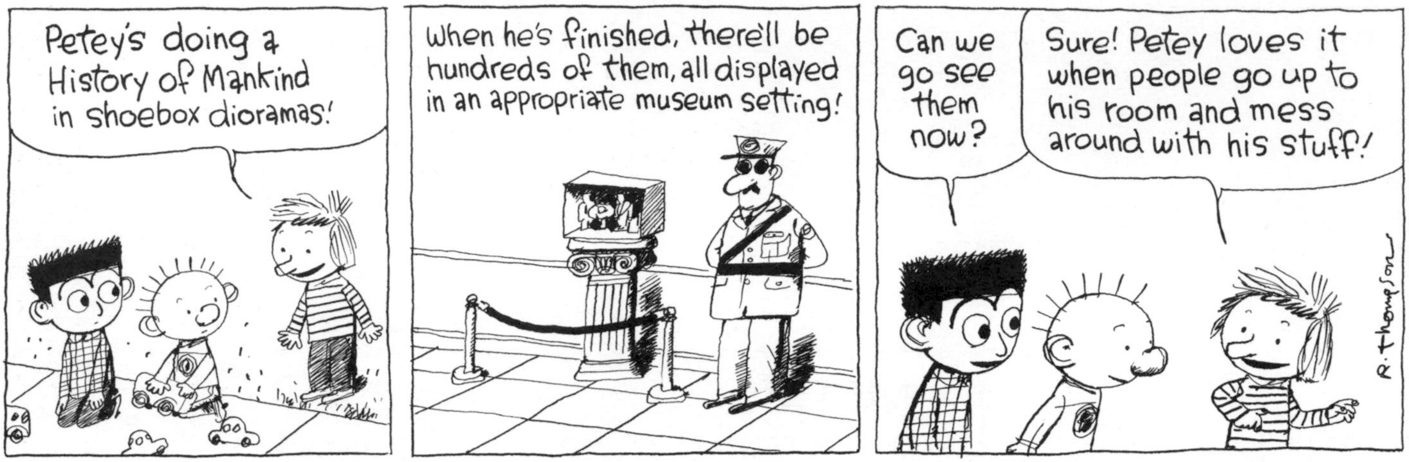
Petey's doing a History of Mankind in shoebox dioramas!
When he's finished, there'll be hundreds of them, all displayed in an appropriate museum setting!
Can we go see them now?
Sure! Petey loves it when people go up to his room and mess around with his stuff!
R. Thompson

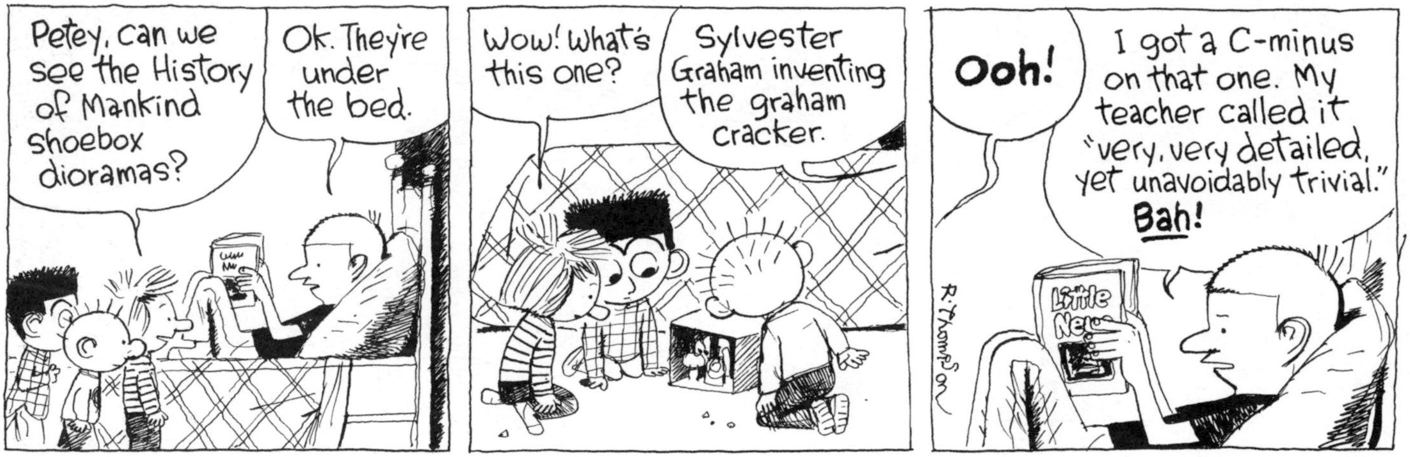
Petey, can we see the History of Mankind shoebox dioramas?
Ok. They're under the bed.
Wow! What's this one?
Sylvester Graham inventing the graham cracker.
Ooh!
I got a C-minus on that one. My teacher called it "very, very detailed, yet unavoidably trivial." Bah!
Little News
R. Thompson

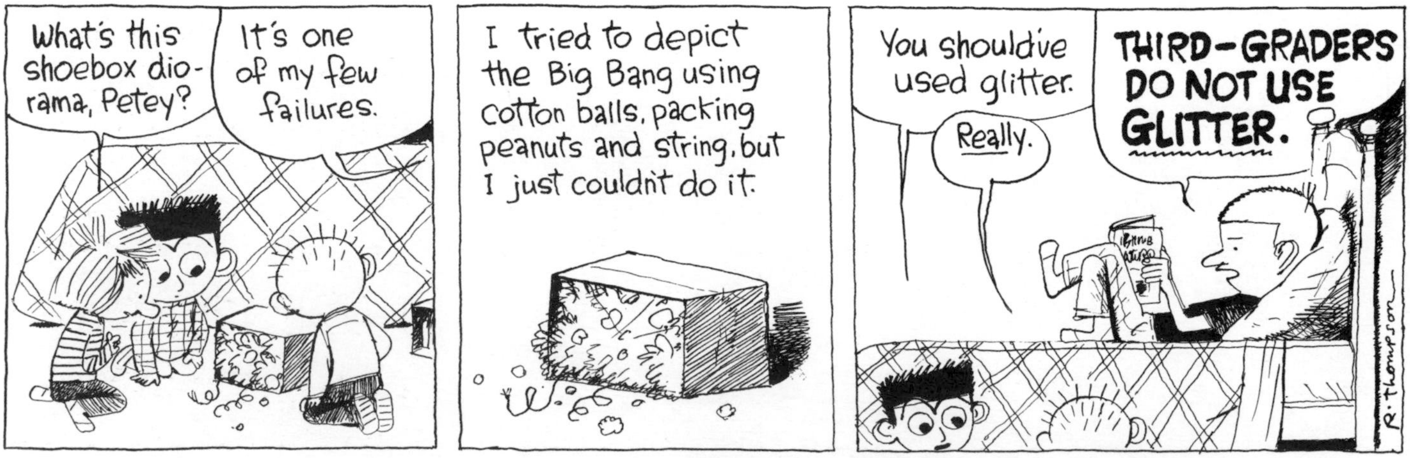
What's this shoebox dio-rama, Petey?
It's one of my few failures.
I tried to depict the Big Bang using cotton balls, packing peanuts and string, but I just couldn't do it.
You should've used glitter.
Really.
THIRD-GRADERS DO NOT USE GLITTER.
R. Thompson

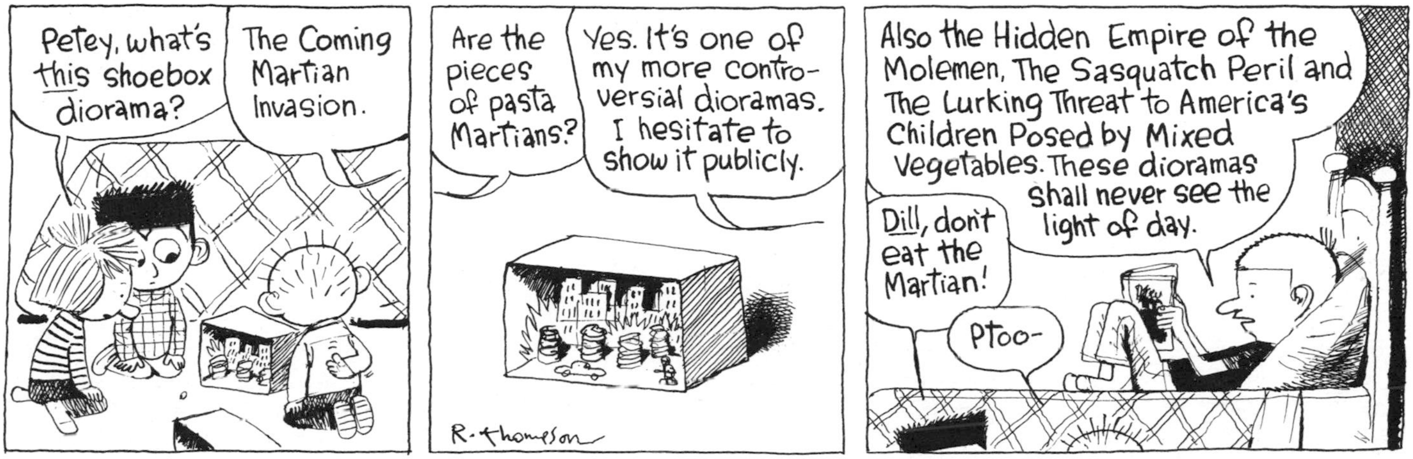
Petey, what's this shoebox diorama?
The Coming Martian Invasion.
Are the pieces of pasta Martians?
Yes. It's one of my more controversial dioramas. I hesitate to show it publicly.
Also the Hidden Empire of the Molemen, The Sasquatch Peril and The Lurking Threat to America's Children Posed by Mixed Vegetables. These dioramas shall never see the light of day.
Dill, don't eat the Martian!
Ptoo-

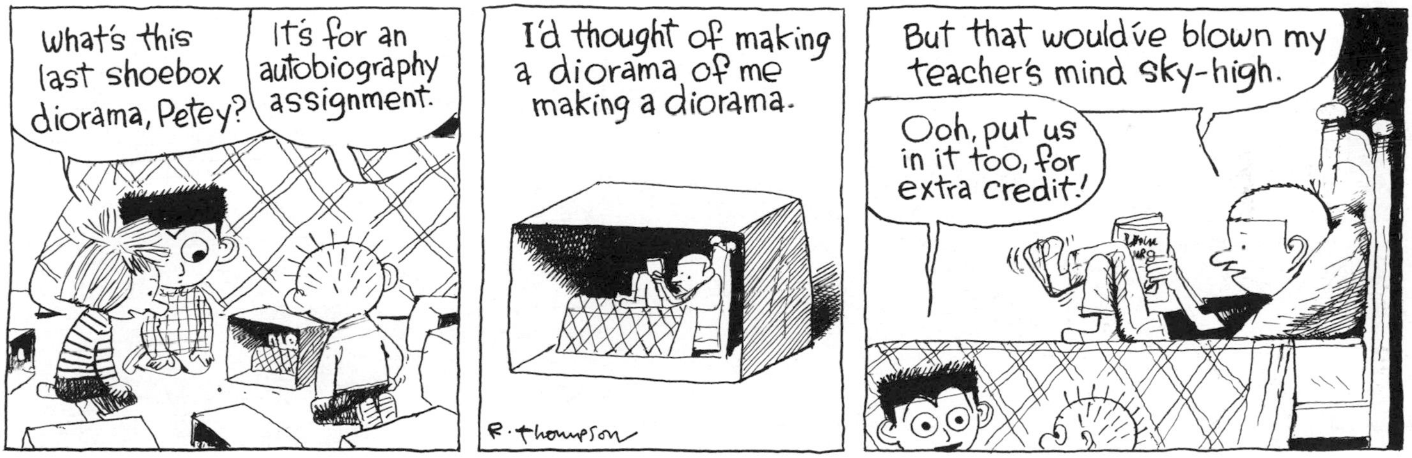
What's this last shoebox diorama, Petey?
It's for an autobiography assignment.
I'd thought of making a diorama of me making a diorama.
But that would've blown my teacher's mind sky-high.
Ooh, put us in it too, for extra credit!

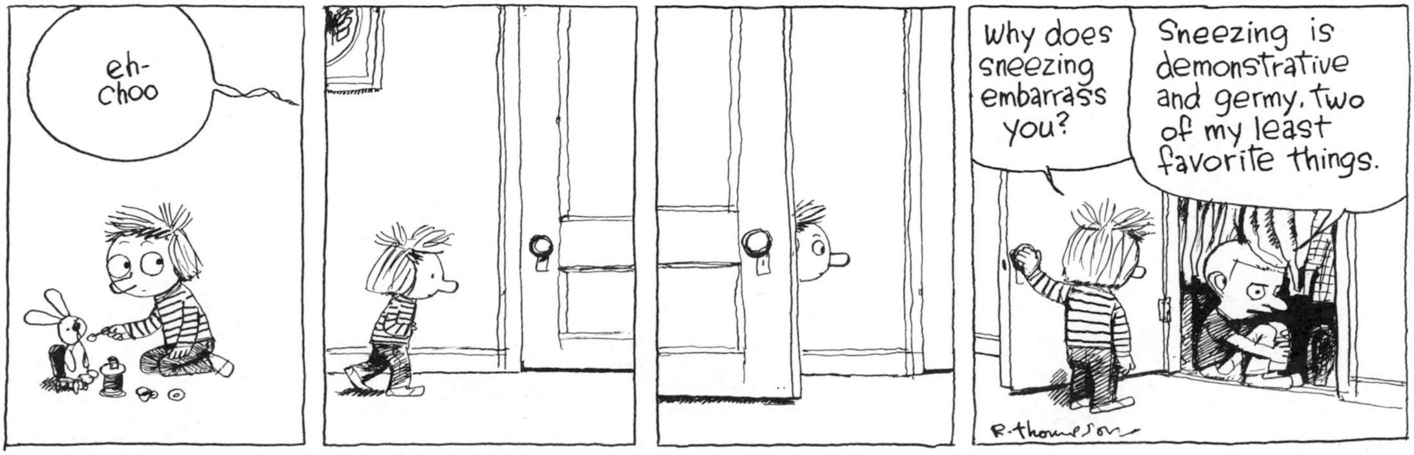
eh-
choo
Why does sneezing embarrass you?
Sneezing is demonstrative and germy, two of my least favorite things.

I dropped my shoe into the under-swing trench. Can you get it?
Okay.
Here, is this it?
That's not it.
This one?
No. How many shoes are down there?
Lots. There are shoes, mittens, a baseball, a tricycle, some socks, some toys, and—
Hi, Dill.
And Kevin! What are you doing down here?
Trying to find my hat. This trench is really deep.
I'll help you. Let's go!
Dill?
Kevin?
CAN SOMEONE CALL THE FIREMEN TO GET ME DOWN OFF THIS SWING?
I'll call them!
R. Thompson

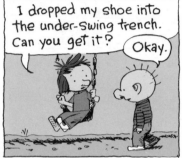

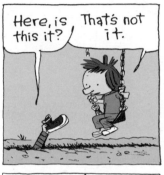

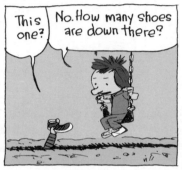

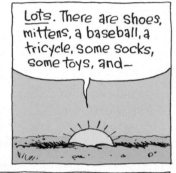

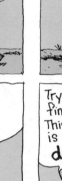

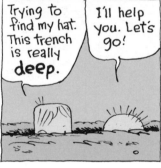

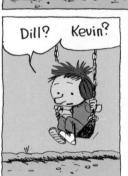

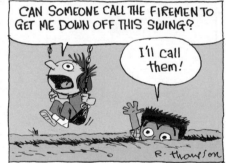

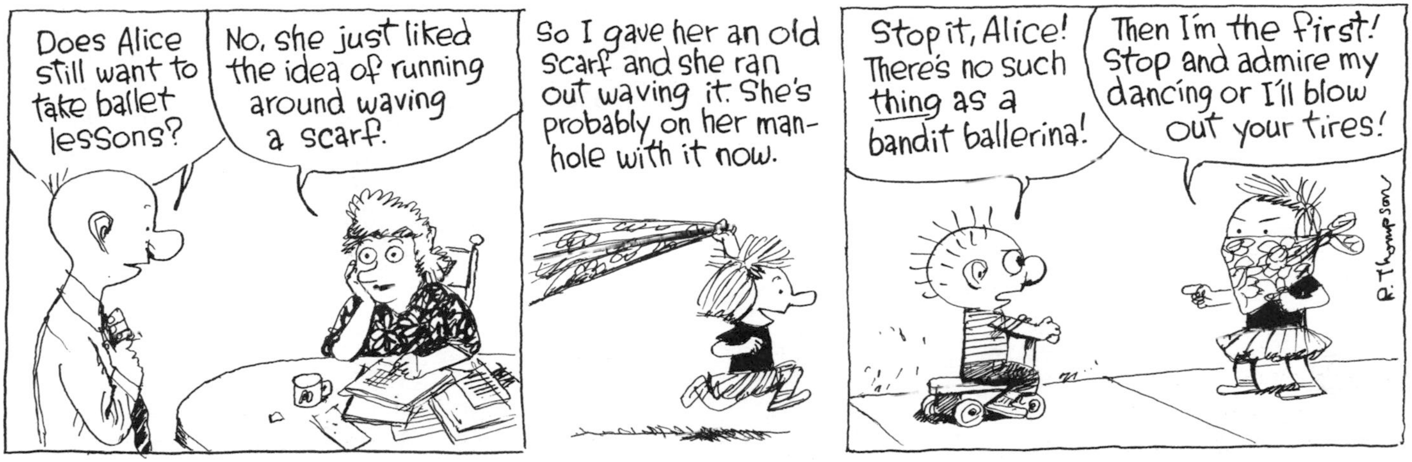
Does Alice still want to take ballet lessons?
No, she just liked the idea of running around waving a scarf.
So I gave her an old scarf and she ran out waving it. She's probably on her man-hole with it now.
Stop it, Alice! There's no such thing as a bandit ballerina!
Then I'm the first! Stop and admire my dancing or I'll blow out your tires!
R. Thompson

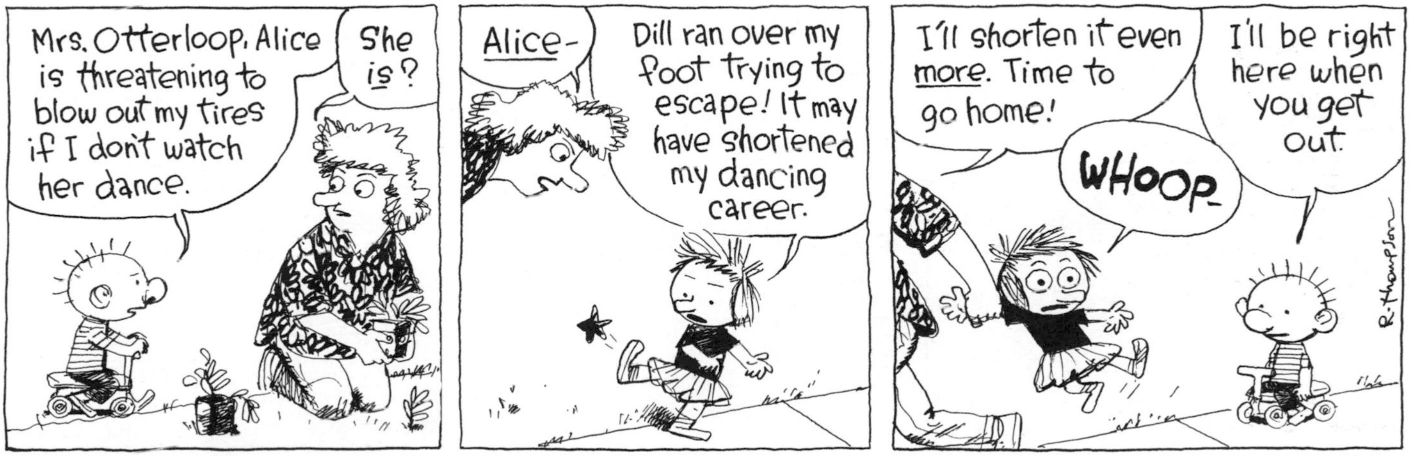
Mrs. Otterloop, Alice is threatening to blow out my tires if I don't watch her dance.
She is?
Alice-
Dill ran over my foot trying to escape! It may have shortened my dancing career.
I'll shorten it even more. Time to go home!
WHOOP-
I'll be right here when you get out.
R. Thompson

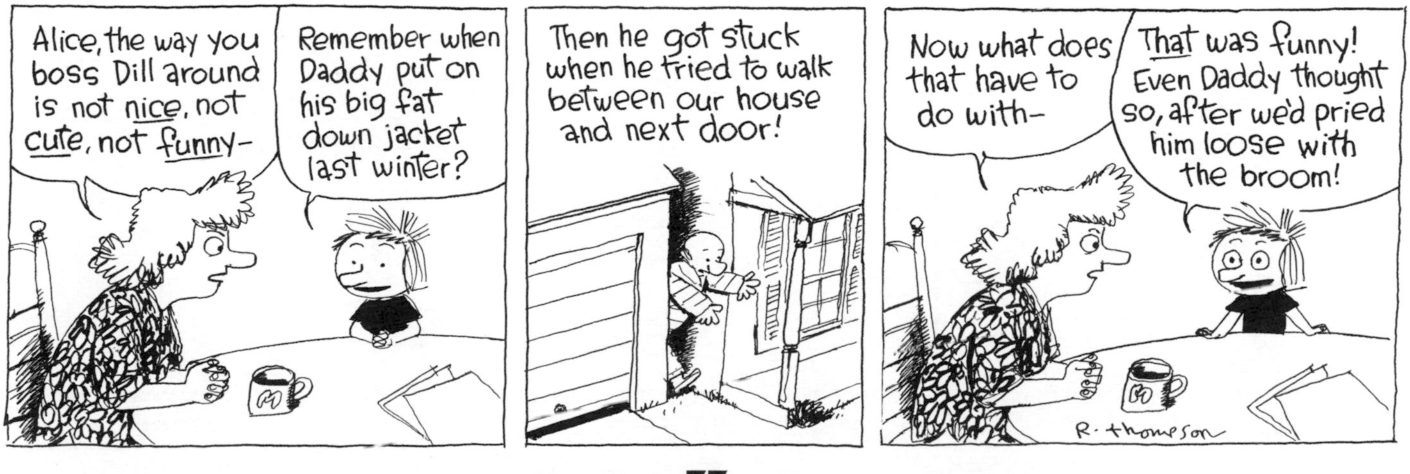
Alice, the way you boss Dill around is not nice, not cute, not funny-
Remember when Daddy put on his big fat down jacket last winter?
Then he got stuck when he tried to walk between our house and next door!
Now what does that have to do with-
That was funny! Even Daddy thought so, after we'd pried him loose with the broom!
R. Thompson

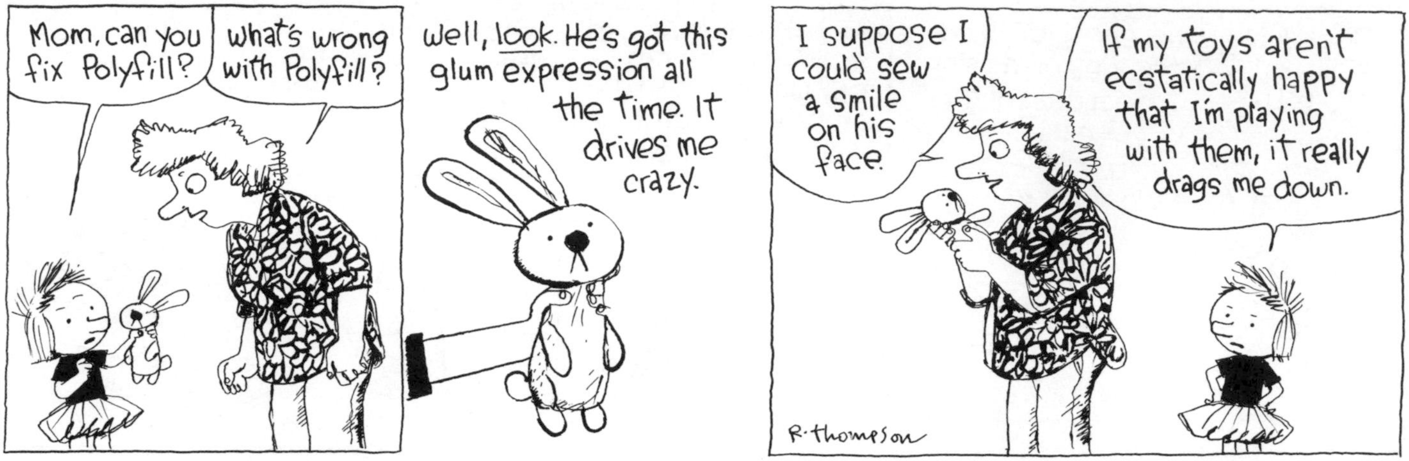
Mom, can you fix Polyfill?
What's wrong with Polyfill?
Well, look. He's got this glum expression all the time. It drives me crazy.
I suppose I could sew a smile on his face.
If my toys aren't ecstatically happy that I'm playing with them, it really drags me down.
R. Thompson

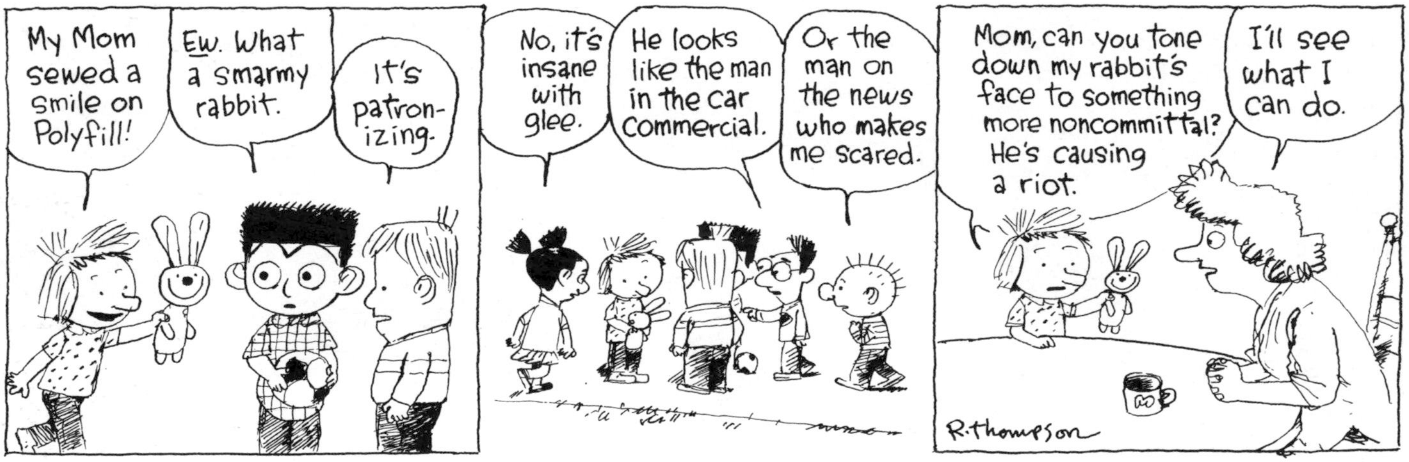
My Mom sewed a smile on Polyfill!
Ew. What a smarmy rabbit.
It's patronizing.
No, it's insane with glee.
He looks like the man in the car commercial.
Or the man on the news who makes me scared.
Mom, can you tone down my rabbit's face to something more noncommittal? He's causing a riot.
I'll see what I can do.
R. Thompson

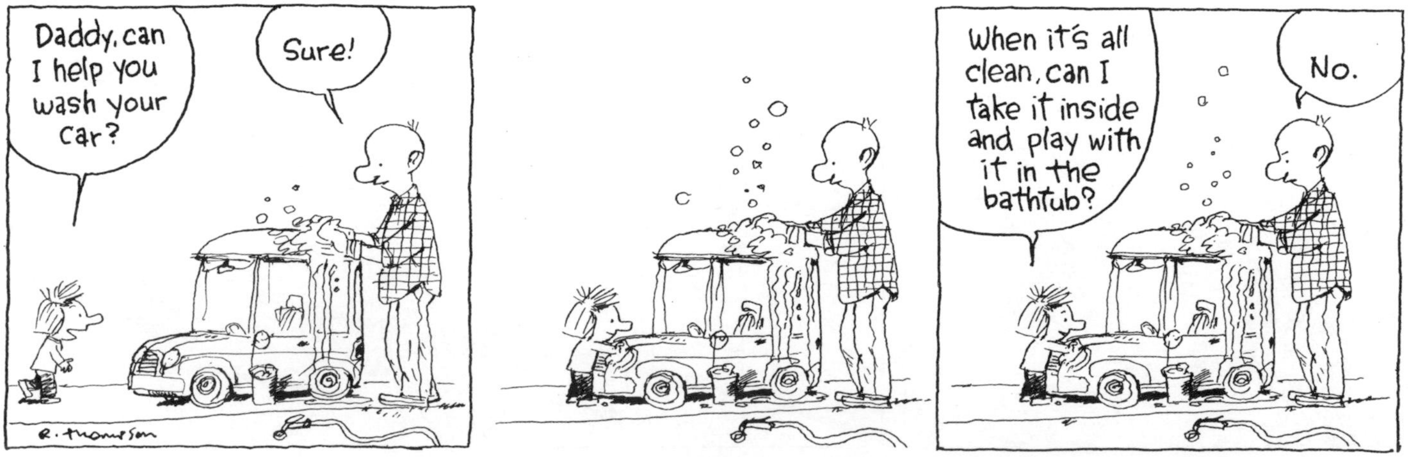
Daddy, can I help you wash your car?
Sure!
When it's all clean, can I take it inside and play with it in the bathtub?
No.
R. Thompson

Here I come, ready or not!
YI-
-KES
ZZ
CRASH
ZIIIIIIING
My Daddy says he used to wax the slide to make it slippery.
If I find your Daddy is behind this, I'm going to hide his little car in the sand-box again.
RThompson

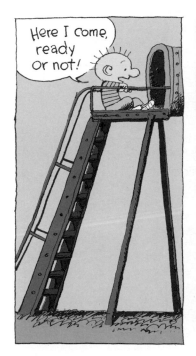

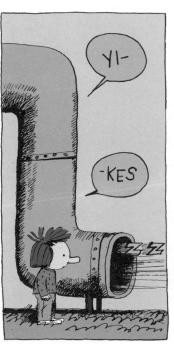

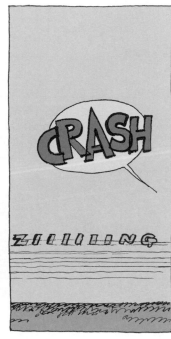

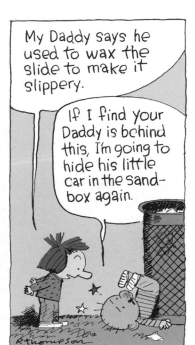

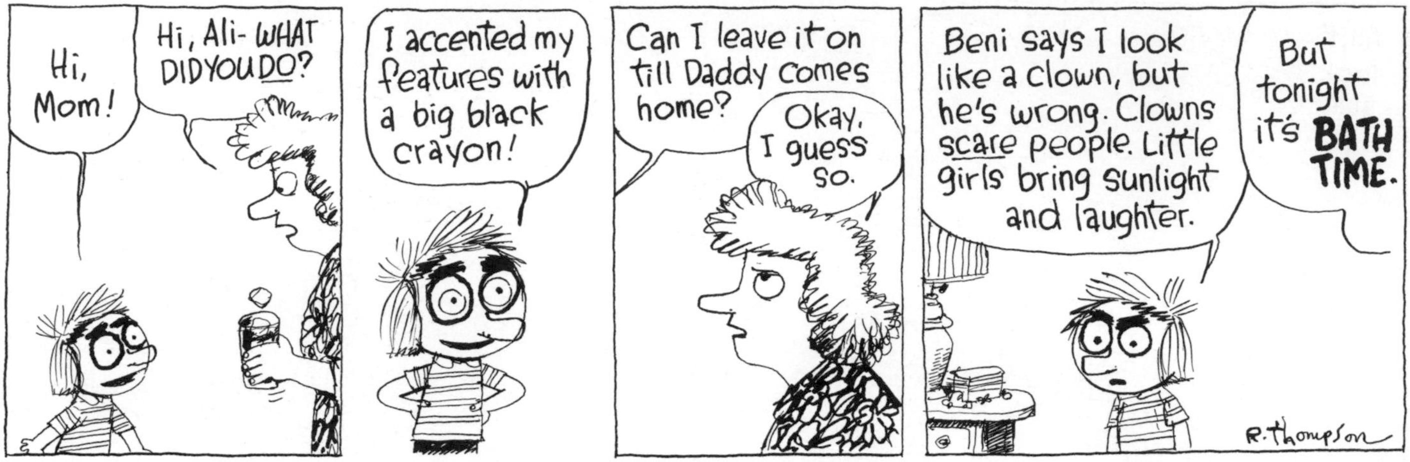
Hi, Mom!
Hi, Ali- WHAT DIDYOUDO?
I accented my features with a big black crayon!
Can I leave it on till Daddy comes home?
Okay, I guess so.
Beni says I look like a clown, but he's wrong. Clowns scare people. Little girls bring sunlight and laughter.
But tonight it's BATH TIME.
R. Thompson

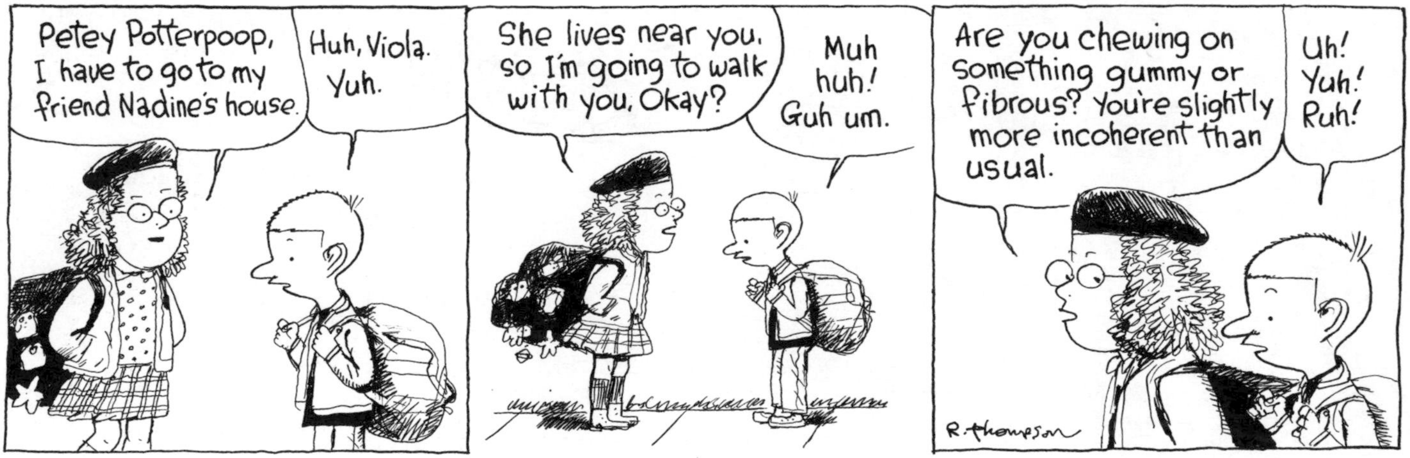
Petey Potterpoop, I have to go to my friend Nadine's house.
Huh, Viola. Yuh.
She lives near you, so I'm going to walk with you, Okay?
Muh huh! Guh um.
Are you chewing on something gummy or fibrous? You're slightly more incoherent than usual.
Uh! Yuh! Ruh!
R. Thompson

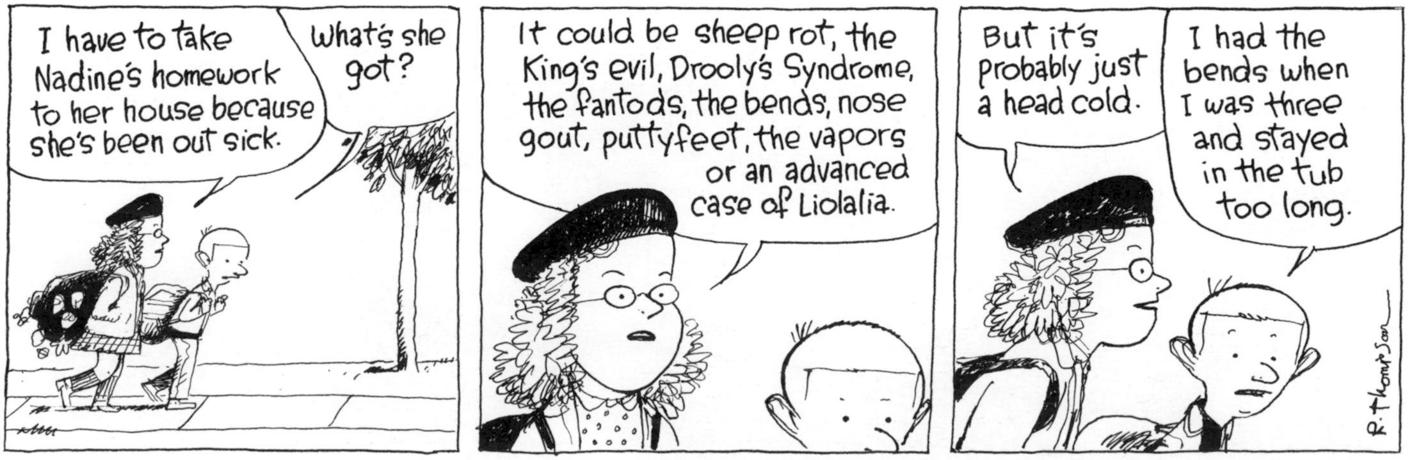
I have to take Nadine's homework to her house because she's been out sick.
What's she got?
It could be sheep rot, the King's evil, Drooly's Syndrome, the fantods, the bends, nose gout, puttyfeet, the vapors or an advanced case of Liolalia.
But it's probably just a head cold.
I had the bends when I was three and stayed in the tub too long.
R. Thompson

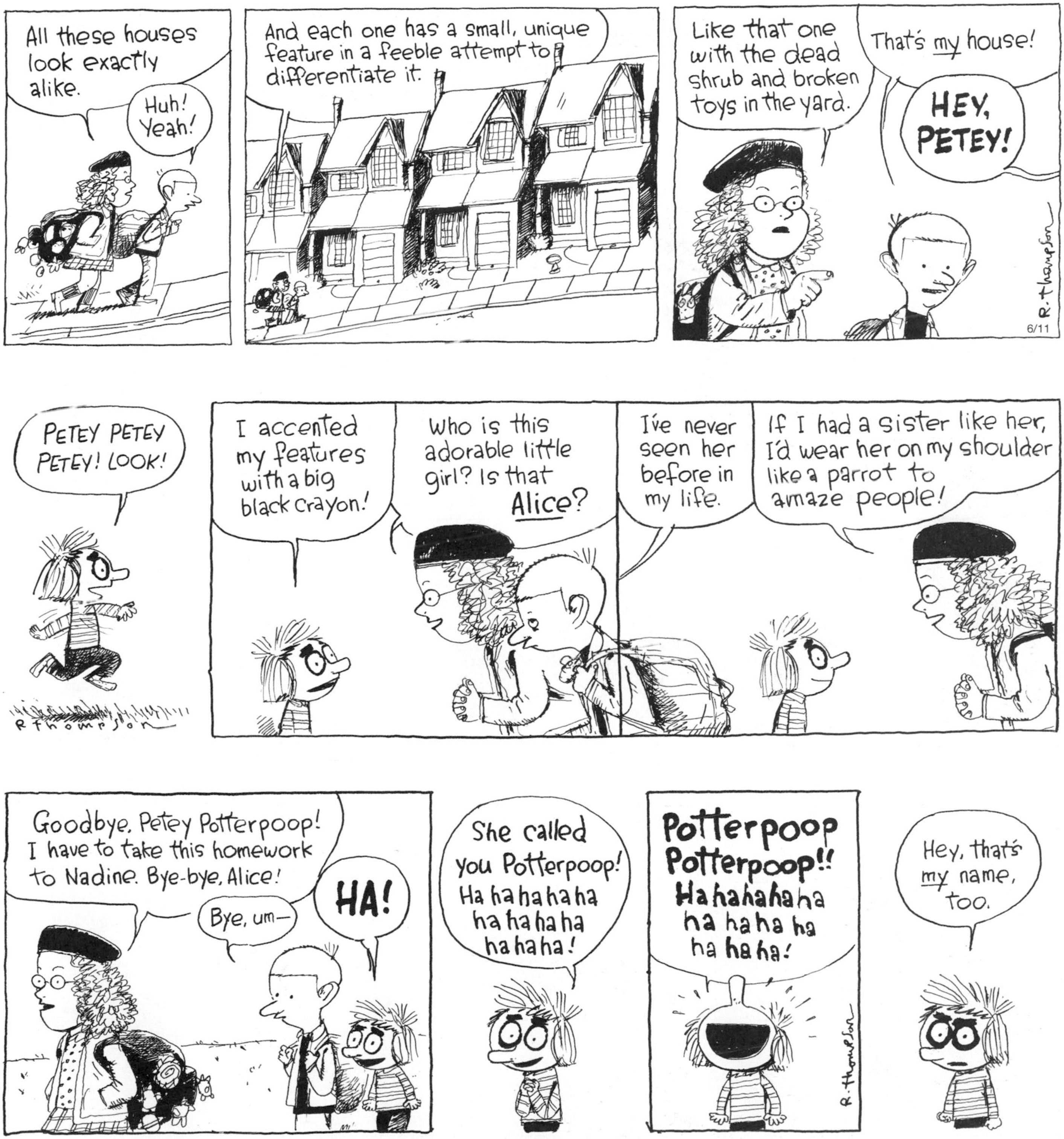
All these houses look exactly alike.
Huh! Yeah!
And each one has a small, unique feature in a feeble attempt to differentiate it.
Like that one with the dead shrub and broken toys in the yard.
That's my house!
HEY, PETEY!
R. Thompson
6/11
PETEY PETEY PETEY! LOOK!
R Thompson
I accented my features with a big black crayon!
Who is this adorable little girl? Is that Alice?
I've never seen her before in my life.
If I had a sister like her, I'd wear her on my shoulder like a parrot to amaze people!
Goodbye, Petey Potterpoop! I have to take this homework to Nadine. Bye-bye, Alice!
Bye, um—
HA!
She called you Potterpoop! Ha ha ha ha ha ha ha ha ha ha ha ha ha ha!
Potterpoop Potterpoop!! Ha ha ha ha ha ha ha ha ha ha ha ha ha!
R. Thompson
Hey, that's my name, too.

SPIDER! SPIDER IN THE SINK!
EEEEEEEEEEEEEEEEEEEEE
Children! That is not a spider!
Come back inside, please!
So a damp piece of fuzz sure looks like a spider.
If we had Spider Drills, this wouldn't have happened.
Or Damp Piece of Fuzz Drills.
R. thompson

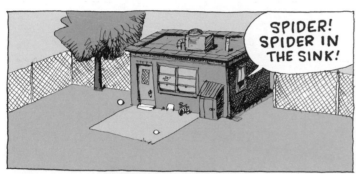

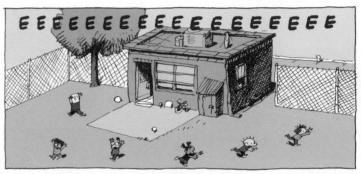

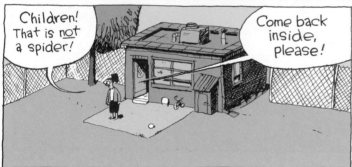

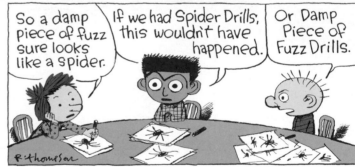

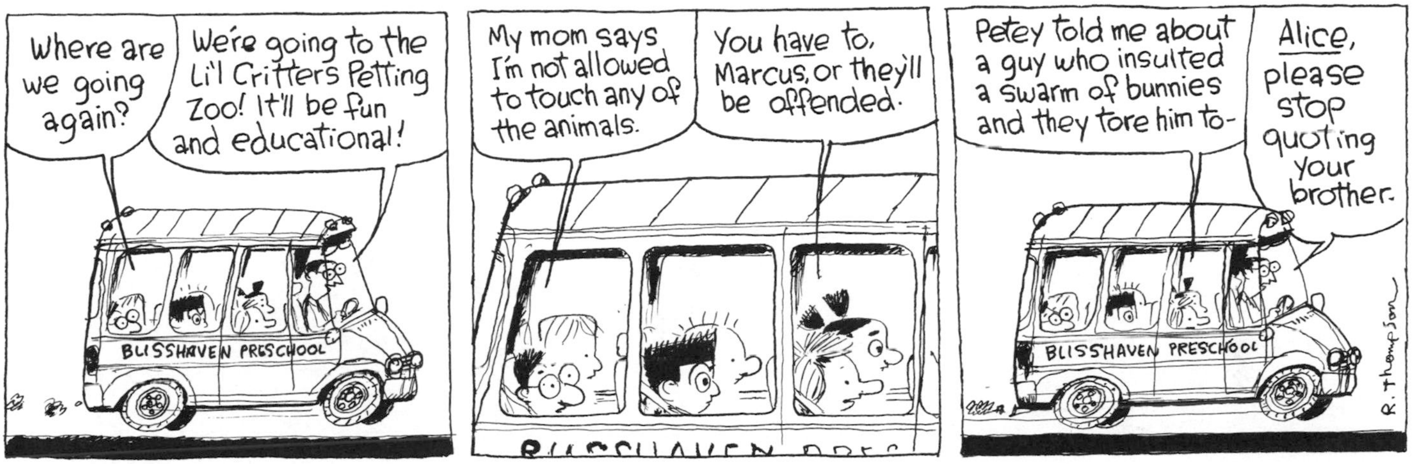
Where are we going again?
We're going to the Li'l Critters Petting Zoo! It'll be fun and educational!
My mom says I'm not allowed to touch any of the animals.
You have to, Marcus, or they'll be offended.
Petey told me about a guy who insulted a swarm of bunnies and they tore him to-
Alice, please stop quoting your brother.
BLISSHAVEN PRESCHOOL
R. Thompson

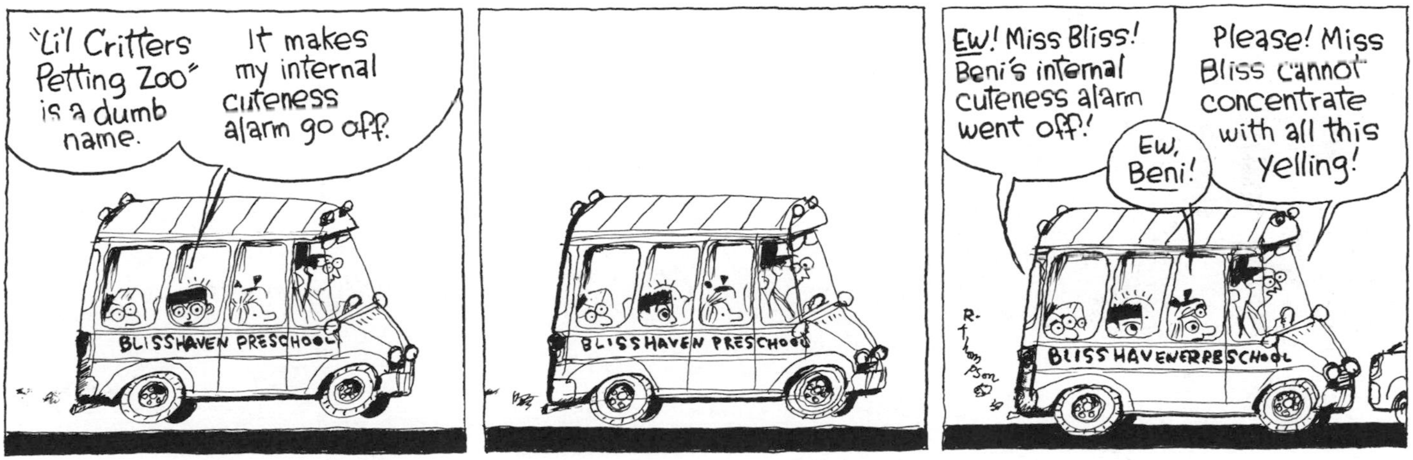
"Li'l Critters Petting Zoo" is a dumb name.
It makes my internal cuteness alarm go off.
Ew! Miss Bliss! Beni's internal cuteness alarm went off!
Ew, Beni!
Please! Miss Bliss cannot concentrate with all this yelling!
BLISSHAVEN PRESCHOOL
R. Thompson

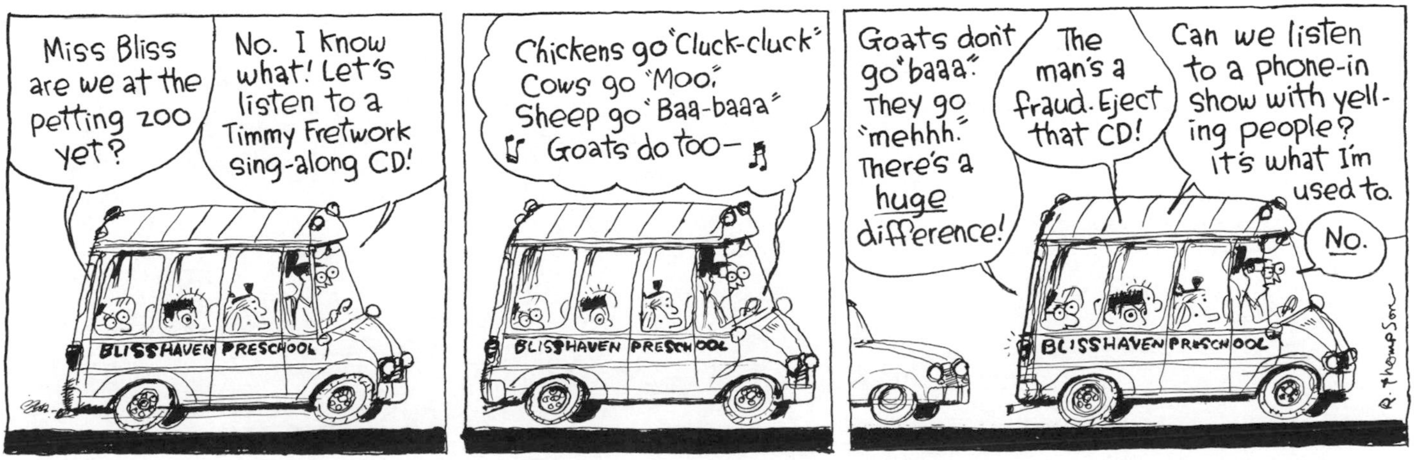
Miss Bliss are we at the petting zoo yet?
No. I know what! Let's listen to a Timmy Fretwork sing-along CD!
Chickens go "Cluck-cluck" Cows go "Moo." Sheep go "Baa-baaa" Goats do too–
Goats don't go "baaa." They go "mehhh." There's a huge difference!
The man's a fraud. Eject that CD!
Can we listen to a phone-in show with yelling people? It's what I'm used to.
No.
BLISSHAVEN PRESCHOOL
R. Thompson

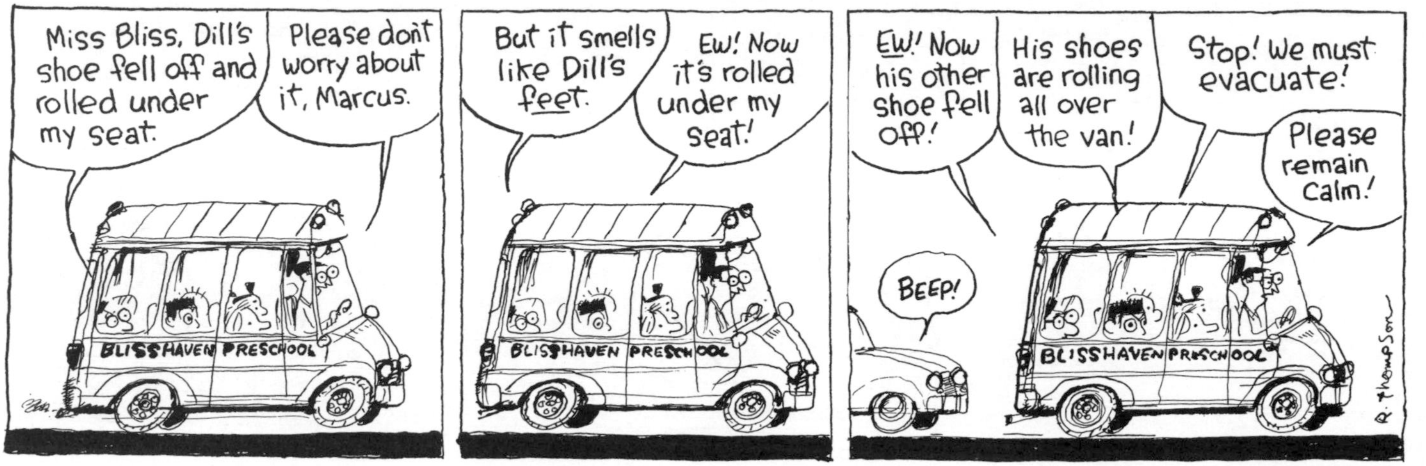
Miss Bliss, Dill's shoe fell off and rolled under my seat.
Please don't worry about it, Marcus.
BLISSHAVEN PRESCHOOL
But it smells like Dill's feet.
Ew! Now it's rolled under my seat!
BLISSHAVEN PRESCHOOL
Ew! Now his other shoe fell off!
His shoes are rolling all over the van!
Stop! We must evacuate!
Please remain calm!
BEEP!
BLISSHAVEN PRESCHOOL

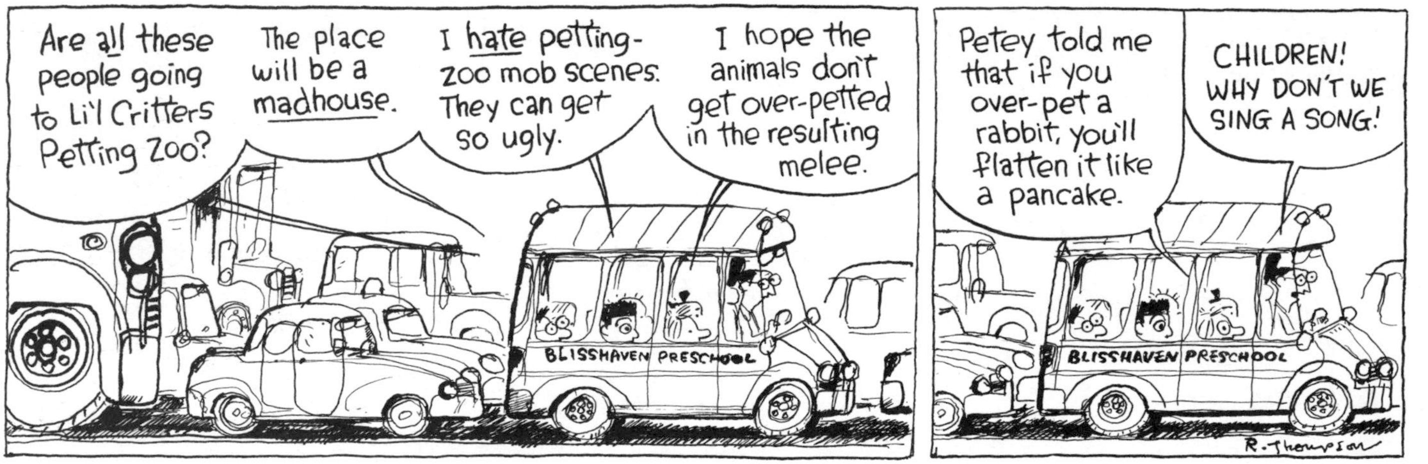
Are all these people going to Li'l Critters Petting Zoo?
The place will be a madhouse.
I hate petting-zoo mob scenes. They can get so ugly.
I hope the animals don't get over-petted in the resulting melee.
BLISSHAVEN PRESCHOOL
Petey told me that if you over-pet a rabbit, you'll flatten it like a pancake.
CHILDREN! WHY DON'T WE SING A SONG!
BLISSHAVEN PRESCHOOL

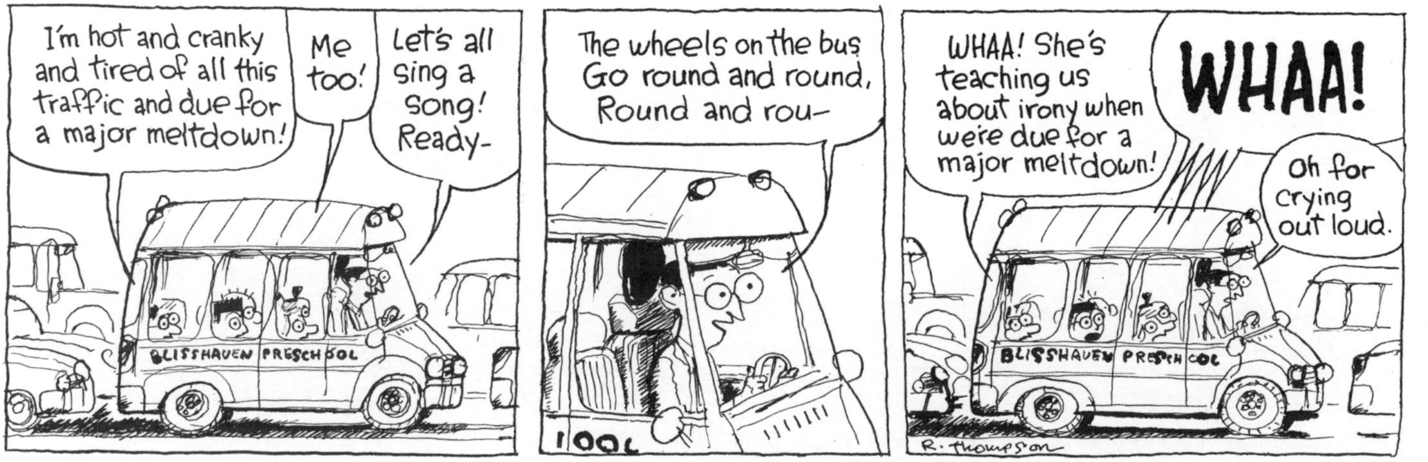
I'm hot and cranky and tired of all this traffic and due for a major meltdown!
Me too!
Let's all sing a song! Ready-
BLISSHAVEN PRESCHOOL
The wheels on the bus Go round and round, Round and rou-
WHAA! She's teaching us about irony when we're due for a major meltdown!
WHAA!
Oh for crying out loud.
BLISSHAVEN PRESCHOOL

Oh, yuck.

What?

There's a green, clown-shaped marshmallow in my cereal.

It's Alice.

There's another one! What's Alice?

She's spreading her dire influence.

She leaves toys everywhere- her stuff seeps inexorably into every corner of the house.

Blocks, stuffed animals, tiny doll shoes, creeping into every nook and cranny, overwhelming all that are not Alice.

R. Thompson

That's just silly.

Marshmallows migrating into your cereal can mean only one thing—

We're out of orange juice. Have one of Alice's juice boxes.

No.

She's in the food chain. We're doomed.

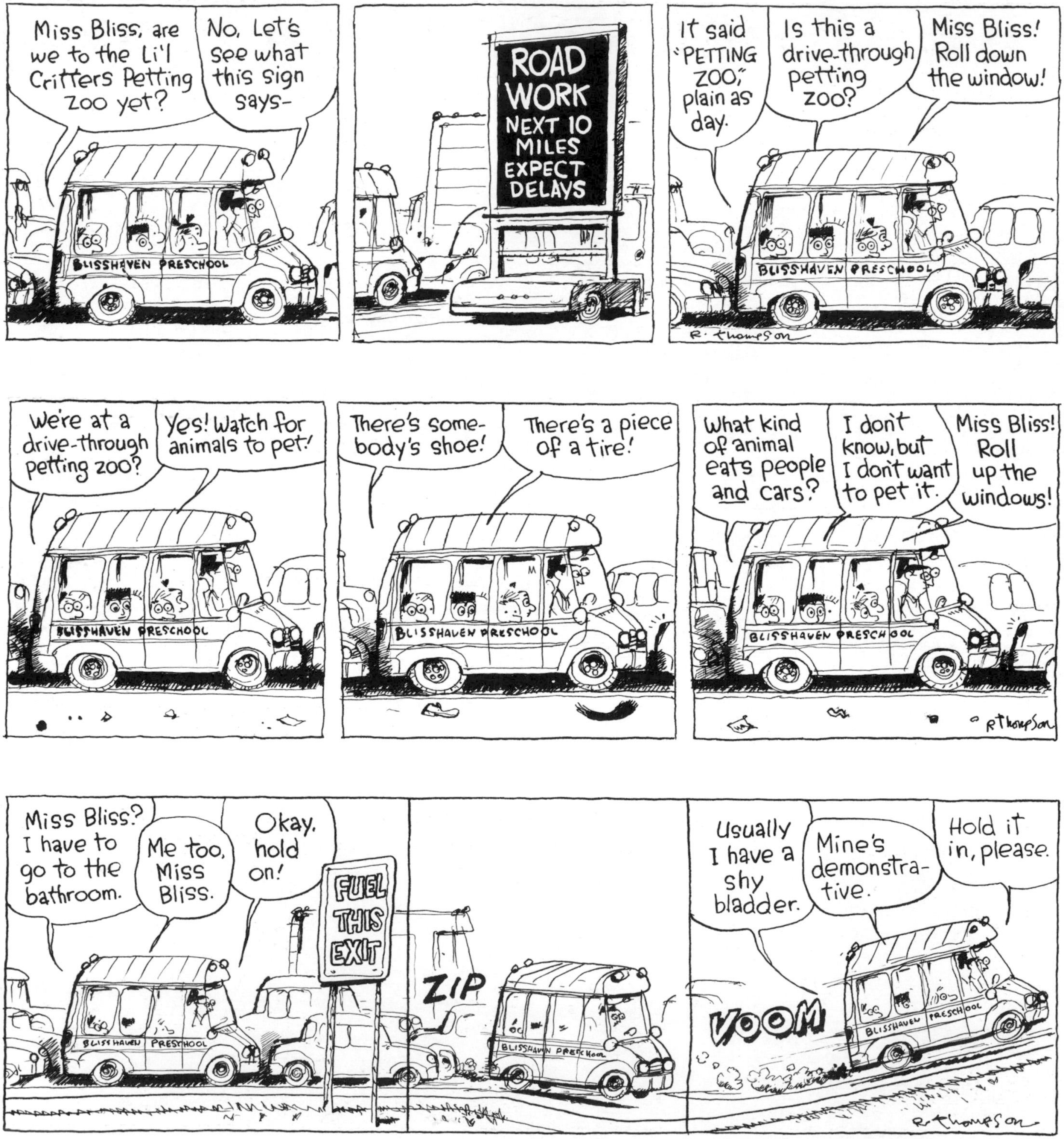

Miss Bliss, are we to the Li'l Critters Petting Zoo yet?
No, Let's see what this sign says-
ROAD WORK NEXT 10 MILES EXPECT DELAYS
It said "PETTING ZOO," plain as day.
Is this a drive-through petting zoo?
Miss Bliss! Roll down the window!
BLISSHAVEN PRESCHOOL
R. Thompson
We're at a drive-through petting zoo?
Yes! Watch for animals to pet!
There's somebody's shoe!
There's a piece of a tire!
What kind of animal eats people and cars?
I don't know, but I don't want to pet it.
Miss Bliss! Roll up the windows!
R Thompson
Miss Bliss? I have to go to the bathroom.
Me too, Miss Bliss.
Okay, hold on!
FUEL THIS EXIT
ZIP
Usually I have a shy bladder.
Mine's demonstrative.
Hold it in, please.
VOOM
R. Thompson

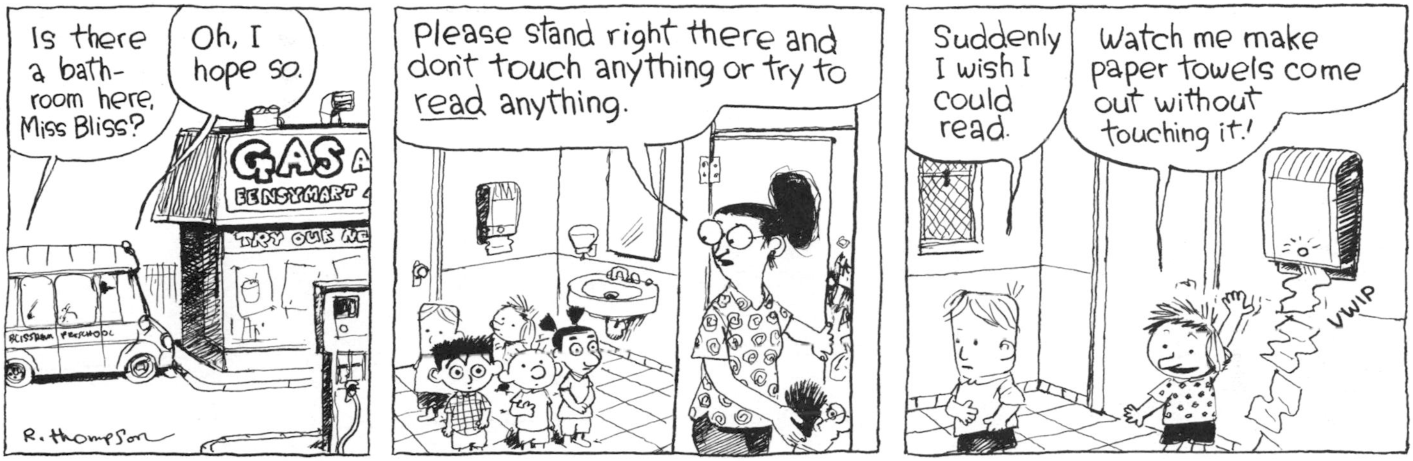
Is there a bathroom here, Miss Bliss?
Oh, I hope so.
GAS
EENSYMART
BLISSHAVEN PRESCHOOL
R. thompson
Please stand right there and don't touch anything or try to read anything.
Suddenly I wish I could read.
Watch me make paper towels come out without touching it!
VWIP

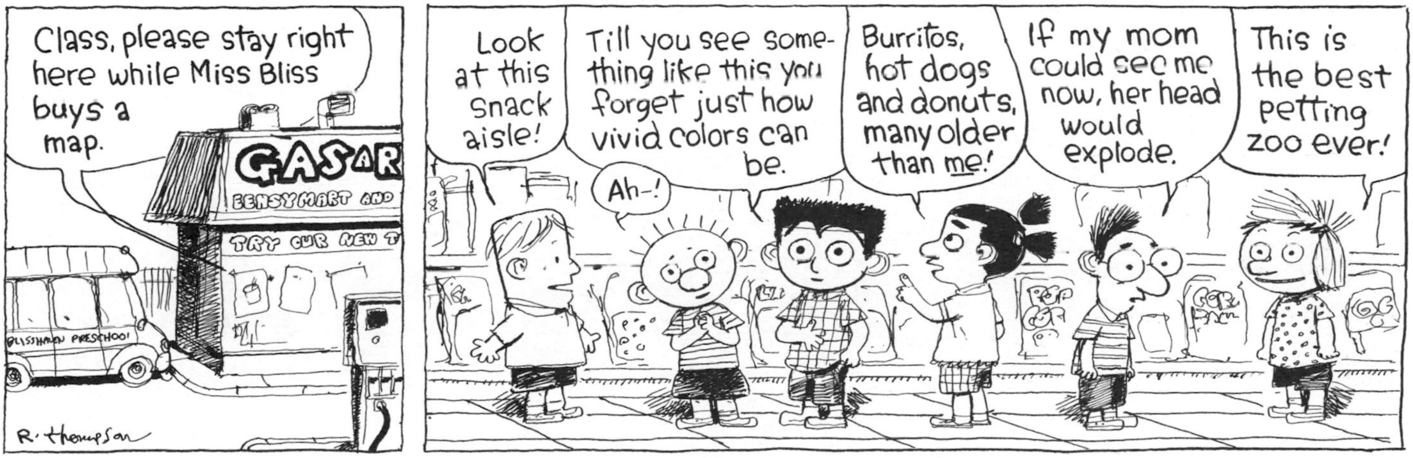
Class, please stay right here while Miss Bliss buys a map.
GAS AR
EENSYMART AND
TRY OUR NEW T
BLISSHAVEN PRESCHOOL
R. thompson
Look at this snack aisle!
Till you see something like this you forget just how vivid colors can be.
Ah-!
Burritos, hot dogs and donuts, many older than me!
If my mom could see me now, her head would explode.
This is the best petting zoo ever!

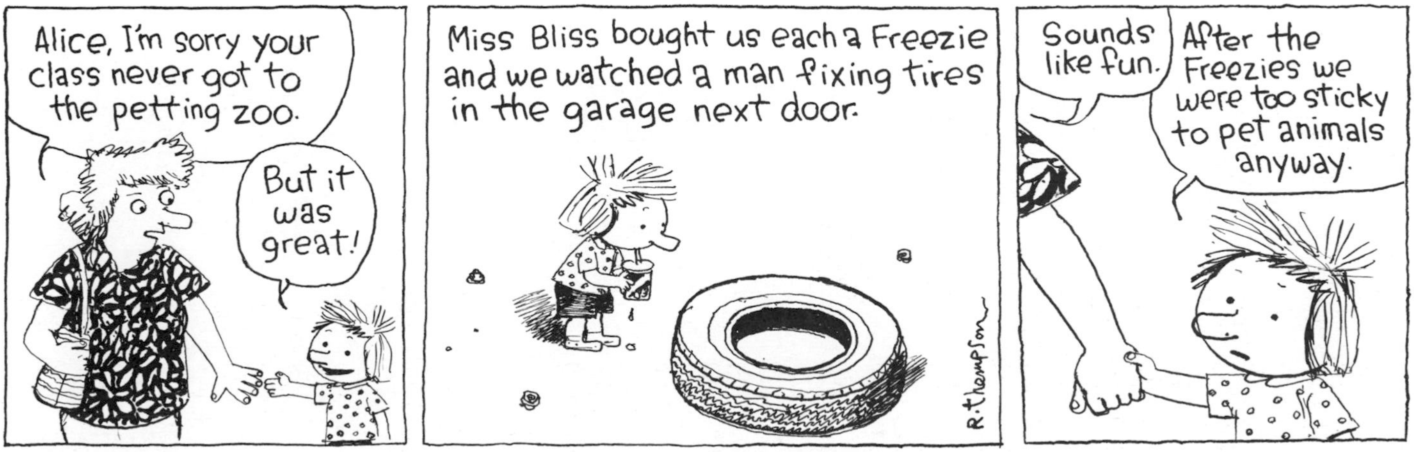
Alice, I'm sorry your class never got to the petting zoo.
But it was great!
Miss Bliss bought us each a Freezie and we watched a man fixing tires in the garage next door.
R. thompson
Sounds like fun.
After the Freezies we were too sticky to pet animals anyway.

Good night, Alice!

MOM! NOT YET.

Alice, we read "Princess Piesmasher and the Ten Angry Bakers." Twice.

We sang the Nighty-Night Song. All sixteen verses, plus choruses.

We did the Hugaboo Dance. Daddy got a bloody nose doing the Oopsie Bedtime Pratfall. What's left?

I'd like to individually thank each of my toys for another day of loyal service to me, Alice. I'll start with Bubsey Clownpants—

GOOD NIGHT.

CLICK

Someday I'm going to extend my bedtime ritual to dawn.

Then she'll be tired and cranky all the time.

Oh, good.

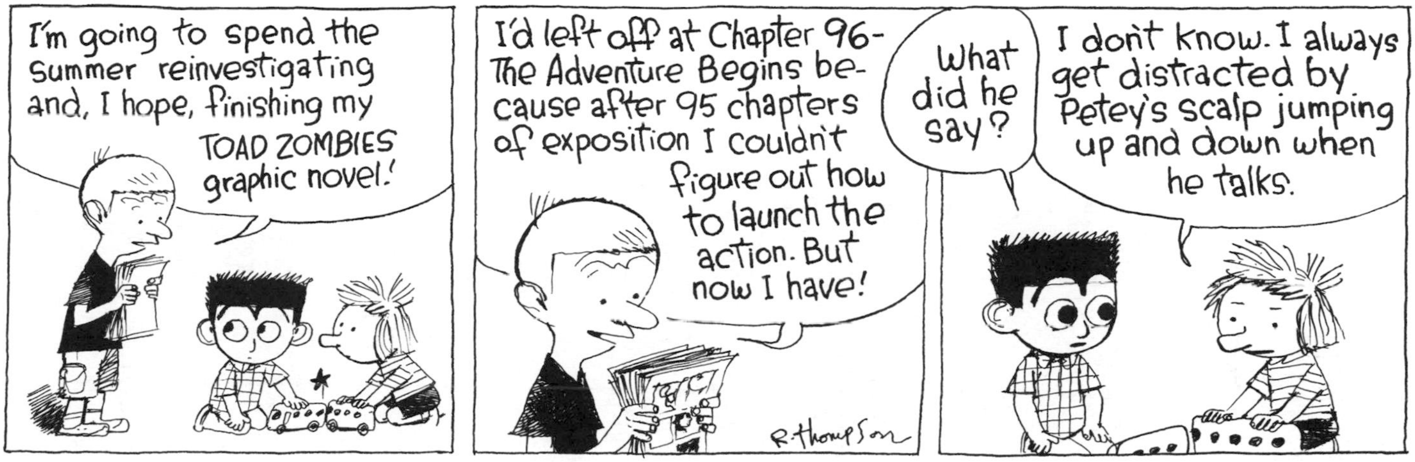
I'm going to spend the summer reinvestigating and, I hope, finishing my TOAD ZOMBIES graphic novel!
I'd left off at Chapter 96-The Adventure Begins because after 95 chapters of exposition I couldn't figure out how to launch the action. But now I have!
What did he say?
I don't know. I always get distracted by Petey's scalp jumping up and down when he talks.
R. Thompson

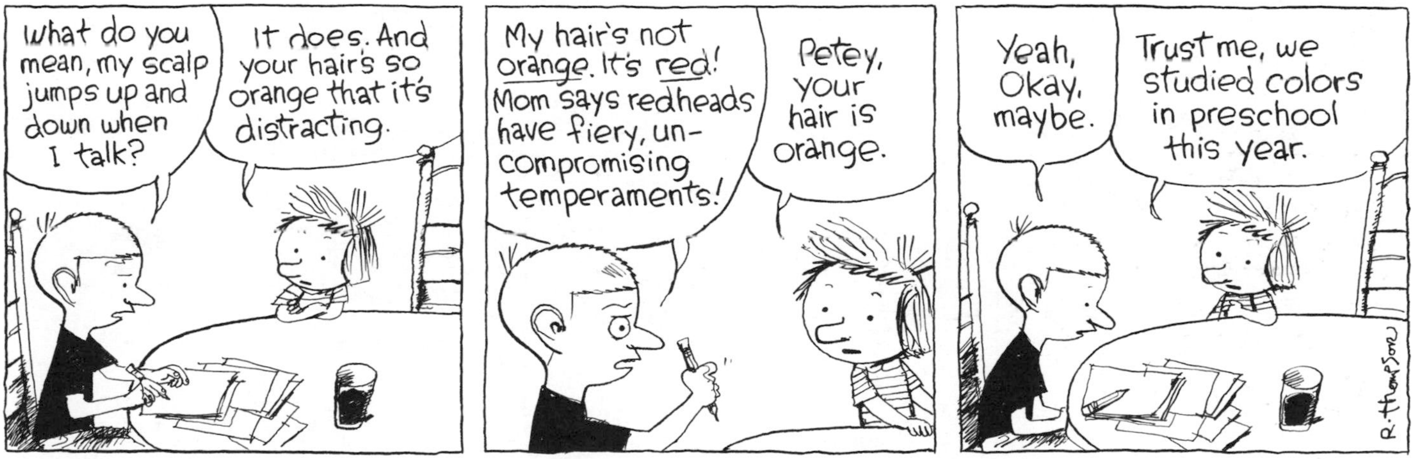
What do you mean, my scalp jumps up and down when I talk?
It does. And your hair's so orange that it's distracting.
My hair's not orange. It's red! Mom says redheads have fiery, uncompromising temperaments!
Petey, your hair is orange.
Yeah, Okay, maybe.
Trust me, we studied colors in preschool this year.
R. Thompson

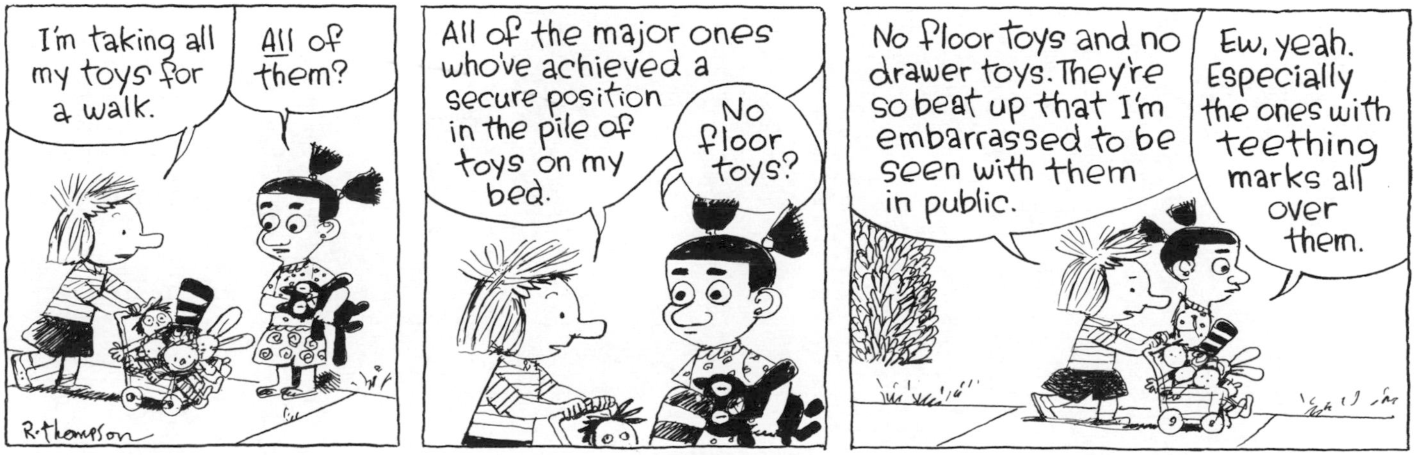
I'm taking all my toys for a walk.
All of them?
R. Thompson
All of the major ones who've achieved a secure position in the pile of toys on my bed.
No floor toys?
No floor toys and no drawer toys. They're so beat up that I'm embarrassed to be seen with them in public.
Ew, yeah. Especially the ones with teething marks all over them.

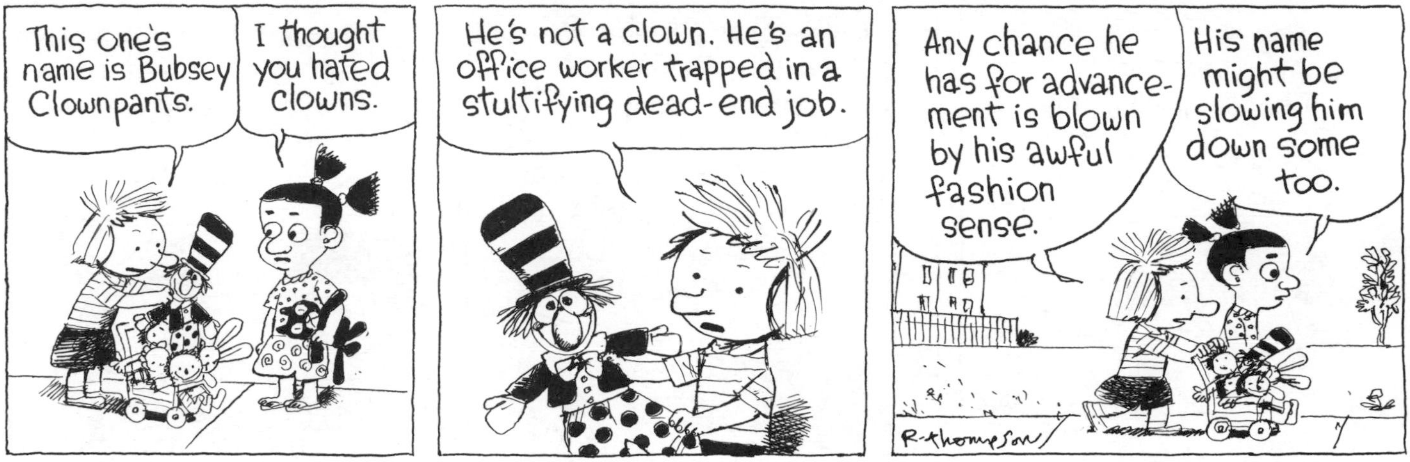
This one's name is Bubsey Clownpants.
I thought you hated clowns.
He's not a clown. He's an office worker trapped in a stultifying dead-end job.
Any chance he has for advancement is blown by his awful fashion sense.
His name might be slowing him down some too.

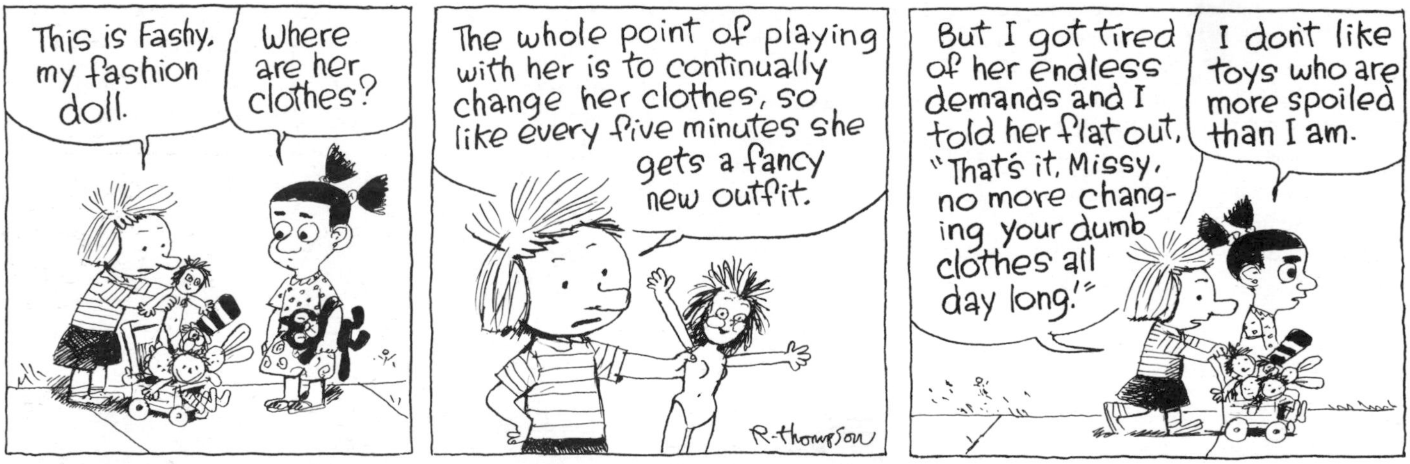
This is Fashy, my fashion doll.
Where are her clothes?
The whole point of playing with her is to continually change her clothes, so like every five minutes she gets a fancy new outfit.
But I got tired of her endless demands and I told her flat out, "That's it, Missy, no more changing your dumb clothes all day long!"
I don't like toys who are more spoiled than I am.

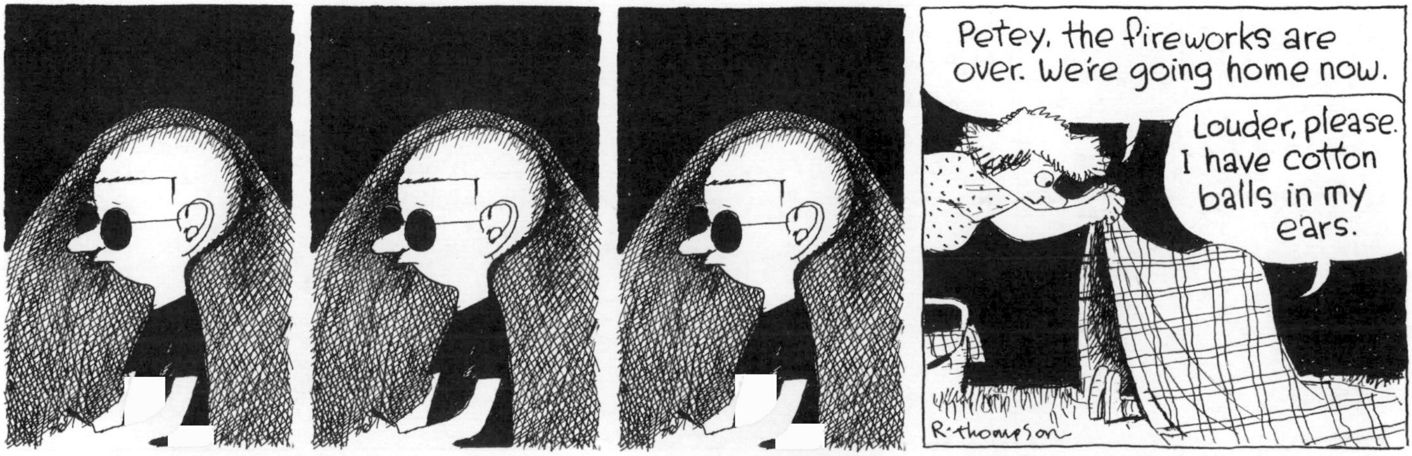
Petey, the fireworks are over. We're going home now.
Louder, please. I have cotton balls in my ears.

Daddy, I'm so glad you're home now. I need help.
What's the matter, Alice?
We're playing Tag and I'm not good at it.
Hey, Tag is my game!
REALLY?
Oh yeah, when I was a kid we played Tag and Freeze Tag.
And TV Tag and Movie Tag, where you have to yell the title of a show so whoever is "It" can't tag you.
R. Thompson
That's like what we're playing.
What are you playing?
Artisanal Cheese Tag. And the only cheese I know is "Orange."
Gruyère!
FONTANEL!
That's not a cheese.
No, I hurt my fontanel.

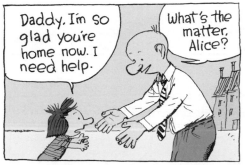

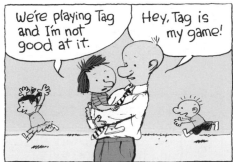

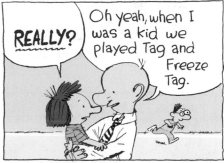

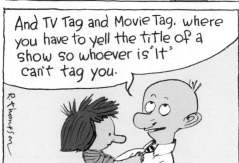

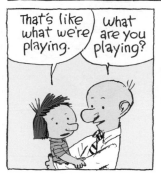

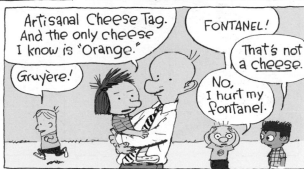

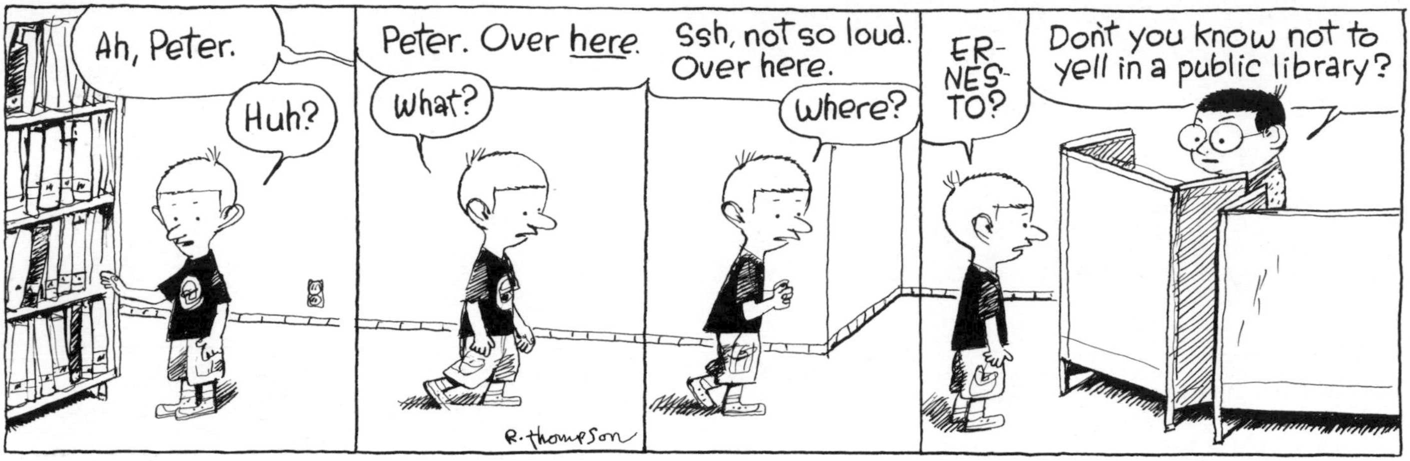
Ah, Peter.
Huh?
Peter. Over here.
What?
Ssh, not so loud. Over here.
Where?
ER-NES-TO?
Don't you know not to yell in a public library?
R. thompson

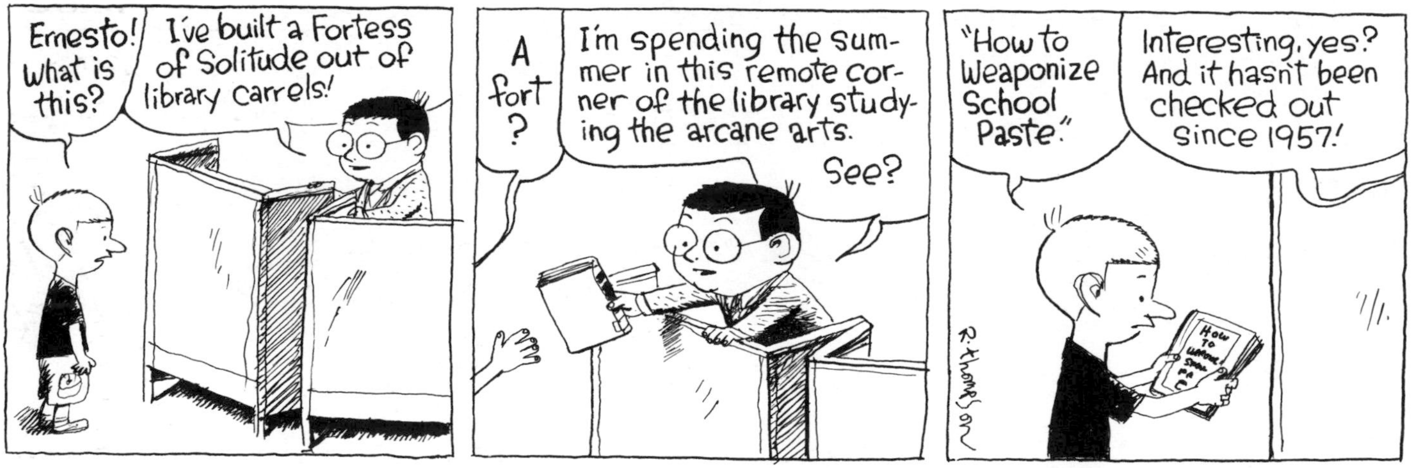
Ernesto! What is this?
I've built a Fortess of Solitude out of library carrels!
A fort?
I'm spending the summer in this remote corner of the library studying the arcane arts.
See?
"How to Weaponize School Paste."
Interesting, yes? And it hasn't been checked out since 1957!
R. thompson

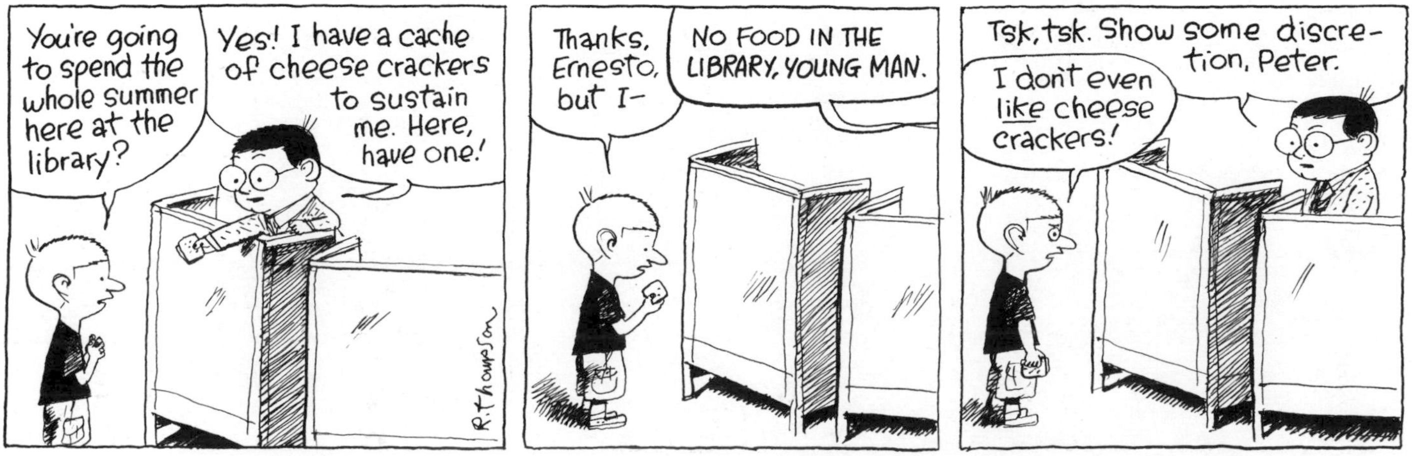
You're going to spend the whole summer here at the library?
Yes! I have a cache of cheese crackers to sustain me. Here, have one!
R. thompson
Thanks, Ernesto, but I-
NO FOOD IN THE LIBRARY, YOUNG MAN.
Tsk, tsk. Show some discretion, Peter.
I don't even like cheese crackers!

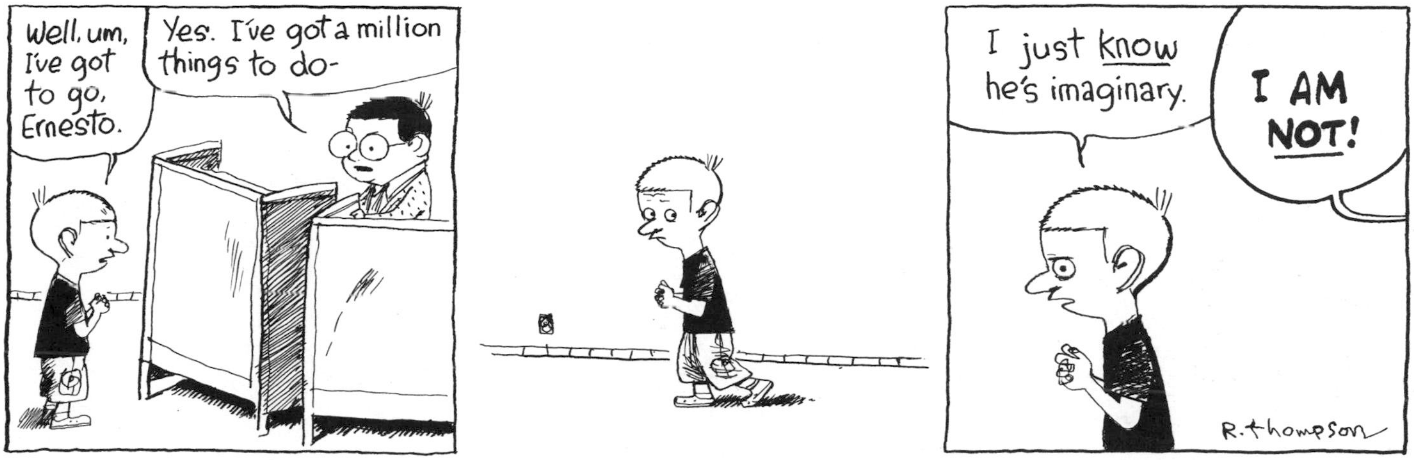
Well, um, I've got to go, Ernesto.
Yes. I've got a million things to do-
I just know he's imaginary.
I AM NOT!
R. Thompson

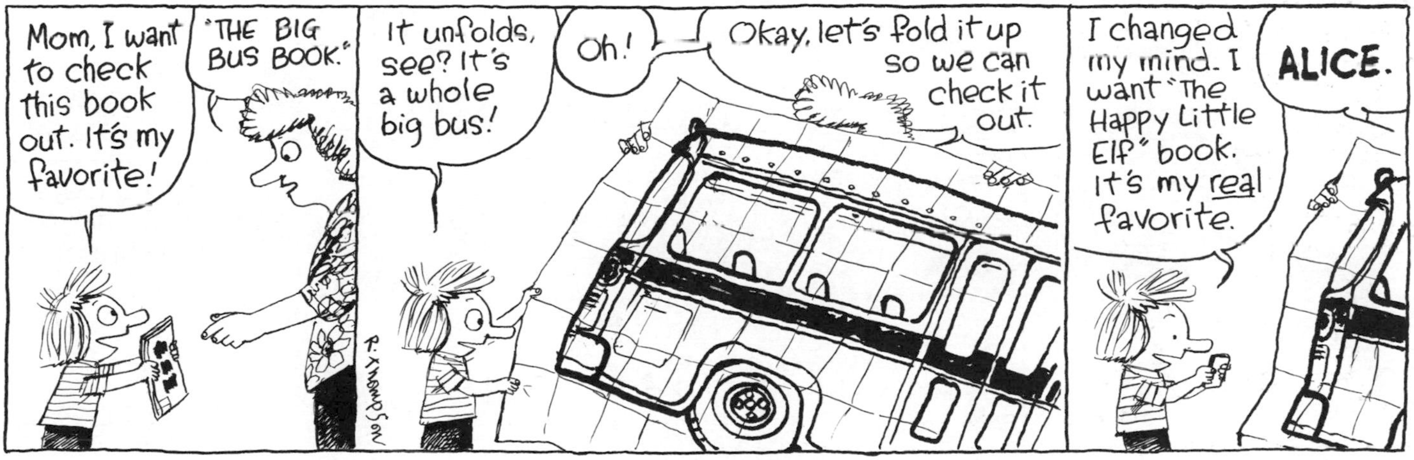
Mom, I want to check this book out. It's my favorite!
"THE BIG BUS BOOK."
R. Thompson
It unfolds, see? It's a whole big bus!
Oh!
Okay, let's fold it up so we can check it out.
I changed my mind. I want "The Happy Little Elf" book. It's my real favorite.
ALICE.

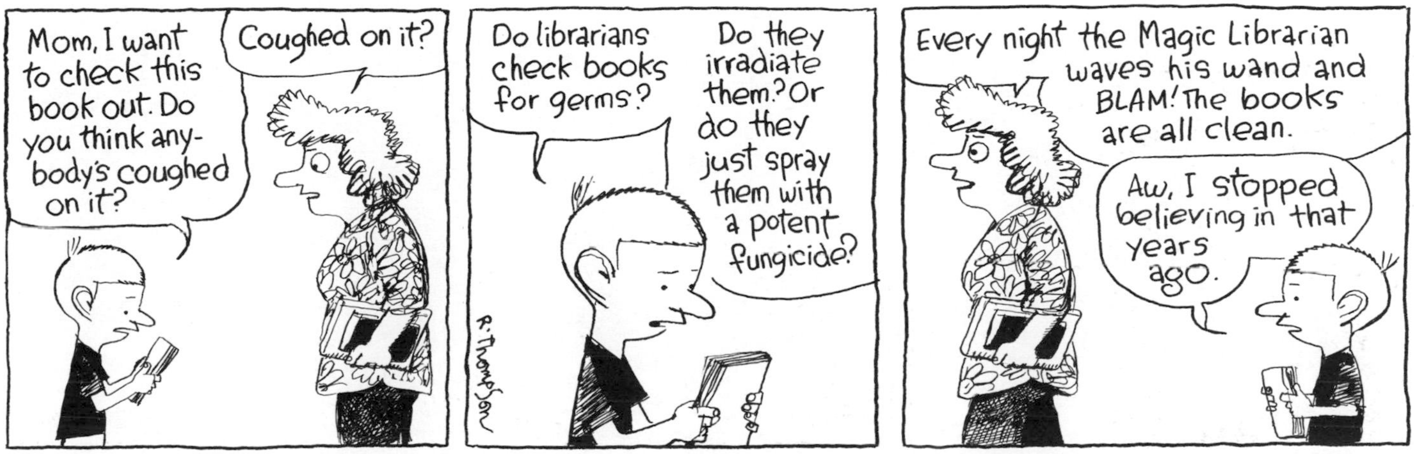
Mom, I want to check this book out. Do you think anybody's coughed on it?
Coughed on it?
Do librarians check books for germs?
Do they irradiate them? Or do they just spray them with a potent fungicide?
R. Thompson
Every night the Magic Librarian waves his wand and BLAM! The books are all clean.
Aw, I stopped believing in that years ago.

Uh-oh. It's that cashier.
Who?
The one who never speaks to me.
So we drove the on Wednesday and stopped
She talks to every-body, but when I speak to her she just grunts and stares.
Let's get in another line, Mom.
Grunt?
Nope, too late! Here we go!
Hi! It's time to buy more groceries! Ha-ha!
Grunt.
Well, we'd better get home and eat these groceries!
Grunt.
R. Thompson
She's talking to the lady behind you! Look, they're hugging!
I must've offended her in a previous existence.
We're having groceries for dinner? BLEAH!

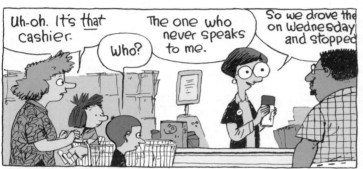

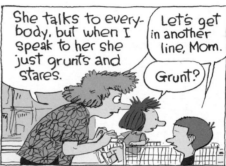

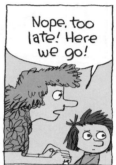

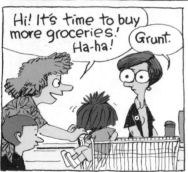

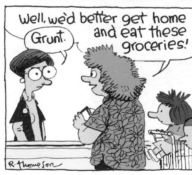

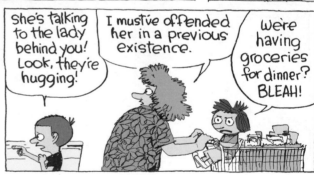

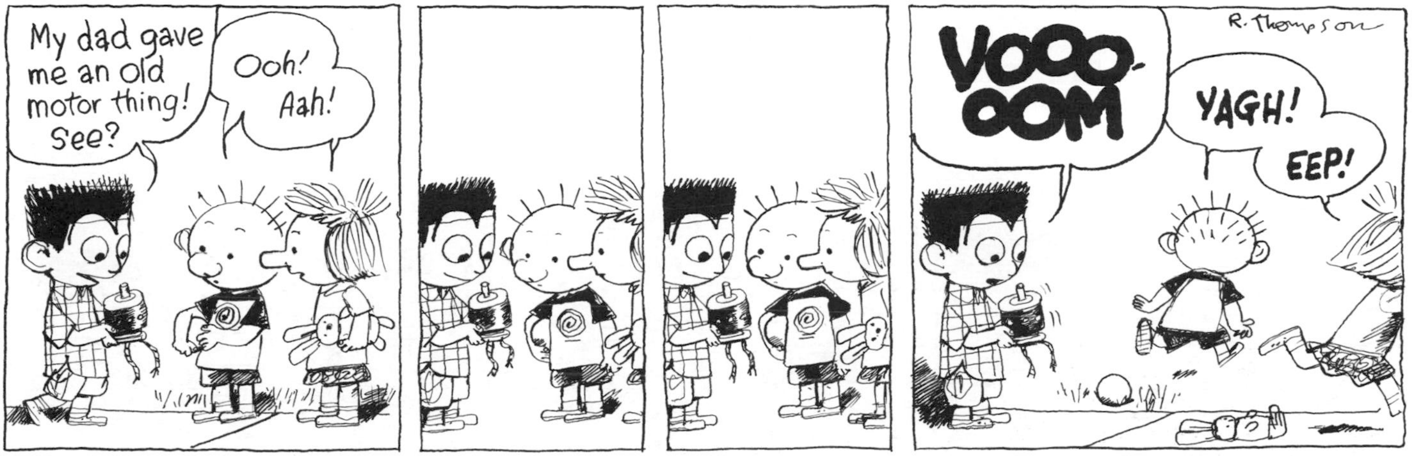
My dad gave me an old motor thing! See?
Ooh! Aah!
R. Thompson
VOOO-OOM
YAGH!
EEP!

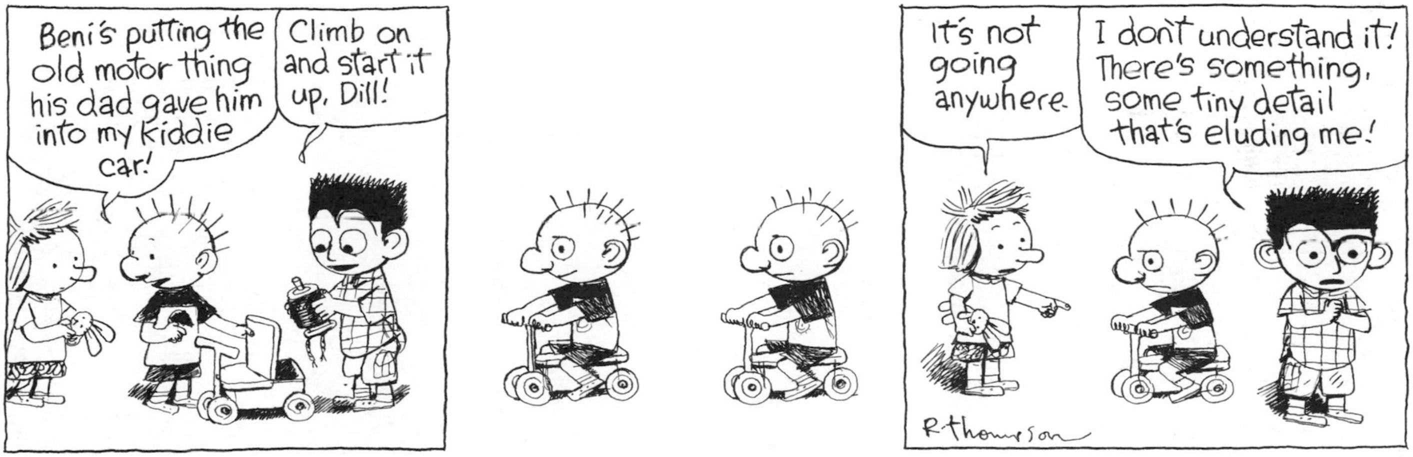
Beni's putting the old motor thing his dad gave him into my kiddie car!
Climb on and start it up, Dill!
It's not going anywhere.
I don't understand it! There's something, some tiny detail that's eluding me!
R. Thompson

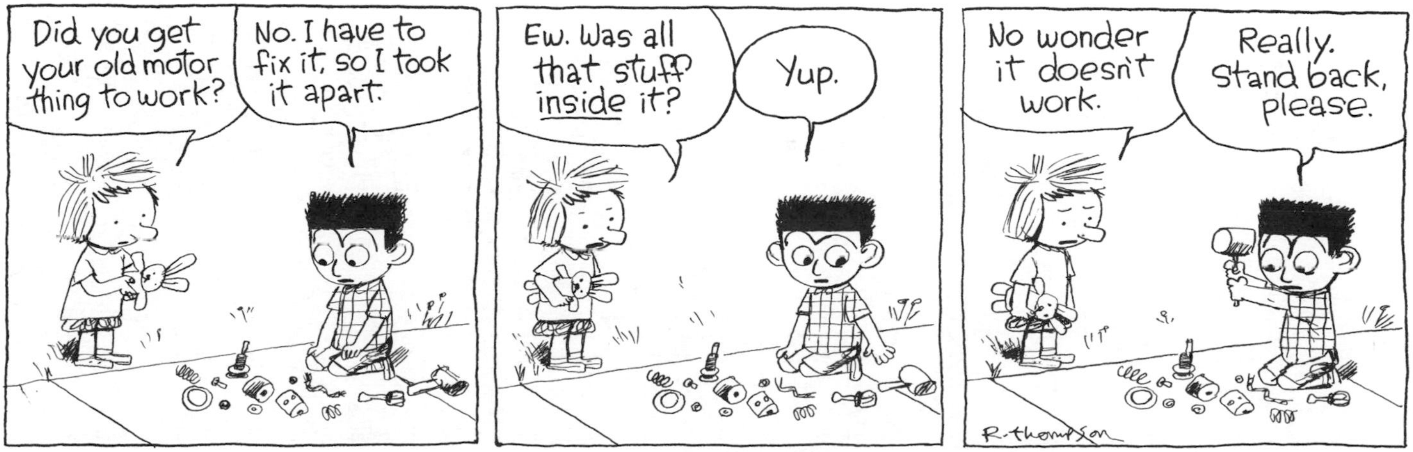
Did you get your old motor thing to work?
No. I have to fix it, so I took it apart.
Ew. Was all that stuff inside it?
Yup.
No wonder it doesn't work.
Really. Stand back, please.
R. Thompson

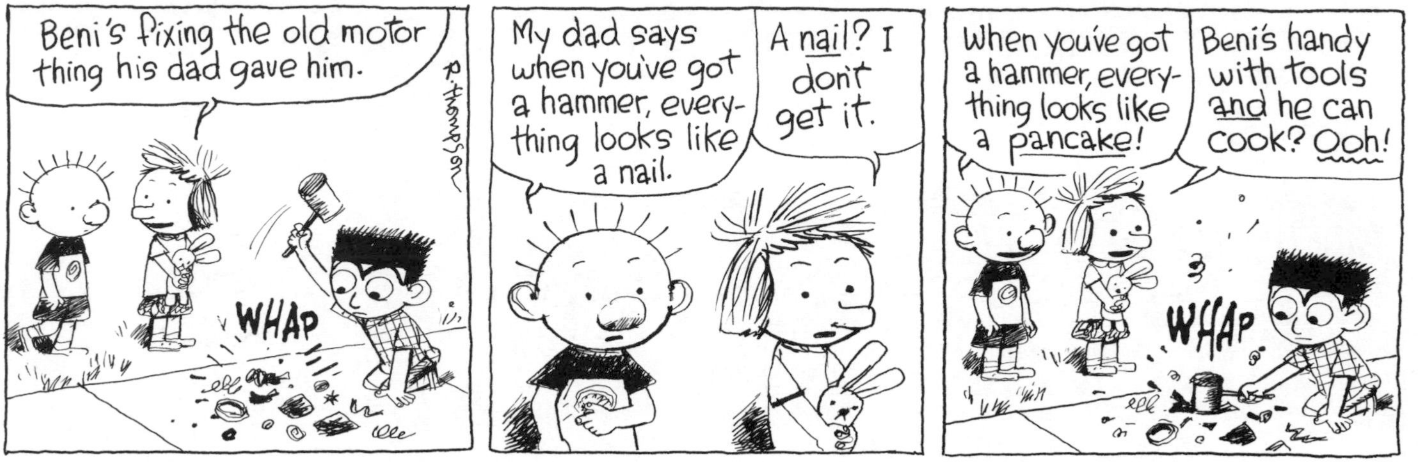
Beni's fixing the old motor thing his dad gave him.
R. Thompson
WHAP
My dad says when you've got a hammer, every-thing looks like a nail.
A nail? I don't get it.
When you've got a hammer, every-thing looks like a pancake!
Beni's handy with tools and he can cook? Ooh!
WHAP

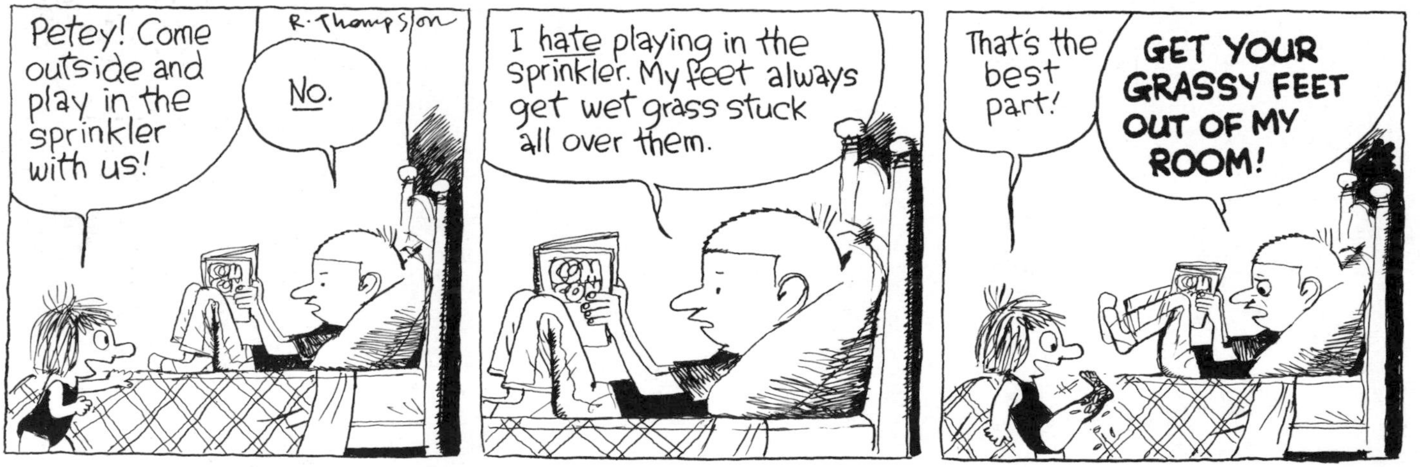
Petey! Come outside and play in the sprinkler with us!
R. Thompson
No.
I hate playing in the sprinkler. My feet always get wet grass stuck all over them.
That's the best part!
GET YOUR GRASSY FEET OUT OF MY ROOM!

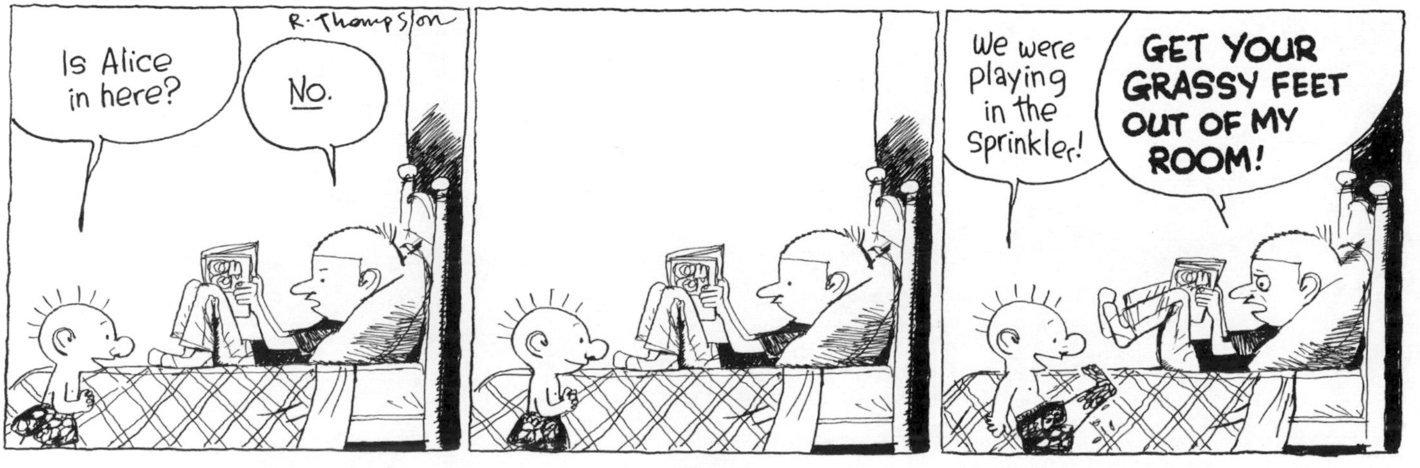
Is Alice in here?
R. Thompson
No.
We were playing in the Sprinkler!
GET YOUR GRASSY FEET OUT OF MY ROOM!

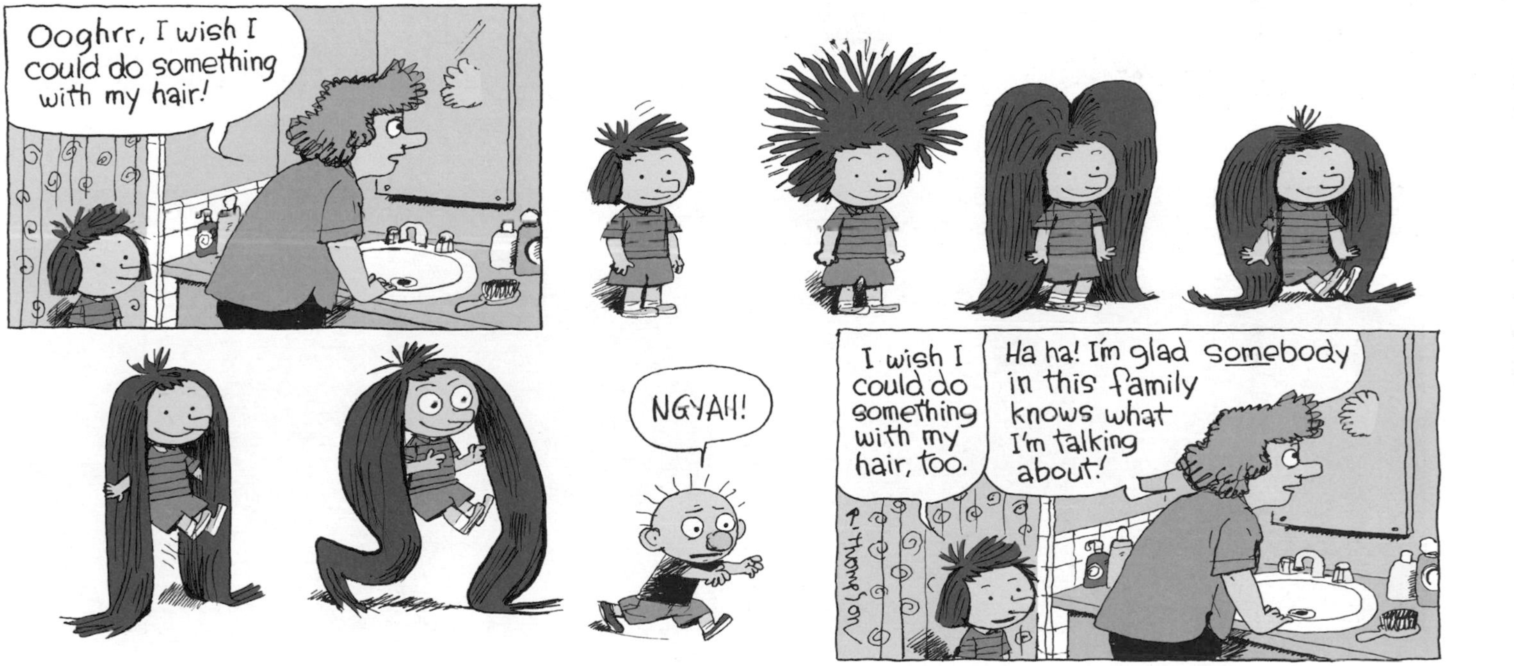
Ooghrr, I wish I could do something with my hair!
NGYAH!
I wish I could do something with my hair, too.
Ha ha! I'm glad somebody in this family knows what I'm talking about!
R. Thompson

Guess what I am-
Dill with a lightning bug on his head?
No... I'm a water tower! Hee hee hee!
What's a water tower?
I never get his jokes.
Hee hee hee!
R. thompson
Stars make me mad.
Why?
They make me feel puny and unnoticed.
Oh.
R. thompson
Let's throw mulch at them!
Is that your answer for everything?
Dill, don't shoot at lightning bugs with a water pistol!
Why?
Petey says it's dangerous! It's like pushing a toaster into the bathtub!
Petey says URLGHK-
AAAG GRRR RRGH!
A little danger can add zest and urgency to an otherwise dull life!
R. thompson

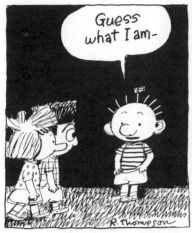

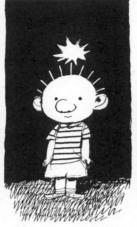

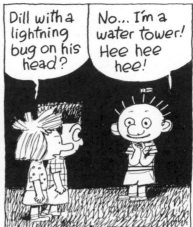

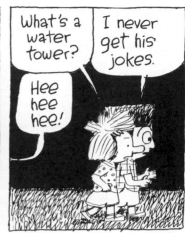

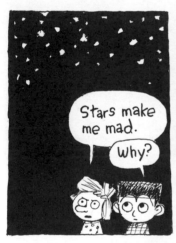

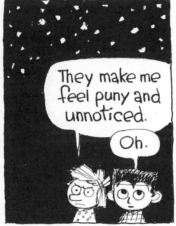

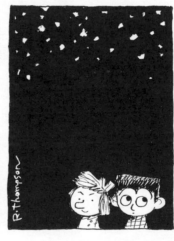

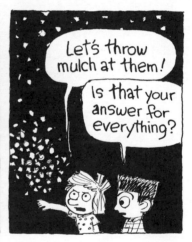

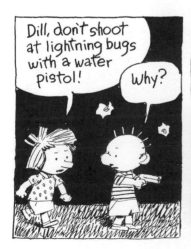

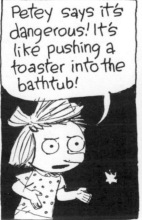

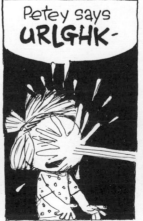

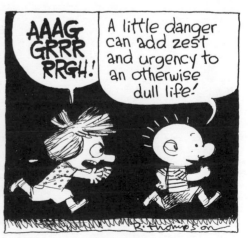

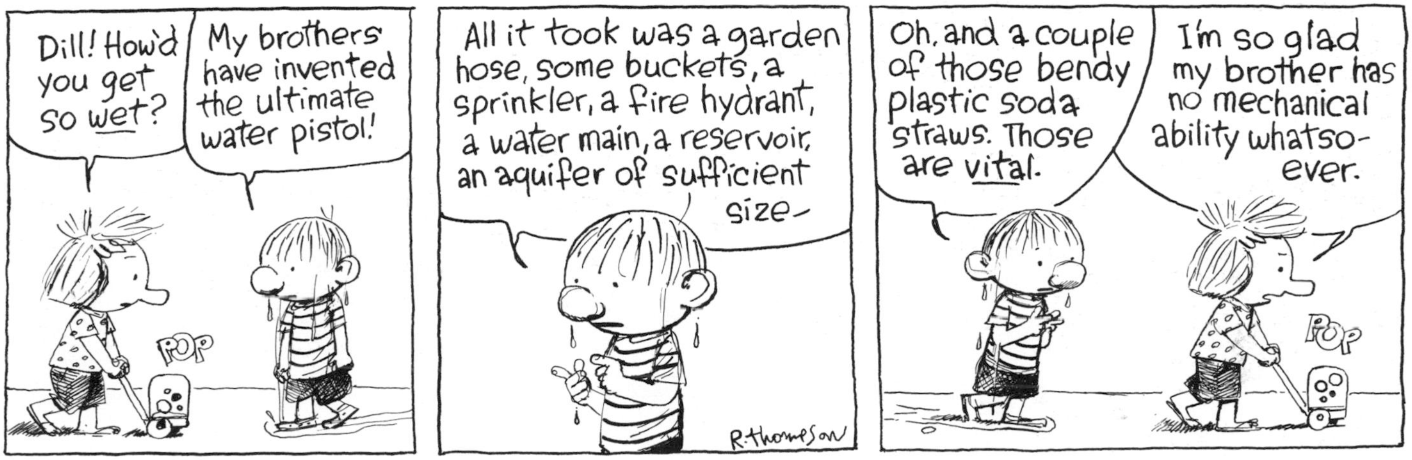
Dill! How'd you get so wet?
My brothers have invented the ultimate water pistol!
POP
All it took was a garden hose, some buckets, a sprinkler, a fire hydrant, a water main, a reservoir, an aquifer of sufficient size-
R. thompson
Oh, and a couple of those bendy plastic soda straws. Those are vital.
I'm so glad my brother has no mechanical ability whatsoever.
POP

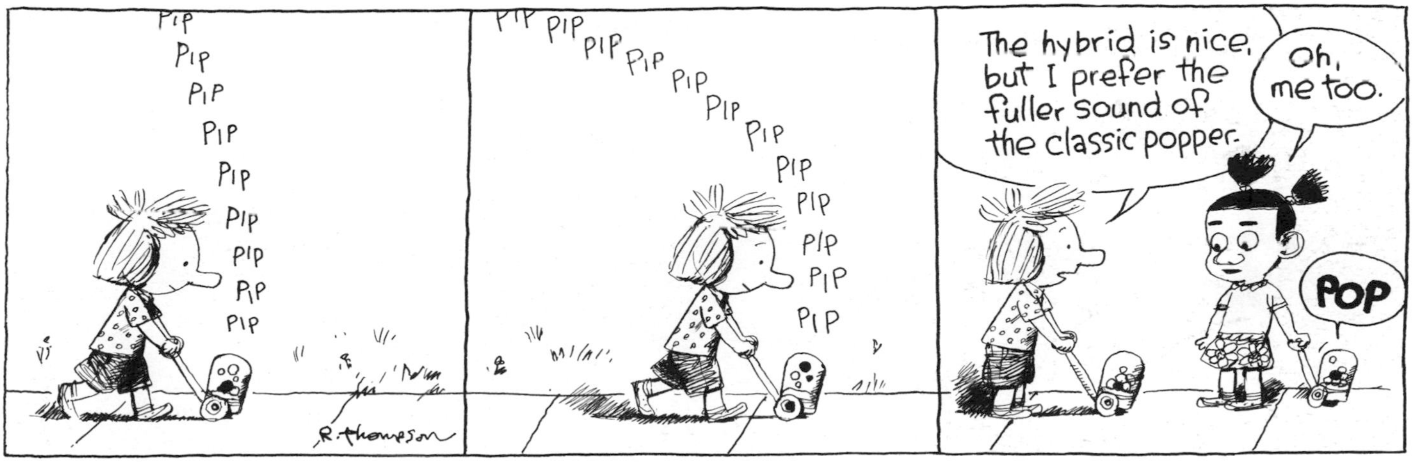
PIP PIP PIP PIP PIP PIP PIP PIP PIP
R. thompson
PIP PIP PIP PIP PIP PIP PIP PIP PIP PIP PIP PIP PIP
The hybrid is nice, but I prefer the fuller sound of the classic popper.
Oh, me too.
POP

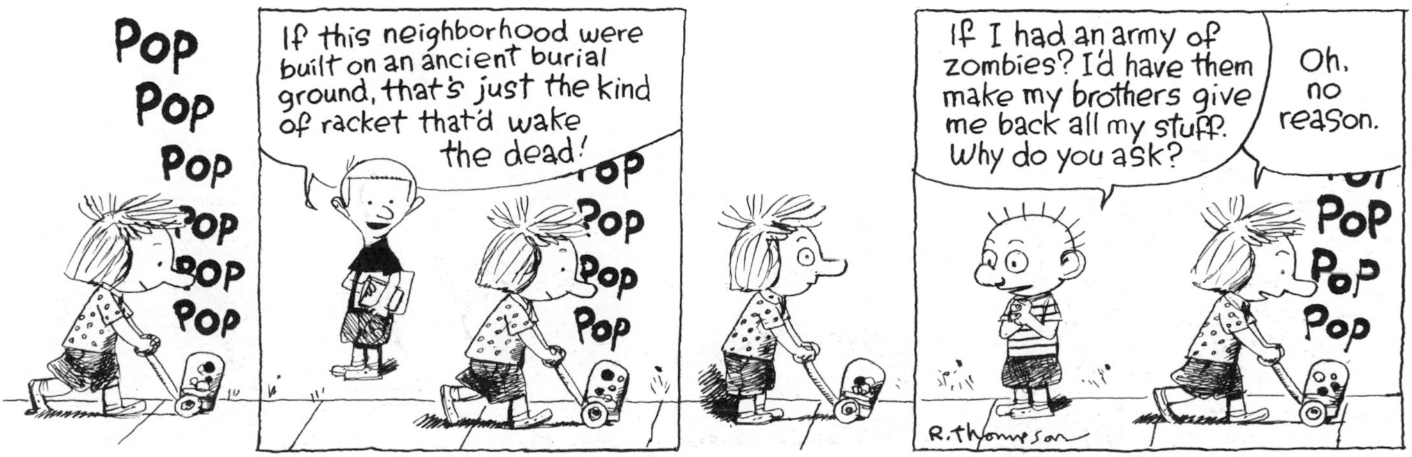
POP POP POP POP POP POP
If this neighborhood were built on an ancient burial ground, that's just the kind of racket that'd wake the dead!
POP POP POP
If I had an army of zombies? I'd have them make my brothers give me back all my stuff. Why do you ask?
Oh. no reason.
POP POP POP
R. thompson

I had a dream about my kiddie car last night.
Did it turn into a horse? Could it fly? Did it go real fast? Did it turn into an elephant? Was it a talking elephant?
CAUTION EDGE OF EARTH
Did the horn really work? Did it turn into a real car? Did you give me a ride? Did you drive to the North Pole? Or to the Moon? Or to my Grandma's?
I have all the wrong dreams.
R. Thompson

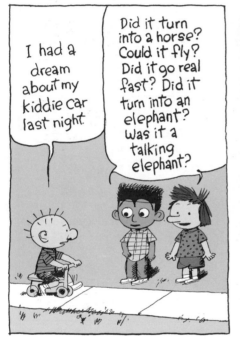

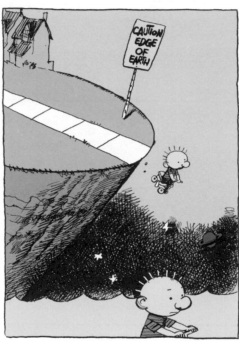

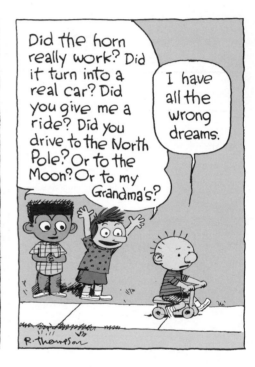

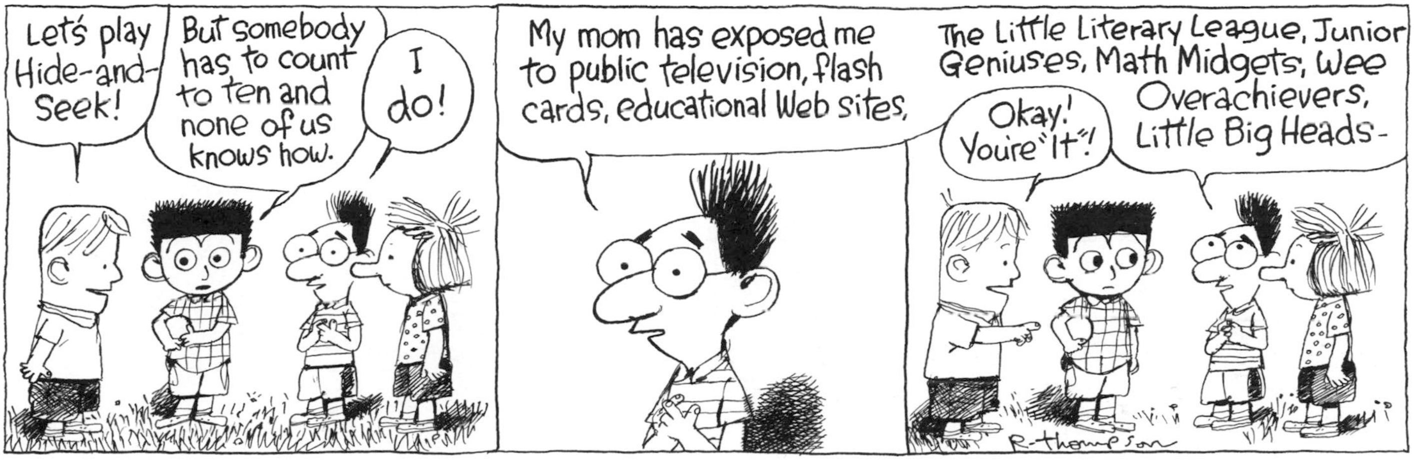
Let's play Hide-and-Seek!
But somebody has to count to ten and none of us knows how.
I do!
My mom has exposed me to public television, flash cards, educational Web sites,
The Little Literary League, Junior Geniuses, Math Midgets, Wee Overachievers, Little Big Heads-
Okay! You're "It"!

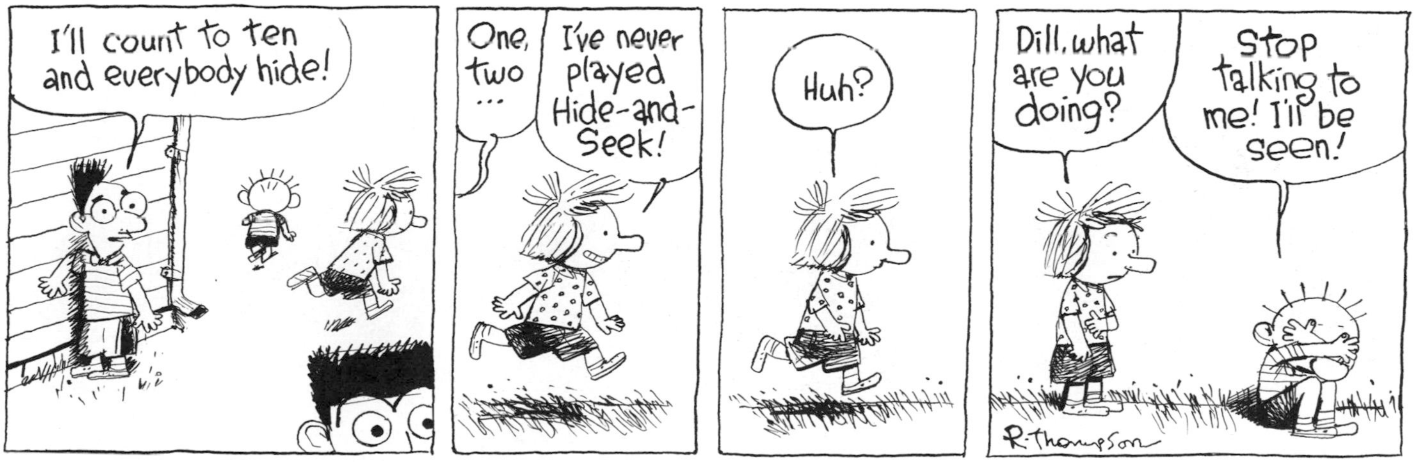
I'll count to ten and everybody hide!
One, two ...
I've never played Hide-and-Seek!
Huh?
Dill, what are you doing?
Stop talking to me! I'll be seen!

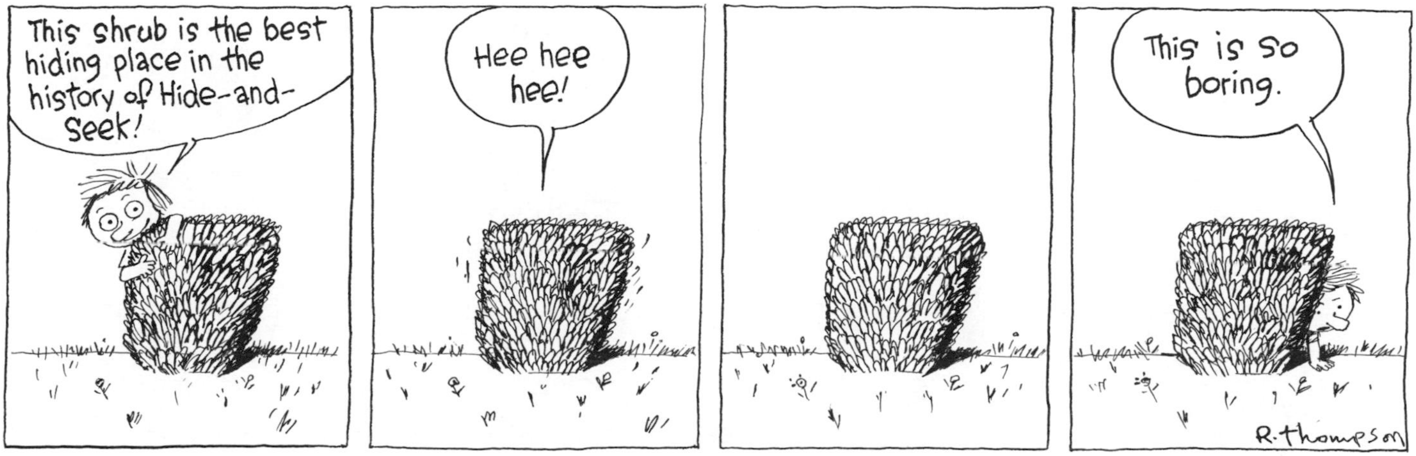
This shrub is the best hiding place in the history of Hide-and-Seek!
Hee hee hee!
This is so boring.

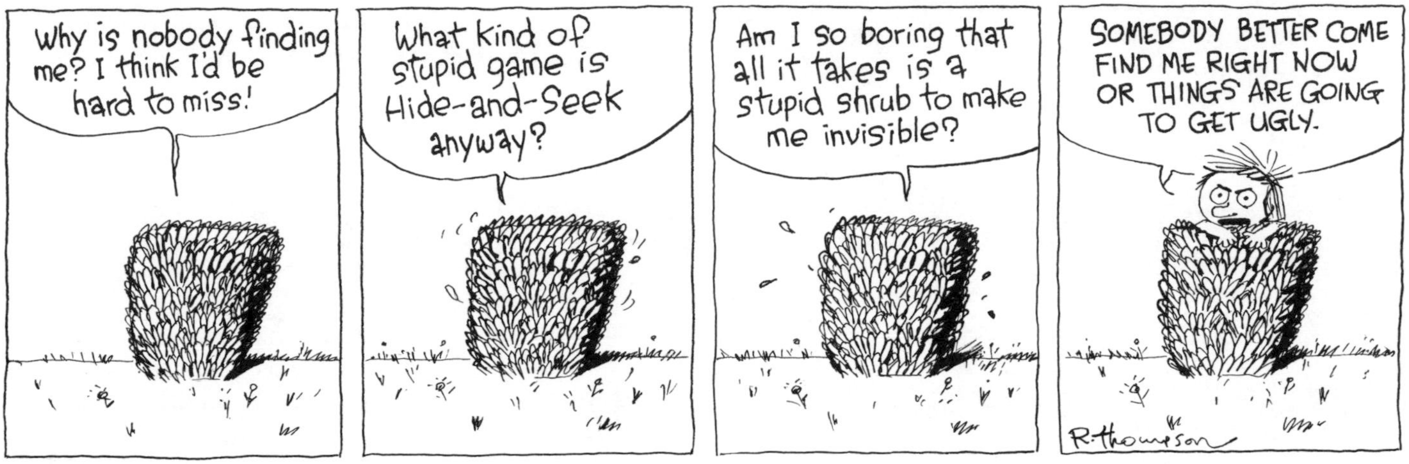
Why is nobody finding me? I think I'd be hard to miss!
What kind of stupid game is Hide-and-Seek anyway?
Am I so boring that all it takes is a stupid shrub to make me invisible?
SOMEBODY BETTER COME FIND ME RIGHT NOW OR THINGS ARE GOING TO GET UGLY.
R. Thompson

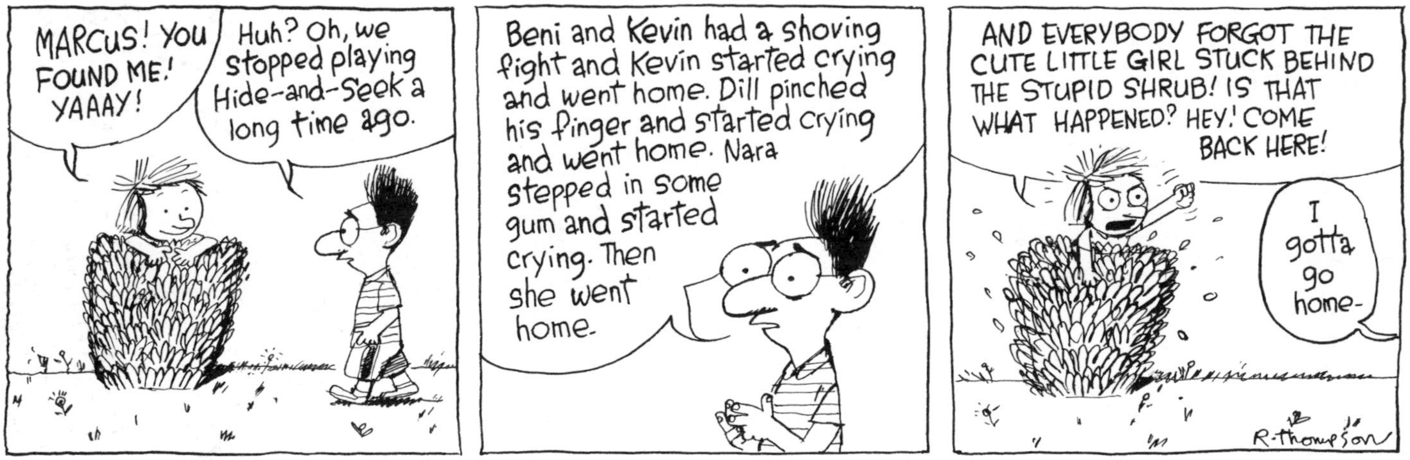
MARCUS! YOU FOUND ME! YAAAY!
Huh? Oh, we stopped playing Hide-and-Seek a long time ago.
Beni and Kevin had a shoving fight and Kevin started crying and went home. Dill pinched his finger and started crying and went home. Nara stepped in some gum and started crying. Then she went home.
AND EVERYBODY FORGOT THE CUTE LITTLE GIRL STUCK BEHIND THE STUPID SHRUB! IS THAT WHAT HAPPENED? HEY! COME BACK HERE!
I gotta go home.
R. Thompson

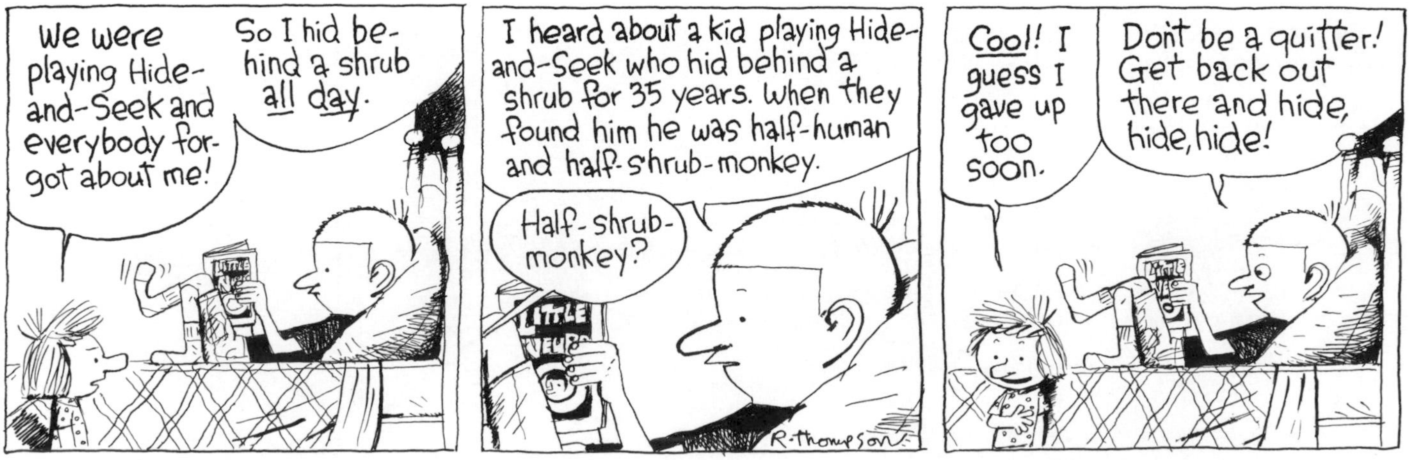
We were playing Hide-and-Seek and everybody forgot about me!
So I hid behind a shrub all day.
LITTLE NEMO
I heard about a kid playing Hide-and-Seek who hid behind a shrub for 35 years. When they found him he was half-human and half-shrub-monkey.
Half-shrub-monkey?
LITTLE NEMO
Cool! I guess I gave up too soon.
Don't be a quitter! Get back out there and hide, hide, hide!
R. Thompson

I got one!
I don't catch lightning bugs any more. Petey says they can go "nova."
They what?
They wait and wait, then they go BLINK! Just like that!
I don't believe it.
That's what Petey says.
BLINK
What else does Petey say?
Ladybugs can smell fear.
R. Thompson

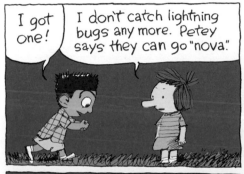

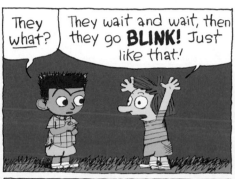

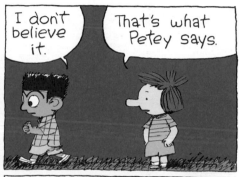

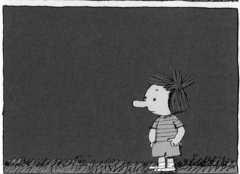

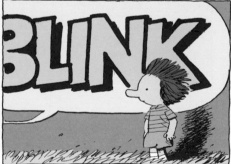

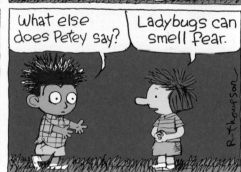

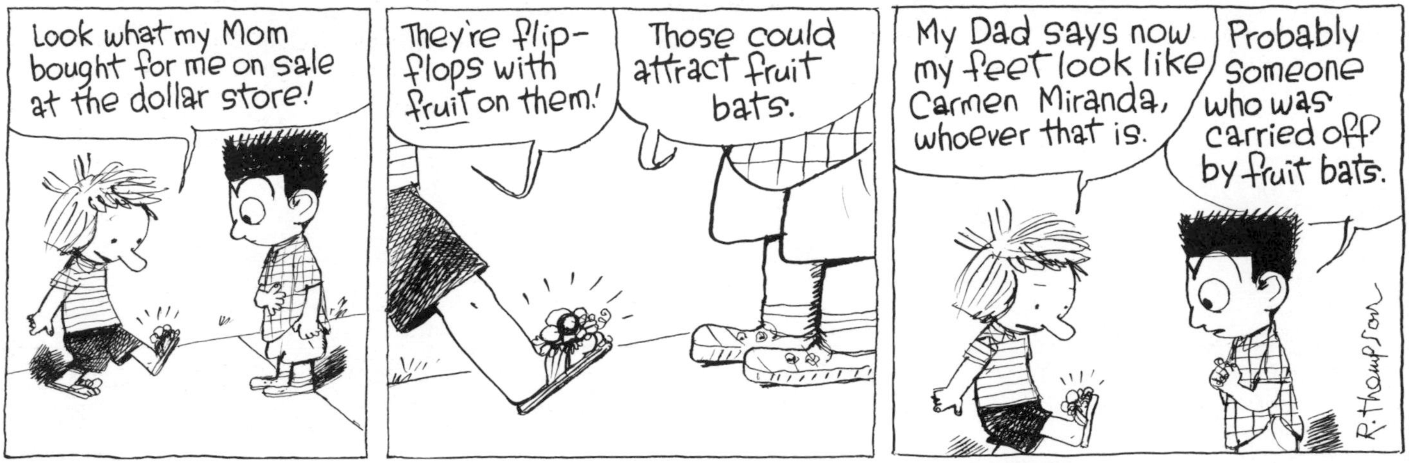

Look what my Mom bought for me on sale at the dollar store!
They're flip-flops with fruit on them!
Those could attract fruit bats.
My Dad says now my feet look like Carmen Miranda, whoever that is.
Probably someone who was carried off by fruit bats.

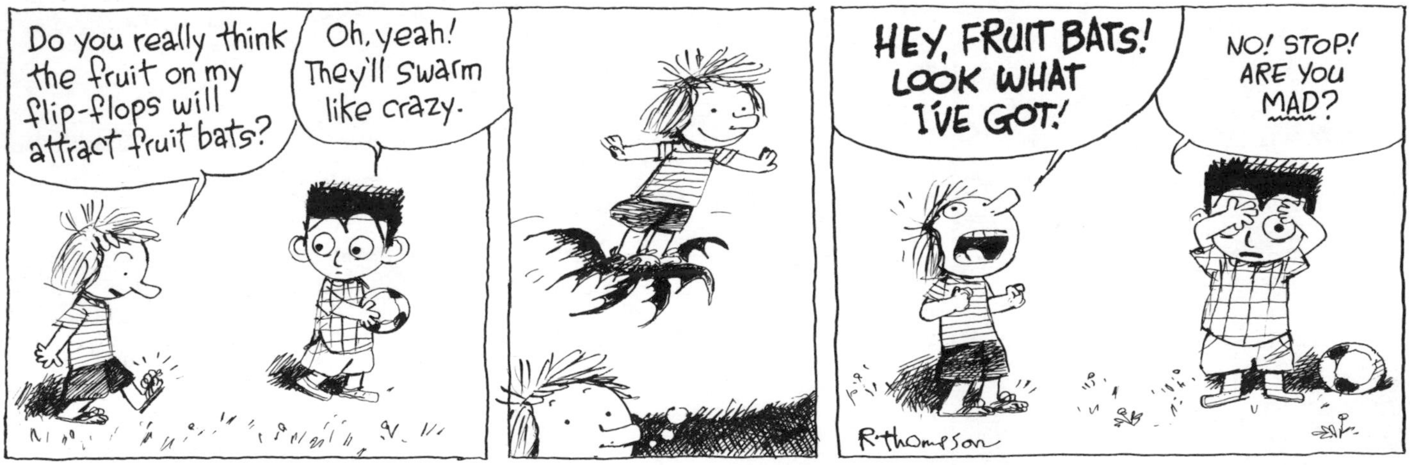

Do you really think the fruit on my flip-flops will attract fruit bats?
Oh, yeah! They'll swarm like crazy.
HEY, FRUIT BATS! LOOK WHAT I'VE GOT!
NO! STOP! ARE YOU MAD?

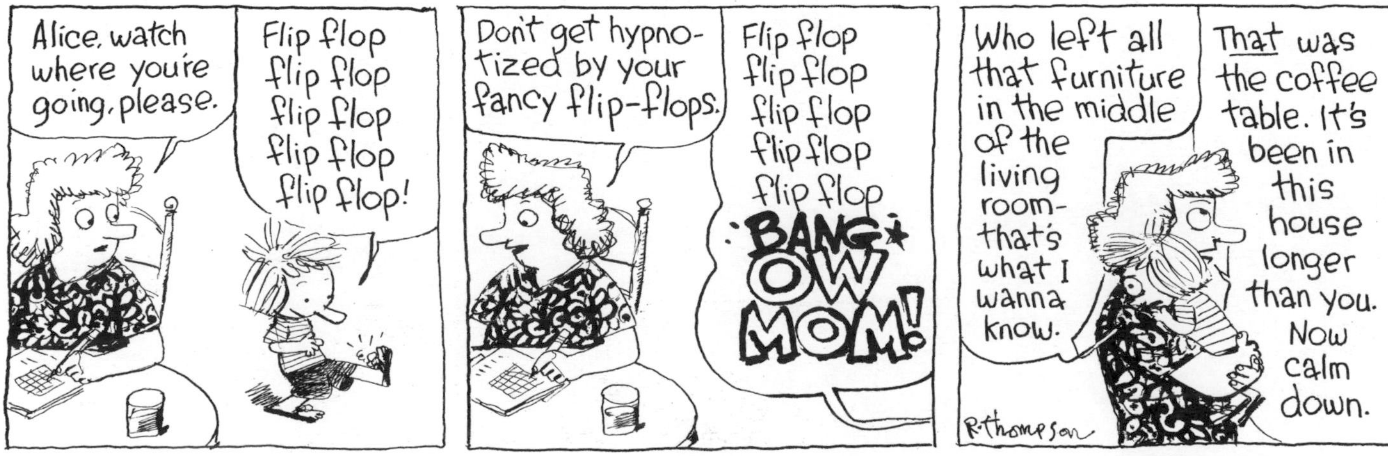

Alice, watch where you're going, please.
Flip flop flip flop flip flop flip flop flip flop!
Don't get hypnotized by your fancy flip-flops.
Flip flop flip flop flip flop flip flop flip flop
BANG
OW MOM!
Who left all that furniture in the middle of the living room—that's what I wanna know.
That was the coffee table. It's been in this house longer than you. Now calm down.

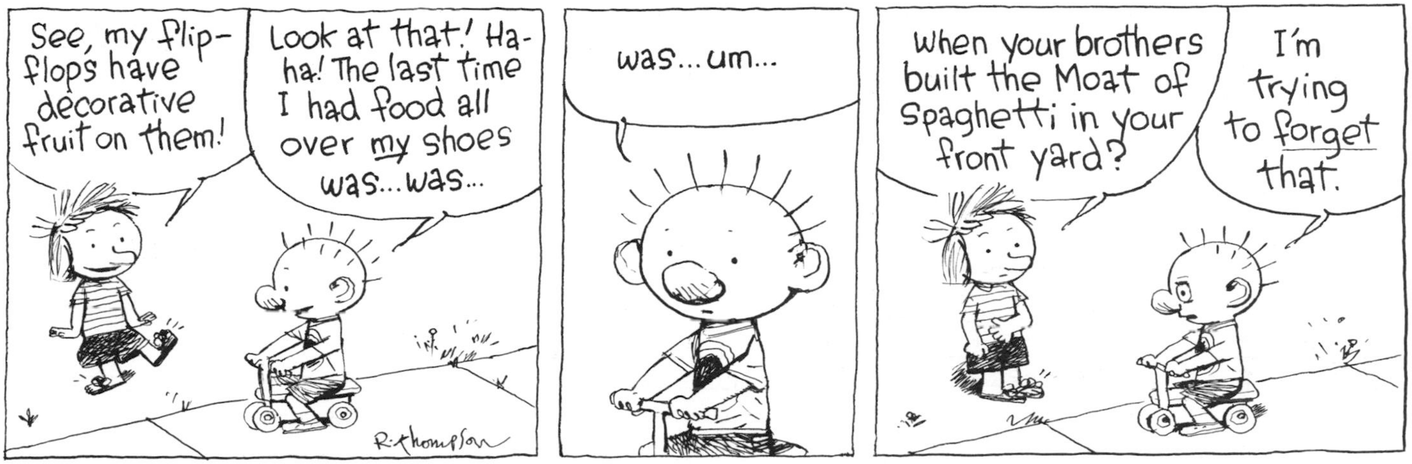
See, my flip-flops have decorative fruit on them!
Look at that! Ha-ha! The last time I had food all over my shoes was...was...
was...um...
When your brothers built the Moat of Spaghetti in your front yard?
I'm trying to forget that.
R. Thompson

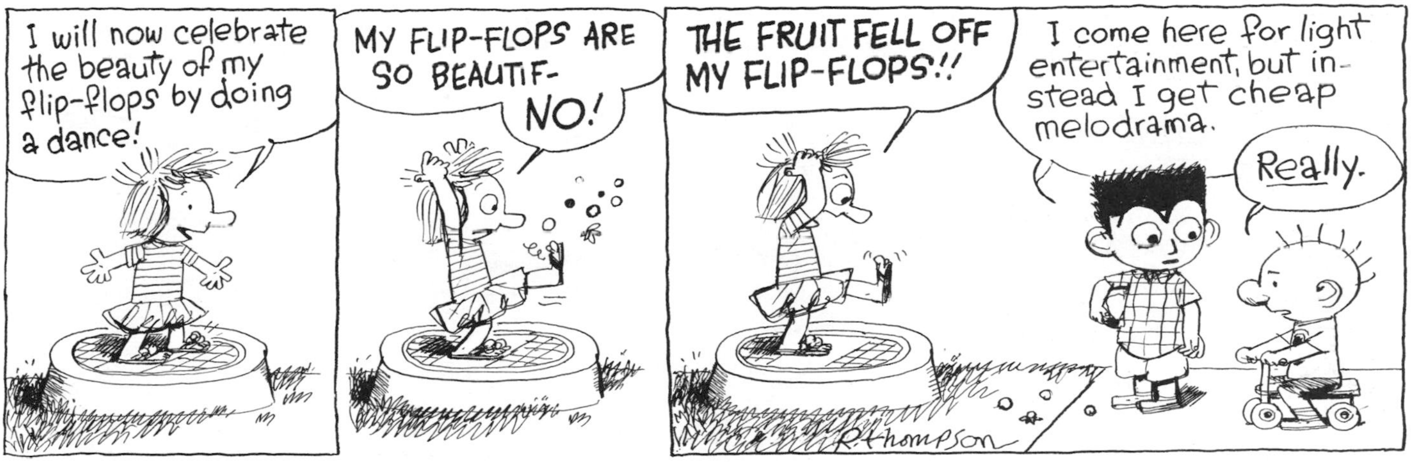
I will now celebrate the beauty of my flip-flops by doing a dance!
MY FLIP-FLOPS ARE SO BEAUTIF-
NO!
THE FRUIT FELL OFF MY FLIP-FLOPS!!
I come here for light entertainment, but instead I get cheap melodrama.
Really.
R. Thompson

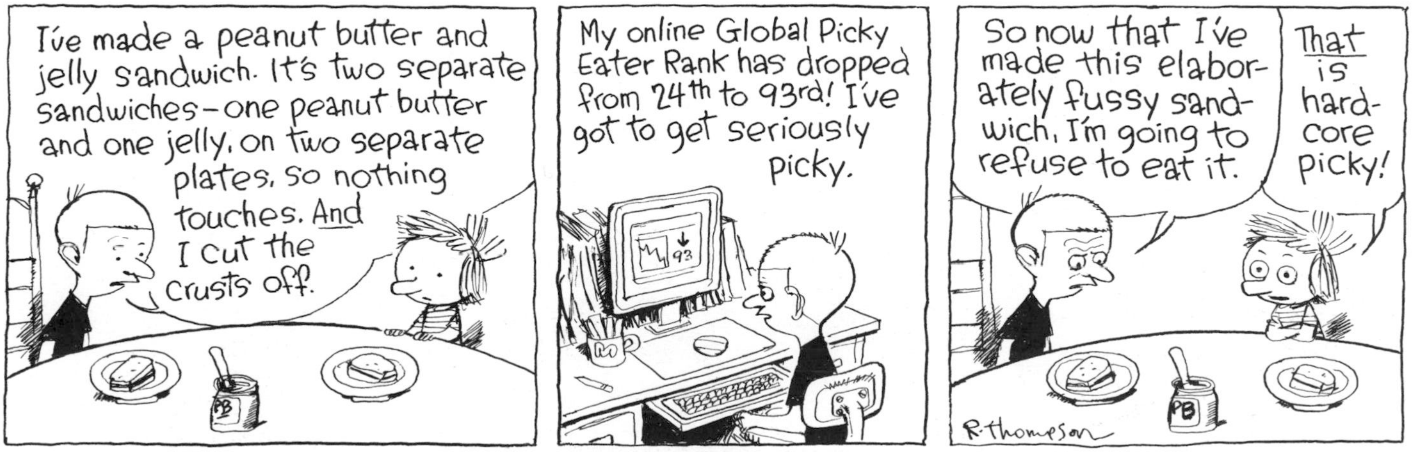
I've made a peanut butter and jelly sandwich. It's two separate sandwiches–one peanut butter and one jelly, on two separate plates, so nothing touches. And I cut the crusts off.
PB
My online Global Picky Eater Rank has dropped from 24th to 93rd! I've got to get seriously picky.
93
So now that I've made this elaborately fussy sandwich, I'm going to refuse to eat it.
That is hard-core picky!
PB
R. Thompson

What's all that stuff in front of your house?
My brothers opened a lemonade stand.
R. thompson
I love lemonade!
Then they expanded into chips, hot dogs, candy and power drinks.
Then bait and tackle, beer and wine, fireworks, souvenirs and automotive supplies.
BAIT
CLOSED
TACKLE
SOUVENIRS
HOT DOGS
LEMONADE $2
BEER + WINE
Then finally car-detailing and a large animal clinic and taxidermy studio.
That's when my dad put his foot down.
Darn! I wanted some lemonade!

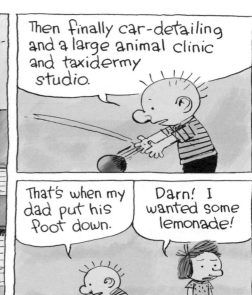

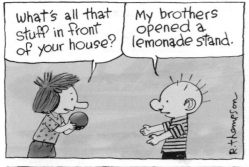

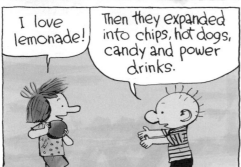

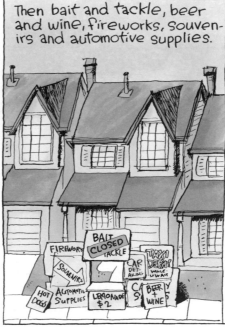

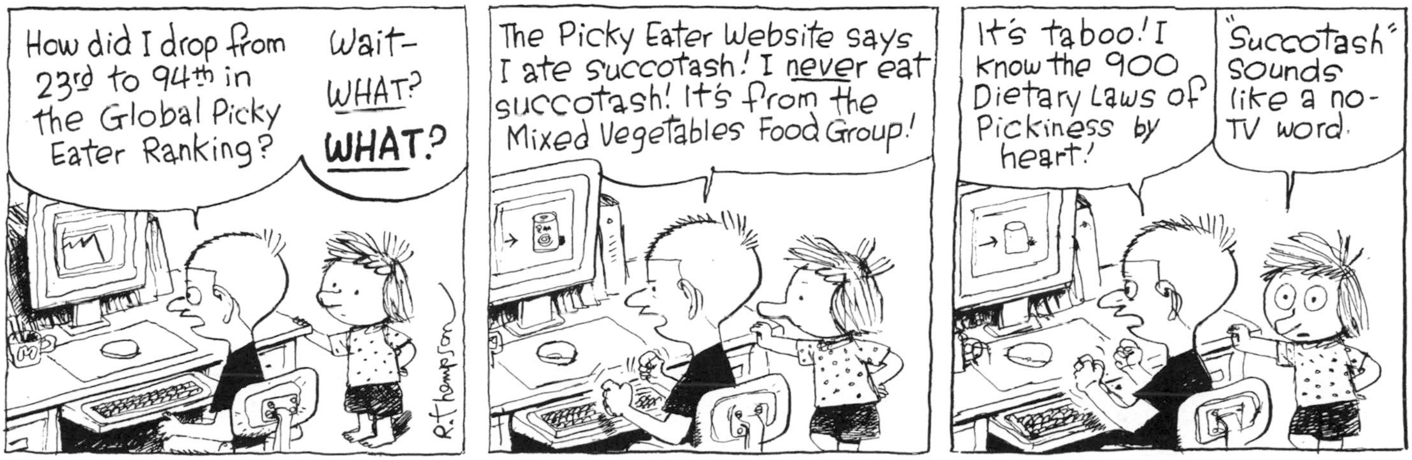
How did I drop from 23rd to 94th in the Global Picky Eater Ranking?
Wait- WHAT? WHAT?
The Picky Eater Website says I ate succotash! I never eat succotash! It's from the Mixed Vegetables Food Group!
It's taboo! I know the 900 Dietary Laws of Pickiness by heart!
"Succotash" sounds like a no-TV word.

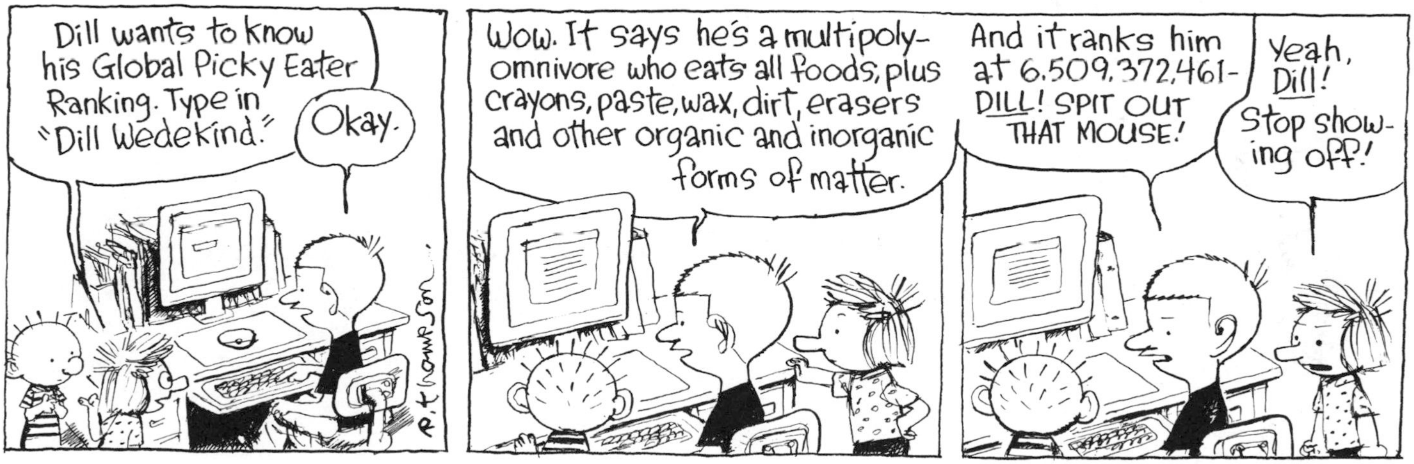
Dill wants to know his Global Picky Eater Ranking. Type in "Dill Wedekind."
Okay.
Wow. It says he's a multipoly-omnivore who eats all foods, plus crayons, paste, wax, dirt, erasers and other organic and inorganic forms of matter.
And it ranks him at 6,509,372,461- DILL! SPIT OUT THAT MOUSE!
Yeah, Dill! Stop showing off!

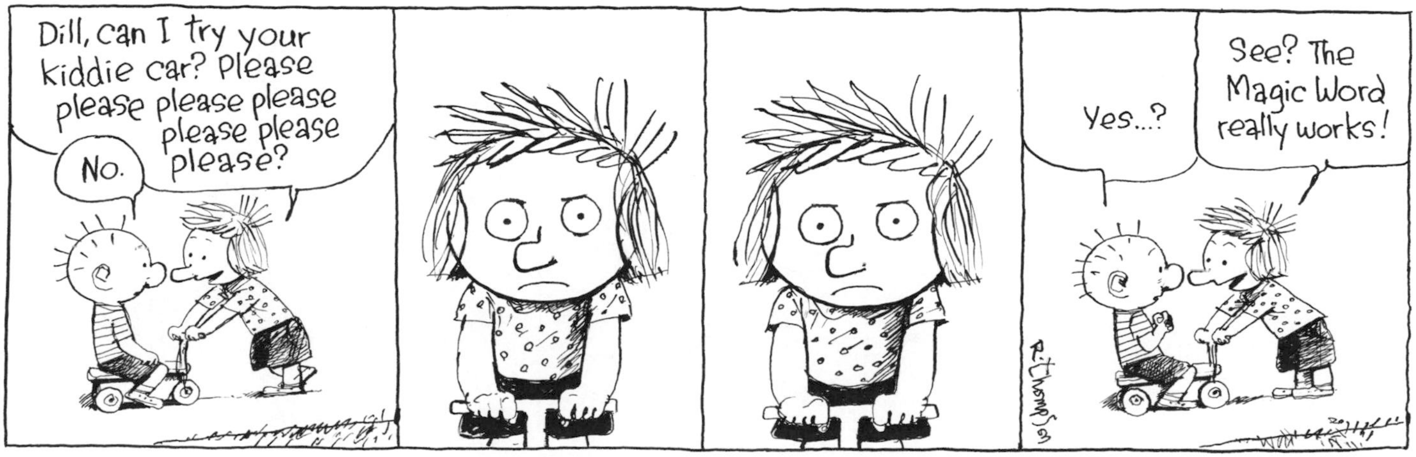
Dill, can I try your kiddie car? Please please please please please please please?
No.
Yes...?
See? The Magic Word really works!

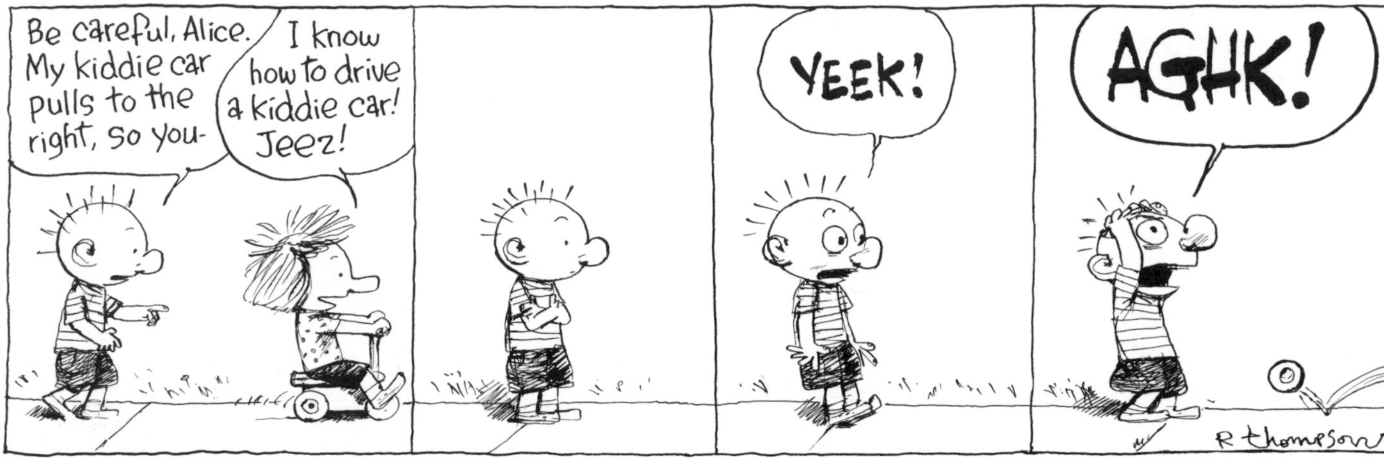
Be careful, Alice. My kiddie car pulls to the right, so you-
I know how to drive a kiddie car! Jeez!
YEEK!
AGHK!
R thompson

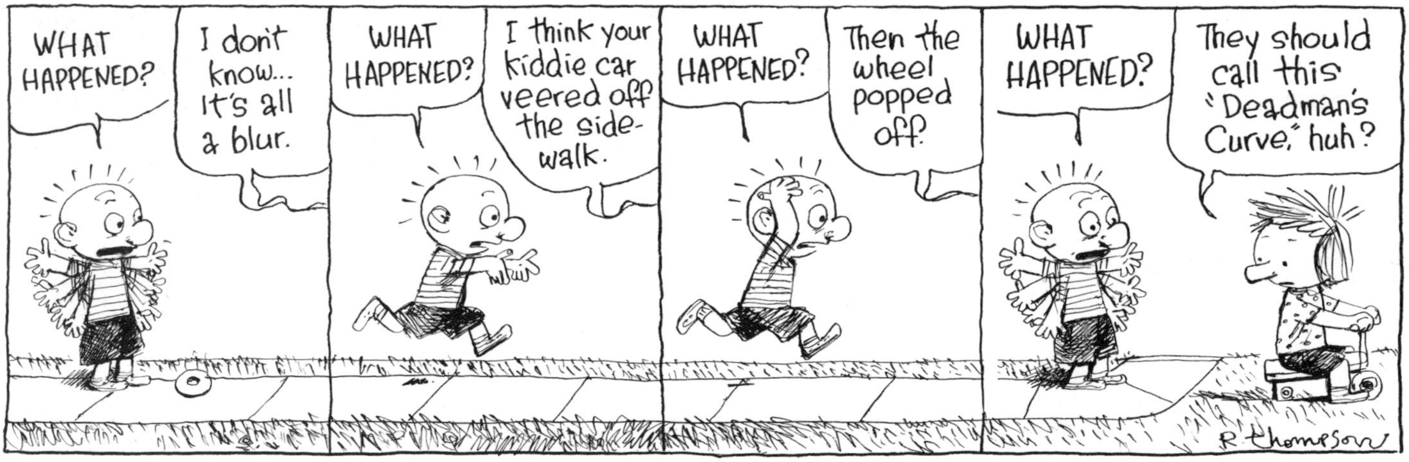
WHAT HAPPENED?
I don't know... It's all a blur.
WHAT HAPPENED?
I think your kiddie car veered off the side-walk.
WHAT HAPPENED?
Then the wheel popped off?
WHAT HAPPENED?
They should call this "Deadman's Curve," huh?
R thompson

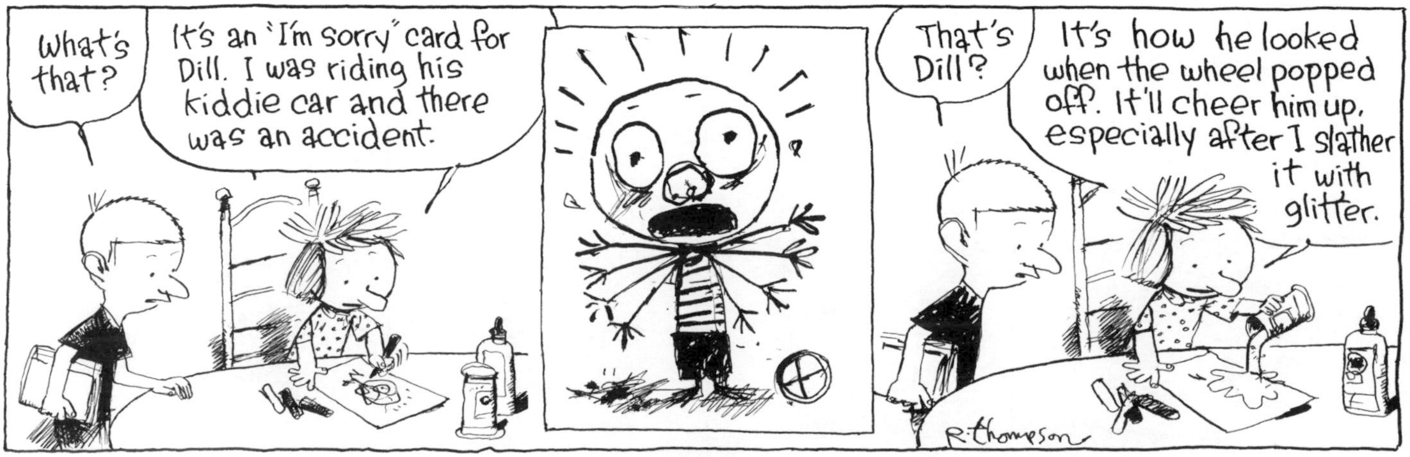
What's that?
It's an "I'm sorry" card for Dill. I was riding his kiddie car and there was an accident.
That's Dill?
It's how he looked when the wheel popped off. It'll cheer him up, especially after I slather it with glitter.
R thompson

POP POP POP POP POP POP
POP POP BANG POP BANG
BANG POP POP BANG BANG
BANG BANG BANG
BANG BANG BANG
BANG BANG POP PFZZZT
SKWIRT
PFZ ZTZ
The matter-antimatter matrix in your popper is higgledy-piggledy. I'll hit it with a hammer and it should be good as new.
I was afraid it was the transmission again.
R. Thompson

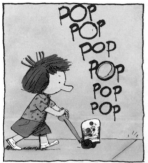

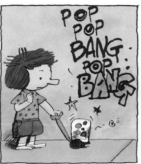

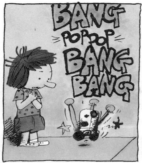

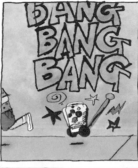

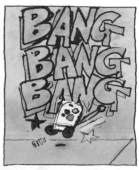

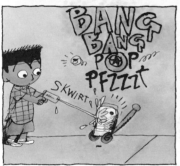

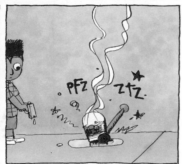

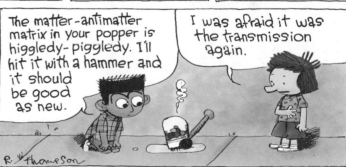

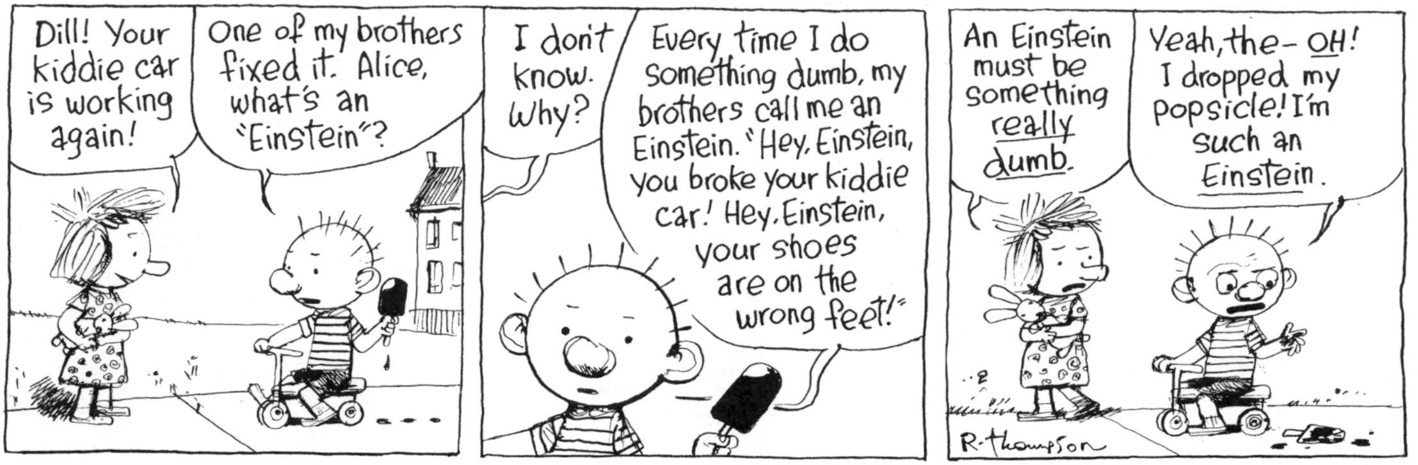

Dill! Your kiddie car is working again!
One of my brothers fixed it. Alice, what's an "Einstein"?
I don't know. Why?
Every time I do something dumb, my brothers call me an Einstein. "Hey, Einstein, you broke your kiddie car! Hey, Einstein, your shoes are on the wrong feet!"
An Einstein must be something really dumb.
Yeah, the– OH! I dropped my popsicle! I'm such an Einstein.
R. Thompson

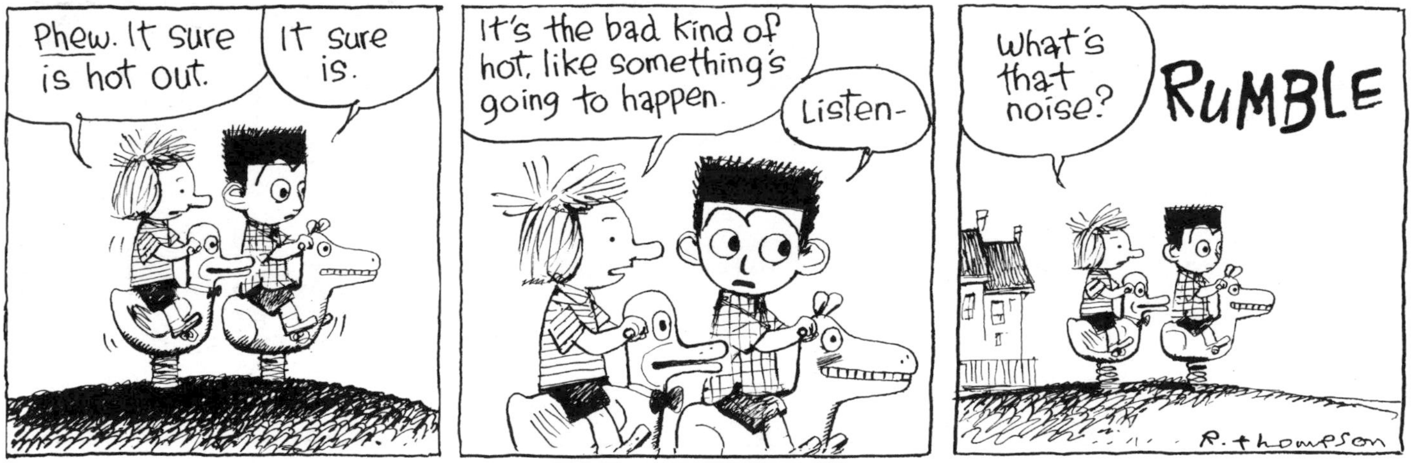

Phew. It sure is hot out.
It sure is.
It's the bad kind of hot, like something's going to happen.
Listen–
What's that noise?
RUMBLE
R. Thompson

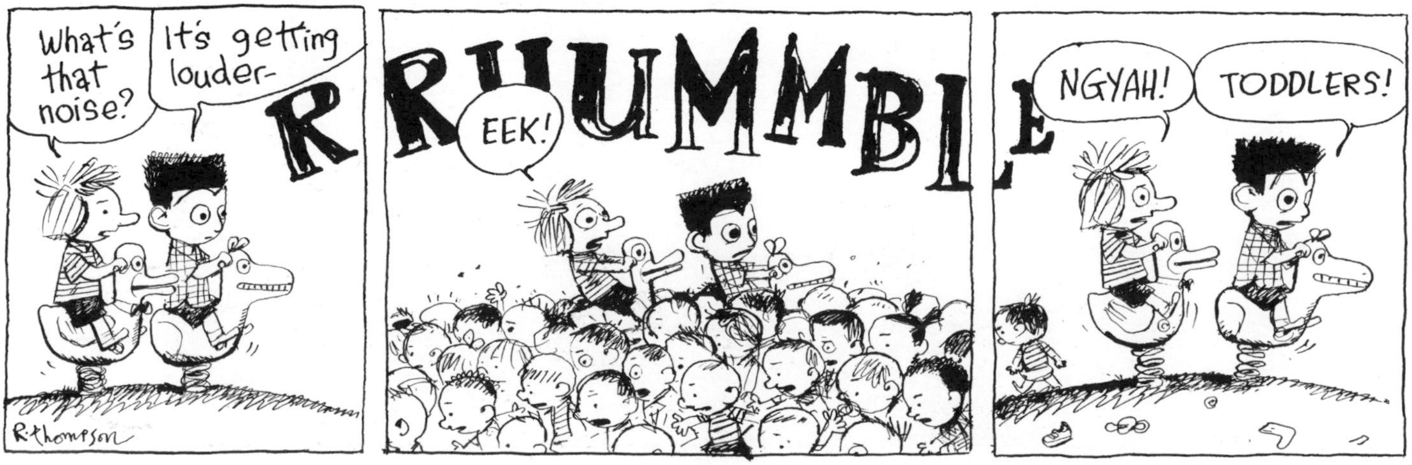

What's that noise?
It's getting louder–
RRUUMMBLE
EEK!
NGYAH!
TODDLERS!
R. Thompson

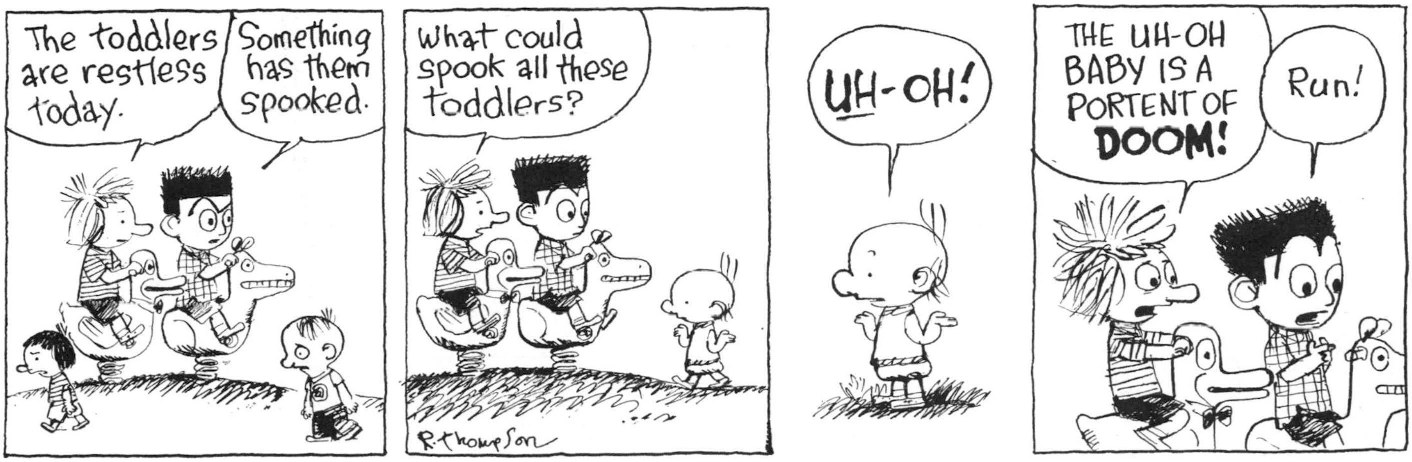
The toddlers are restless today.
Something has them spooked.
What could spook all these toddlers?
UH-OH!
THE UH-OH BABY IS A PORTENT OF DOOM!
Run!
R. thompson

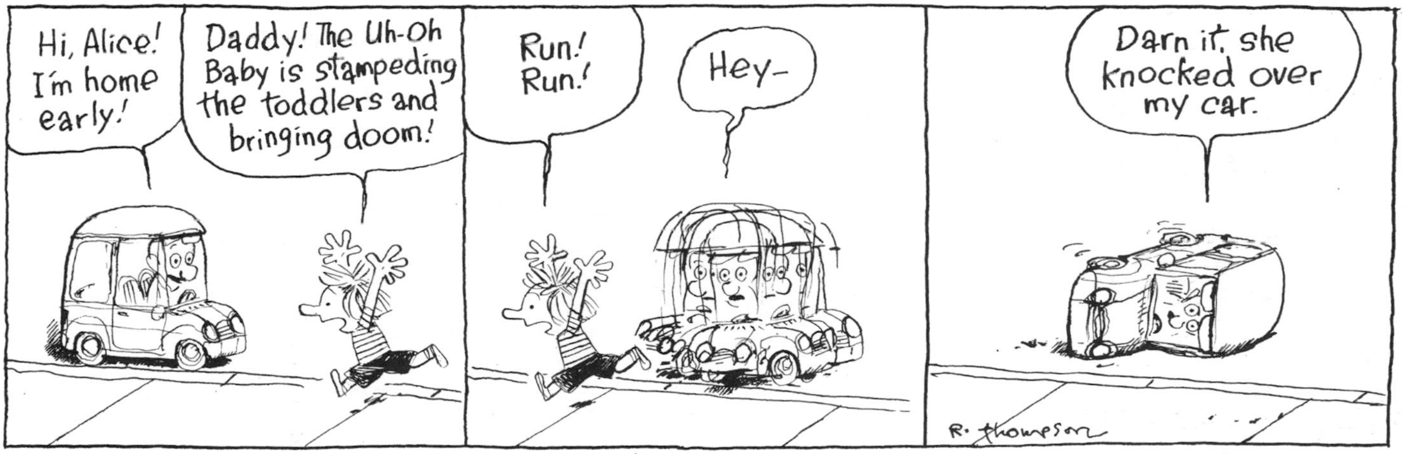
Hi, Alice! I'm home early!
Daddy! The Uh-Oh Baby is stampeding the toddlers and bringing doom!
Run! Run!
Hey-
Darn it, she knocked over my car.
R. thompson

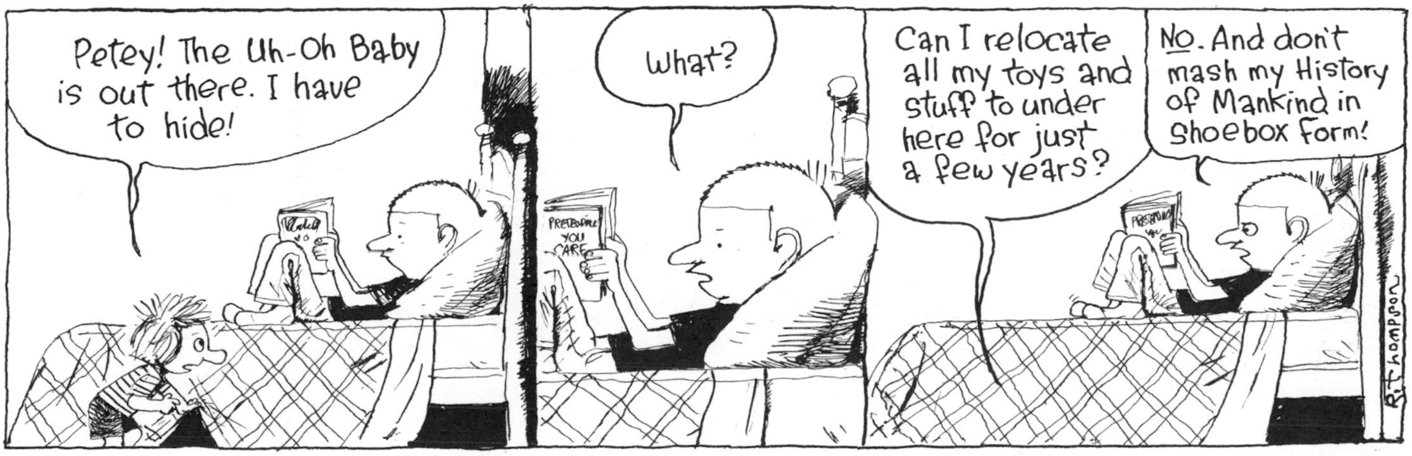
Petey! The Uh-Oh Baby is out there. I have to hide!
What?
Can I relocate all my toys and stuff to under here for just a few years?
NO. And don't mash my History of Mankind in Shoebox Form!
R. thompson

What are you reading, Petey?

"Little Neuro and the Magic Dragon."

What's it about?

Little Neuro is sitting in bed when a dragon sticks its head in the window.

It tells him it'll grant his every wish.

R. Thompson

Cool!

But Little Neuro's dragon allergy acts up and he sneezes all over it, so it leaves.

Why doesn't the stupid dragon just eat him?

Take your gory imagination and get out of my room.

Everybody ready for three days of fun and sun in fabulous GEEK'S NECK?

Fun in the sun, here we come! YIPPIE!

GNRR RRRR RRR

Petey's chewing his arm off!

Petey! Spit it out.

Or I'll turn this van around before we even leave the driveway!

R. thompson

Here we are!

Why is it raining?

KOMFY INN GEEK'S NECK

WELCOME ICE MACHINE REPAIRMAN

R. thompson

Room's a bit small.

The TV's a bit huge.

Is it supposed to be raining?

Why is it still raining?

Let's find a postcard for Grandma!

GEEK'S NECK GIFT-A-TERIA

END OF SEASON SALE!

Here's one!

"BEACH BUMS." Let's find a nice card.

Mom, the cage of hermit crabs is freaking me out. Can we go?

Here's one!

"BOTTOMS UP." No, a nice card.

R. thompson

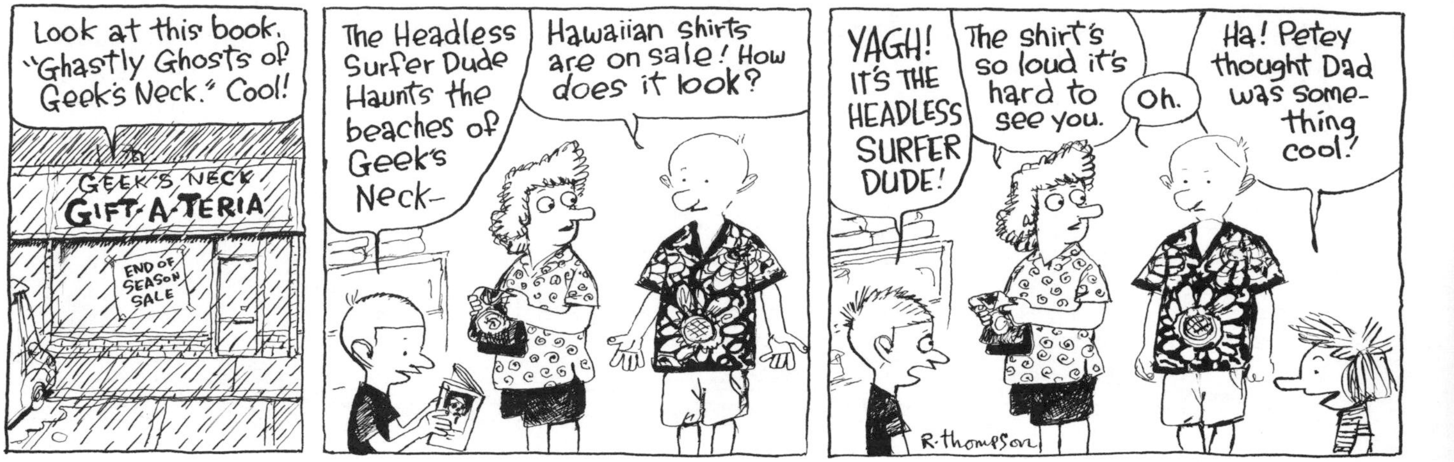
Look at this book, "Ghastly Ghosts of Geek's Neck." Cool!
GEEK'S NECK
GIFT-A-TERIA
END OF SEASON SALE
The Headless Surfer Dude Haunts the beaches of Geek's Neck–
Hawaiian shirts are on sale! How does it look?
YAGH! IT'S THE HEADLESS SURFER DUDE!
The shirt's so loud it's hard to see you.
Oh.
Ha! Petey thought Dad was something cool!
R. thompson

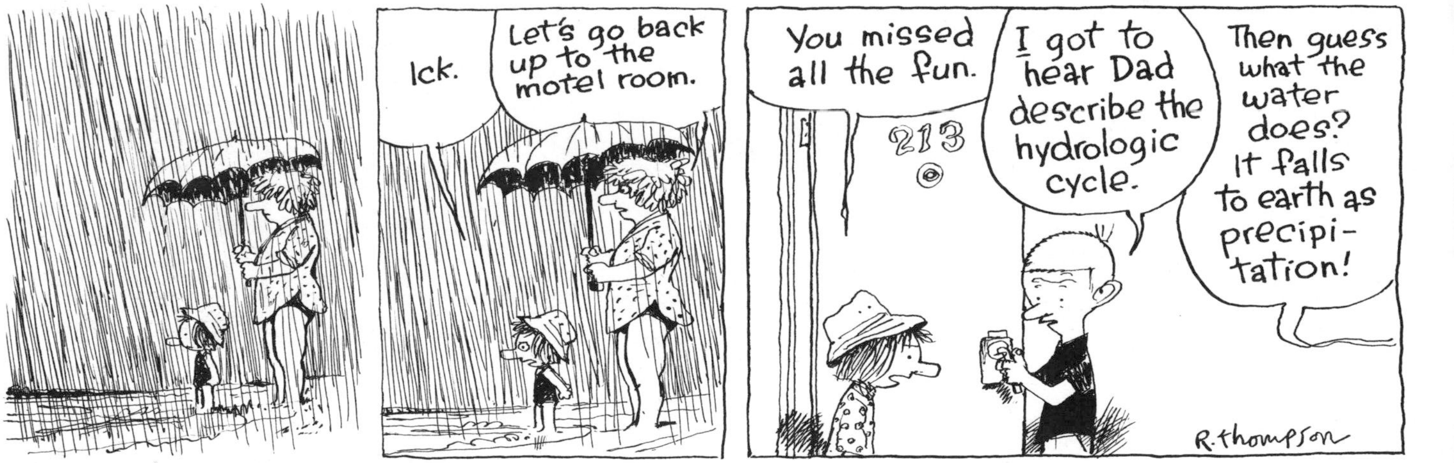
Ick.
Let's go back up to the motel room.
You missed all the fun.
213
I got to hear Dad describe the hydrologic cycle.
Then guess what the water does? It falls to earth as precipitation!
R. thompson

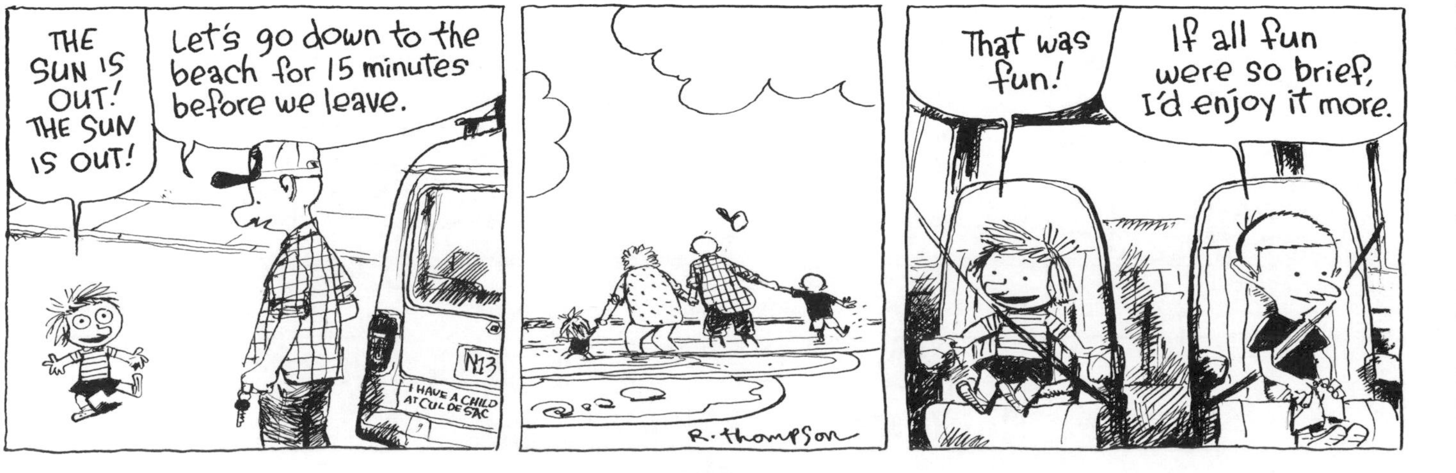
THE SUN IS OUT! THE SUN IS OUT!
Let's go down to the beach for 15 minutes before we leave.
N13
I HAVE A CHILD AT CUL DE SAC
R. thompson
That was fun!
If all fun were so brief, I'd enjoy it more.

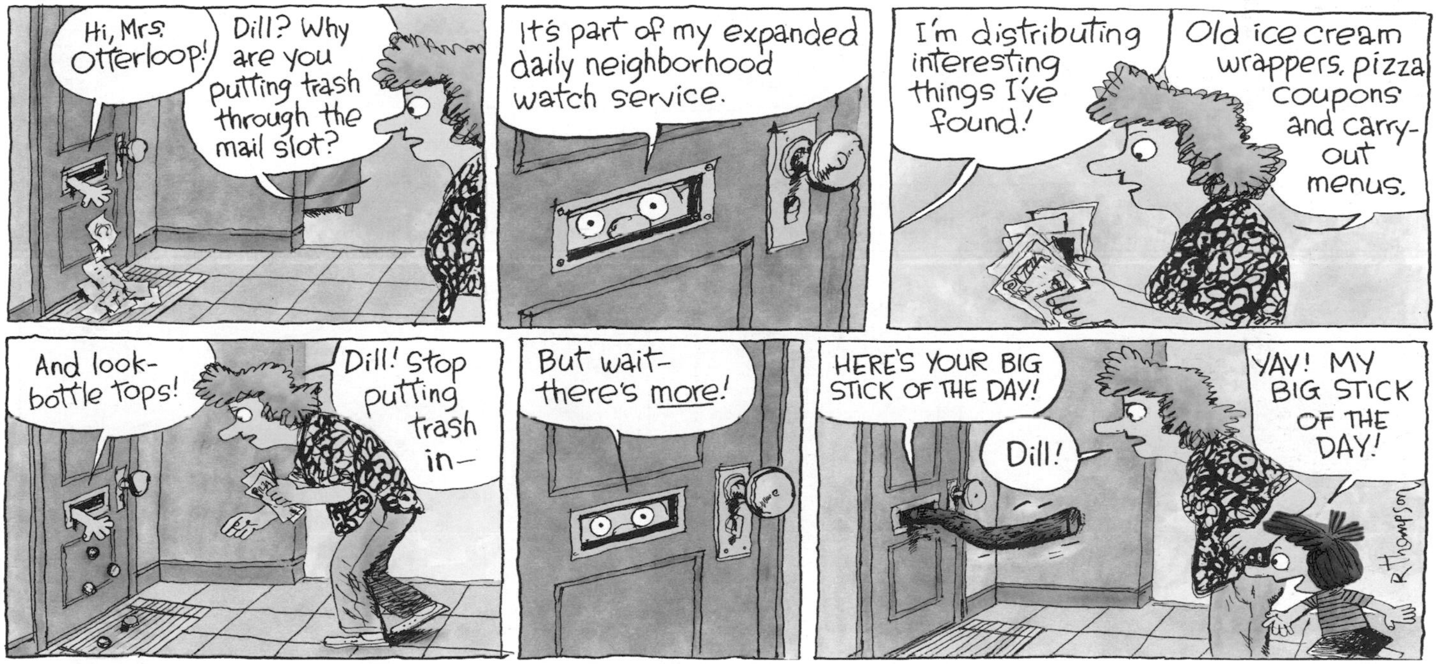
Hi, Mrs. Otterloop!
Dill? Why are you putting trash through the mail slot?
It's part of my expanded daily neighborhood watch service.
I'm distributing interesting things I've found!
Old ice cream wrappers, pizza coupons and carry-out menus.
And look- bottle tops!
Dill! Stop putting trash in—
But wait- there's more!
HERE'S YOUR BIG STICK OF THE DAY!
Dill!
YAY! MY BIG STICK OF THE DAY!
R Thompson

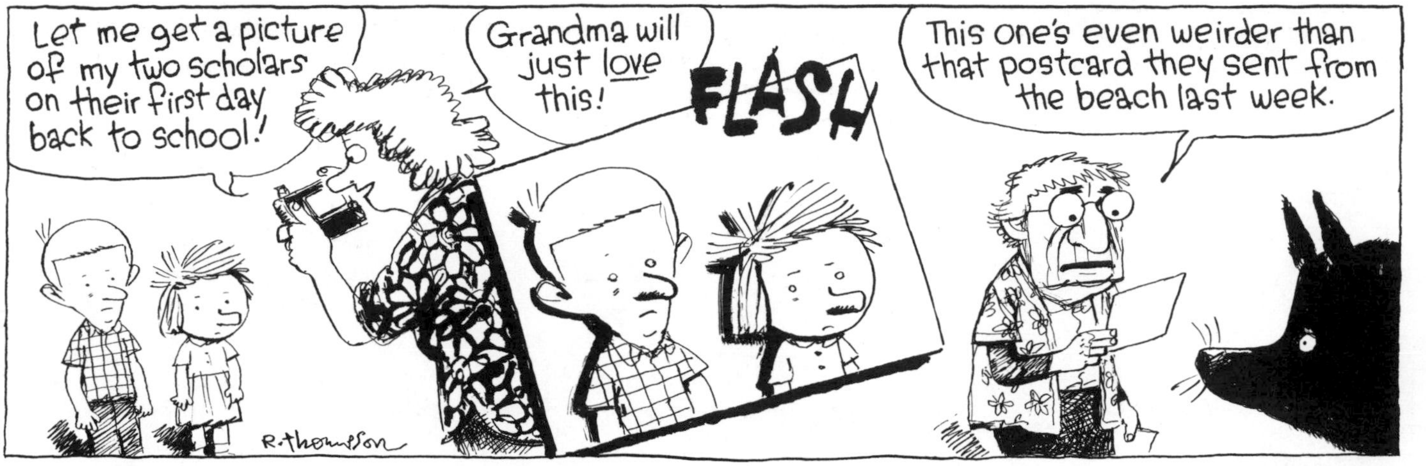
Let me get a picture of my two scholars on their first day back to school!
Grandma will just love this!
FLASH
This one's even weirder than that postcard they sent from the beach last week.
R. Thompson

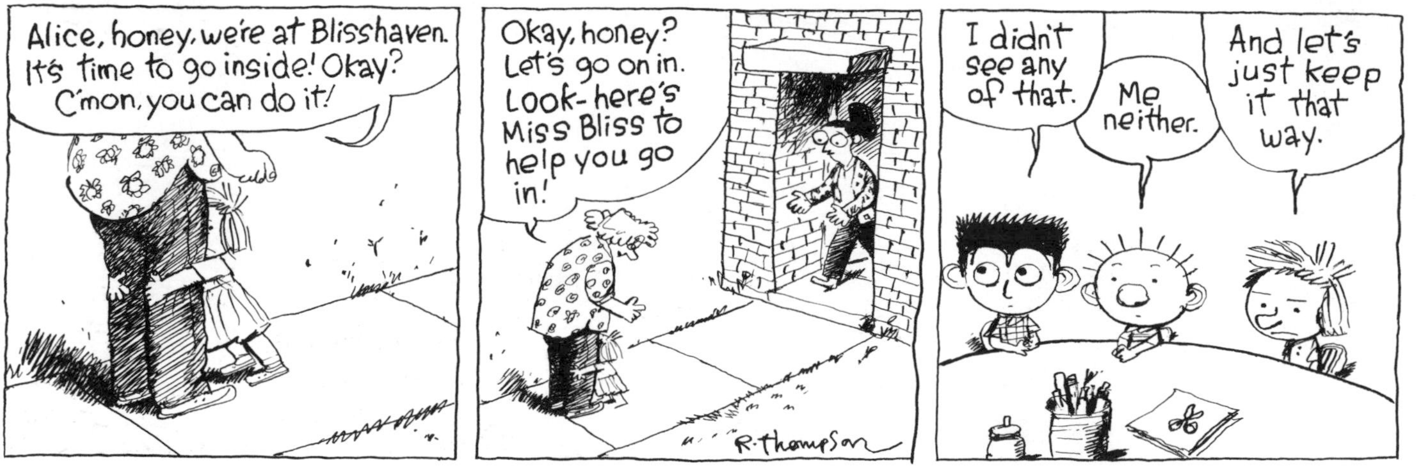
Alice, honey, we're at Blisshaven. It's time to go inside! Okay? C'mon, you can do it!
Okay, honey? Let's go on in. Look- here's Miss Bliss to help you go in!
R. Thompson
I didn't see any of that.
Me neither.
And let's just keep it that way.

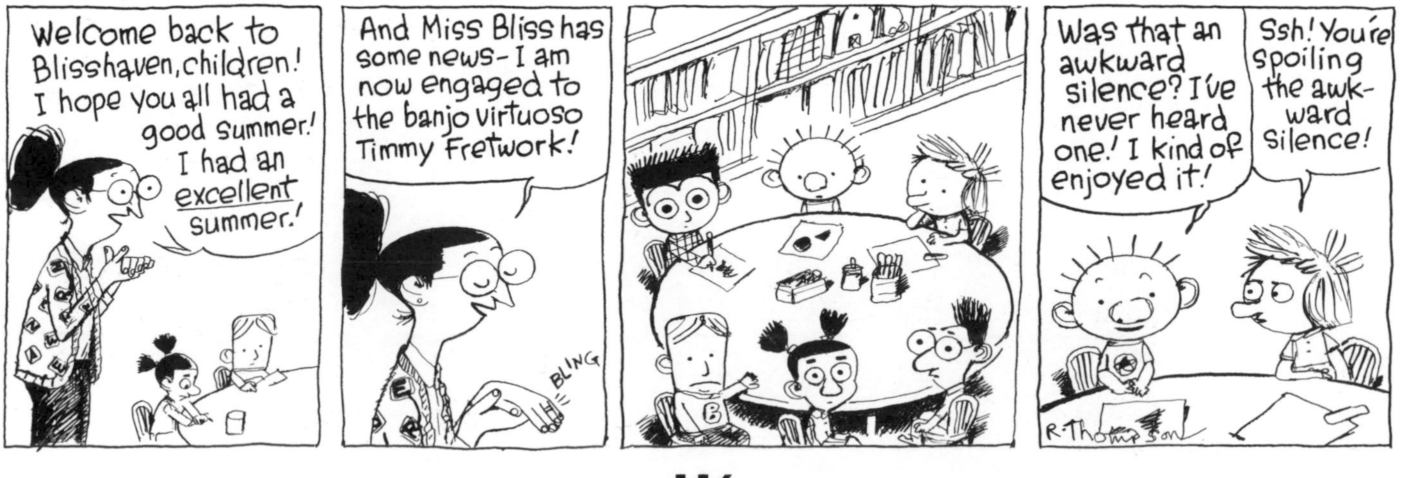
Welcome back to Blisshaven, children! I hope you all had a good summer! I had an excellent summer!
And Miss Bliss has some news- I am now engaged to the banjo virtuoso Timmy Fretwork!
BLING
Was that an awkward silence? I've never heard one! I kind of enjoyed it!
Ssh! You're spoiling the awkward silence!
R. Thompson

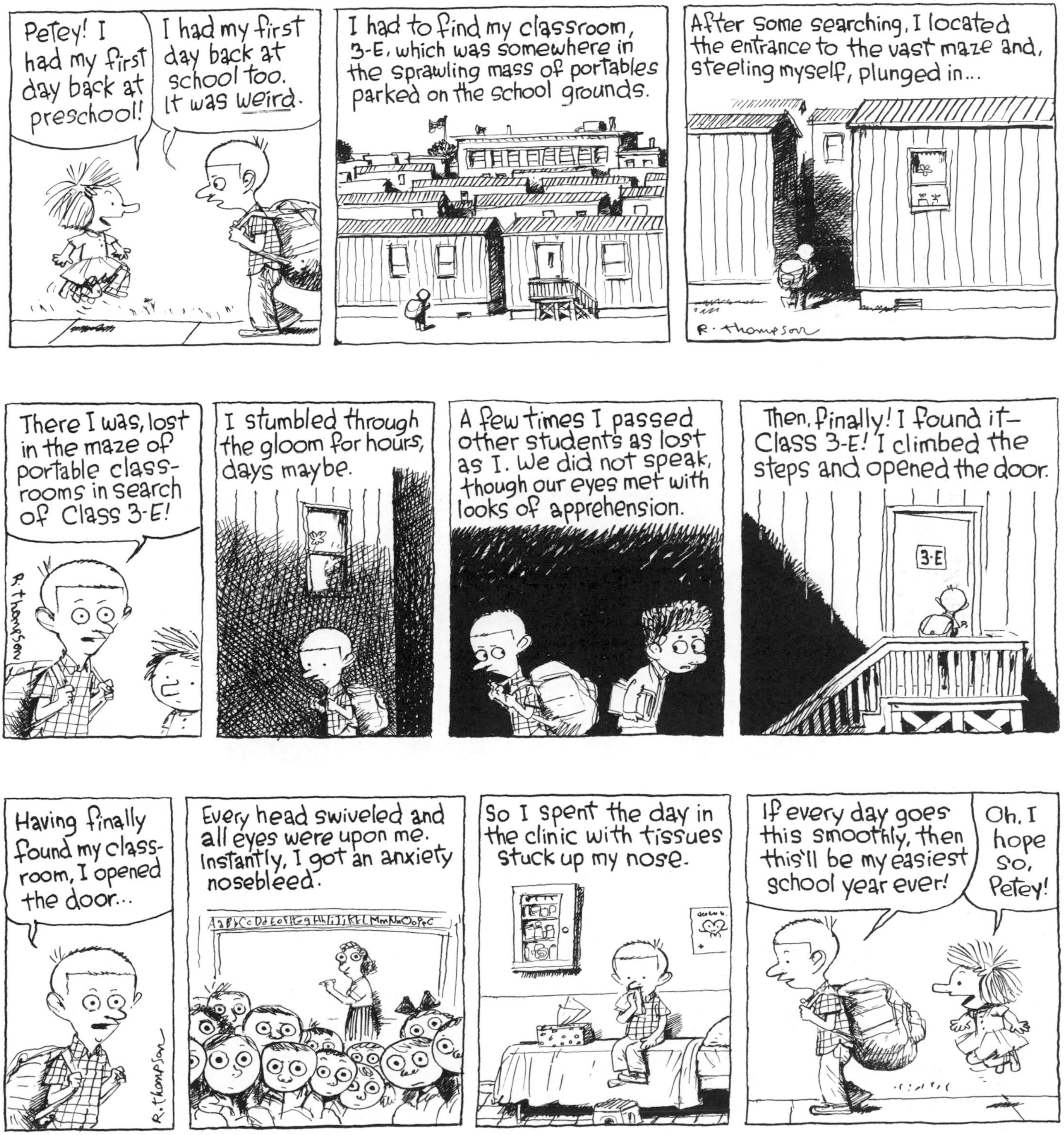
Petey! I had my first day back at preschool!
I had my first day back at school too. It was weird.
I had to find my classroom, 3-E, which was somewhere in the sprawling mass of portables parked on the school grounds.
After some searching, I located the entrance to the vast maze and, steeling myself, plunged in...
R. Thompson
There I was, lost in the maze of portable classrooms in search of Class 3-E!
R. Thompson
I stumbled through the gloom for hours, days maybe.
A few times I passed other students as lost as I. We did not speak, though our eyes met with looks of apprehension.
Then, finally! I found it—Class 3-E! I climbed the steps and opened the door.
3·E
Having finally found my classroom, I opened the door...
R. Thompson
Every head swiveled and all eyes were upon me. Instantly, I got an anxiety nosebleed.
So I spent the day in the clinic with tissues stuck up my nose.
If every day goes this smoothly, then this'll be my easiest school year ever!
Oh, I hope so, Petey!

Guess what? I was in the Rocket to Mars at the Food Pyramid waiting for my mom.
And I saw Miss Bliss walk out of the store carrying groceries!
PARKING
ROCKET TO MARS
Then she got in a car with stickers all over it and drove away.
Wow! Did she see you?
No. It would have been awkward.
Wow. Miss Bliss with groceries and a car!
It was so weird.
And another thing. No matter how long I sit in it, the Rocket to Mars never actually goes to Mars.
PUD
You have to put money in it, Einstein.
R. thompson

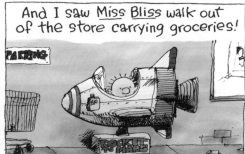

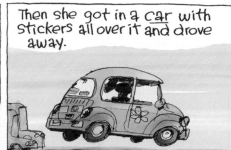

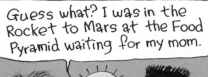

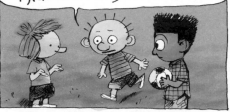

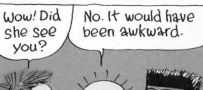

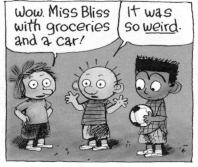

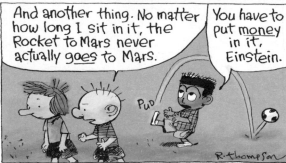

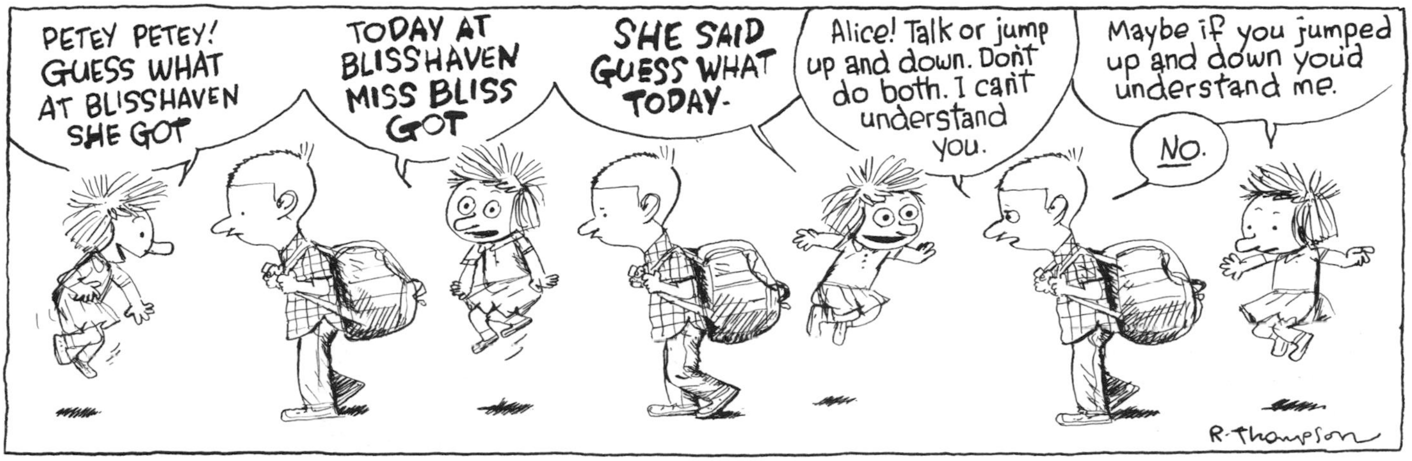
PETEY PETEY! GUESS WHAT AT BLISSHAVEN SHE GOT
TODAY AT BLISSHAVEN MISS BLISS GOT
SHE SAID GUESS WHAT TODAY-
Alice! Talk or jump up and down. Don't do both. I can't understand you.
Maybe if you jumped up and down you'd understand me.
NO.
R. Thompson

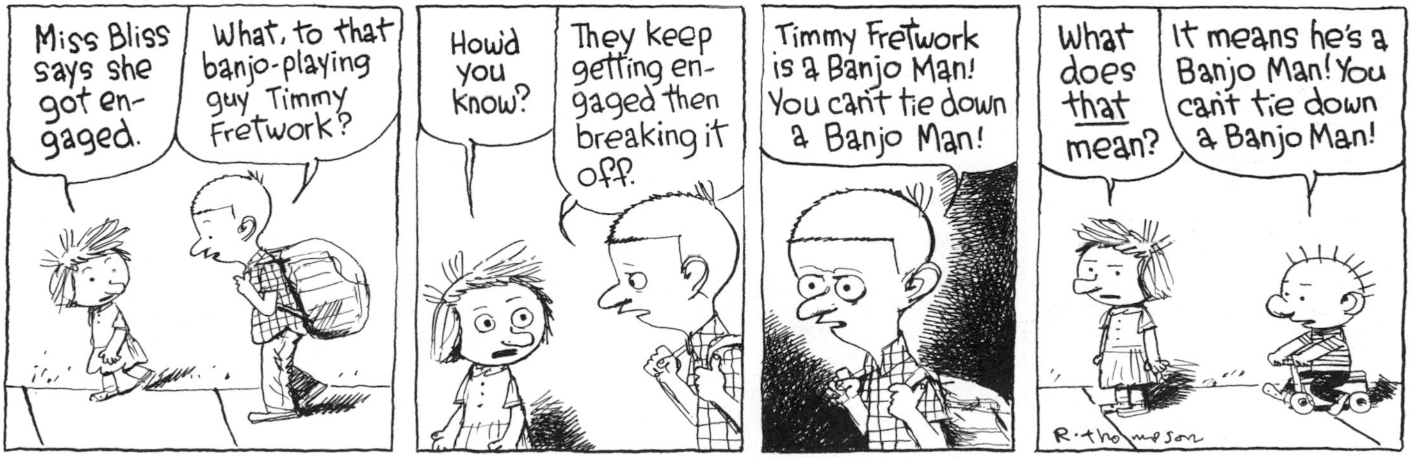
Miss Bliss says she got engaged.
What, to that banjo-playing guy Timmy Fretwork?
How'd you know?
They keep getting engaged then breaking it off.
Timmy Fretwork is a Banjo Man! You can't tie down a Banjo Man!
What does that mean?
It means he's a Banjo Man! You can't tie down a Banjo Man!
R. Thompson

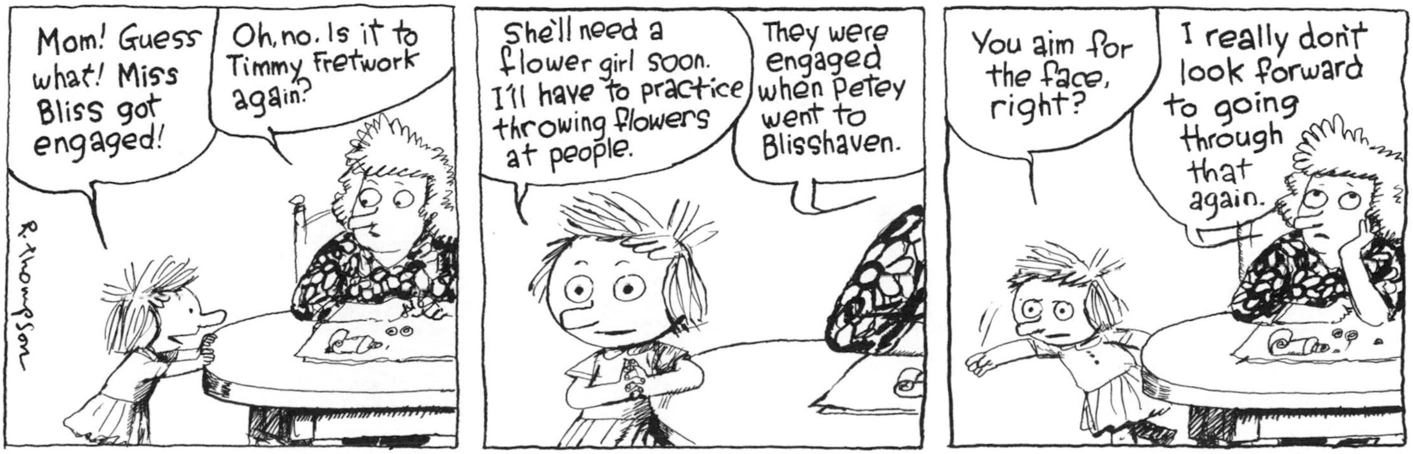
Mom! Guess what! Miss Bliss got engaged!
Oh, no. Is it to Timmy Fretwork again?
R. Thompson
She'll need a flower girl soon. I'll have to practice throwing flowers at people.
They were engaged when Petey went to Blisshaven.
You aim for the face, right?
I really don't look forward to going through that again.

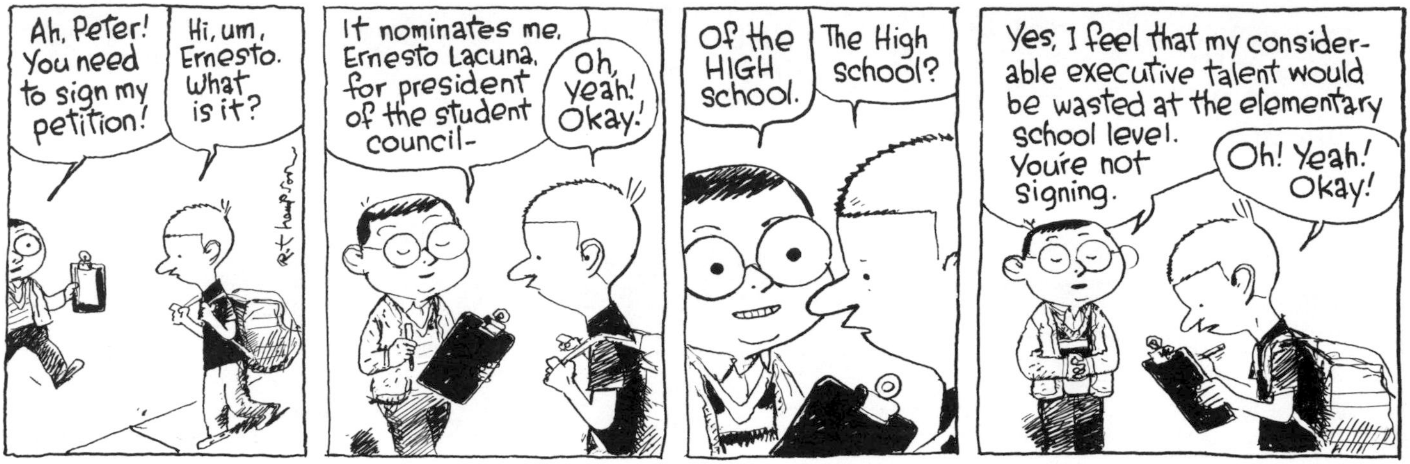
Ah, Peter! You need to sign my petition!
Hi, um, Ernesto. What is it?
It nominates me, Ernesto Lacuna, for president of the student council-
Oh, yeah! Okay!
Of the HIGH school.
The High school?
Yes, I feel that my considerable executive talent would be wasted at the elementary school level. You're not signing.
Oh! Yeah! Okay!

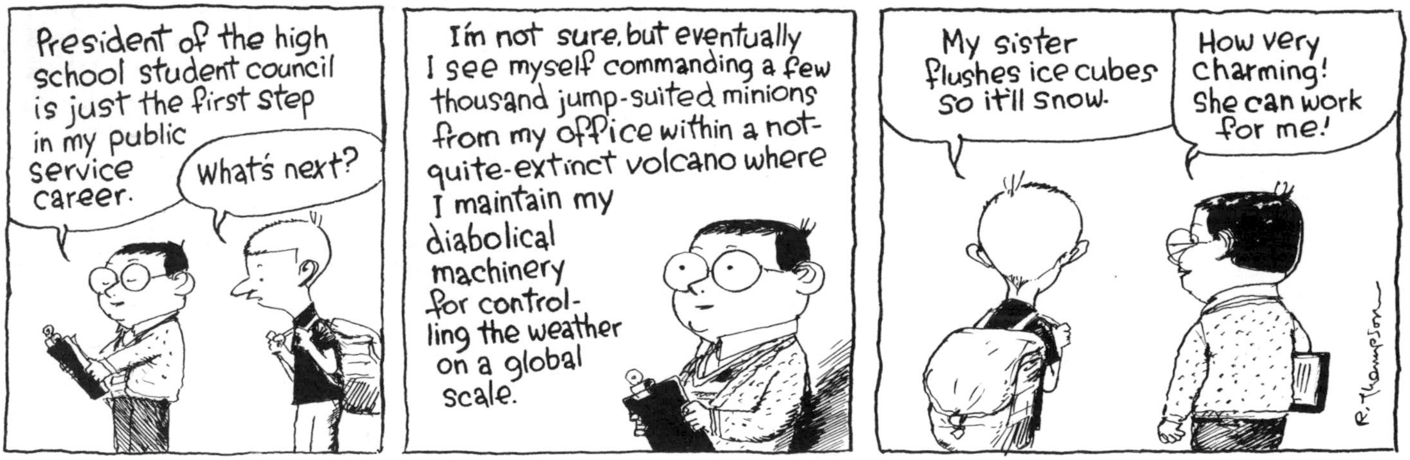
President of the high school student council is just the first step in my public service career.
What's next?
I'm not sure, but eventually I see myself commanding a few thousand jump-suited minions from my office within a not-quite-extinct volcano where I maintain my diabolical machinery for controlling the weather on a global scale.
My sister flushes ice cubes so it'll snow.
How very charming! She can work for me!
R. thompson

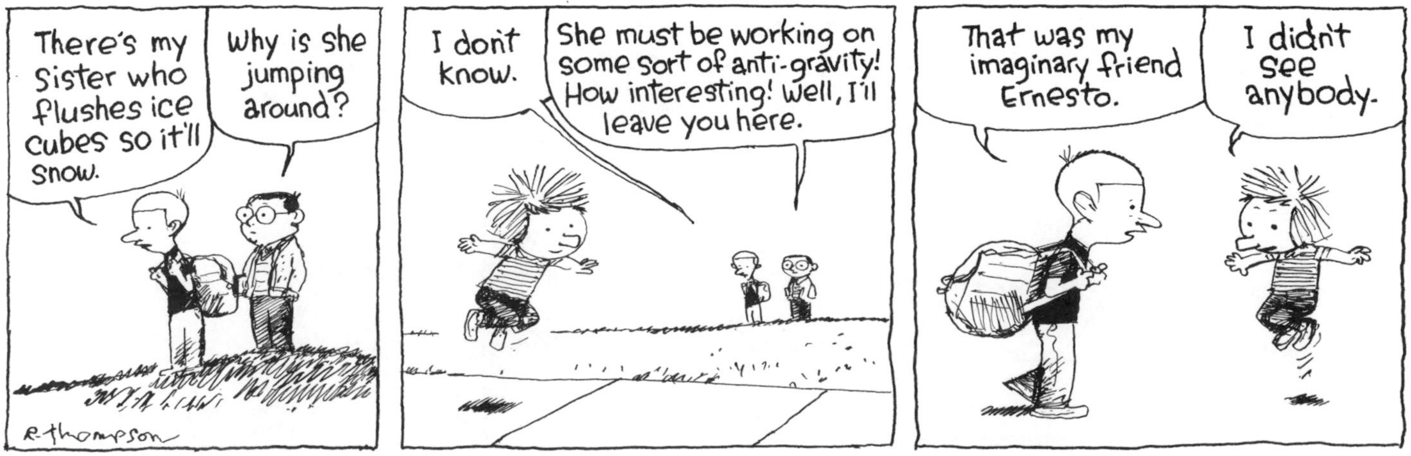
There's my sister who flushes ice cubes so it'll snow.
Why is she jumping around?
I don't know.
She must be working on some sort of anti-gravity! How interesting! Well, I'll leave you here.
That was my imaginary friend Ernesto.
I didn't see anybody.
R. thompson

As breakfast is the most important meal, I put a lot of thought into choosing my cereal.
When scanning the cereal aisle, I'm careful to avoid earth tones, subdued fonts or any hint of restraint in packaging design.
DULLARDS WITH RAISINS
BLAND O'S
FIBROUS CLUMPS
GOOD FOR YOU
These are warning signs of a boring cereal. I look for radio-active colors, eye-watering fonts and obsessive animal mascots.
SWEET EZ
An obsessive animal mascot— rabbit, bumblebee, bear, monkey, squid, etc.— is a key indicator of a good cereal.
S
Even better is an obsessive imaginary creature, say a fanatical leprechaun or a rabid unicorn.
Hey, Alice, did you know hot dogs are merely a vehicle for the condiments?
Daddy! I'm still discussing cereal!
RThompson

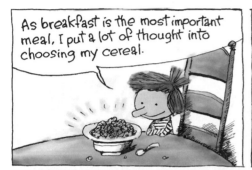

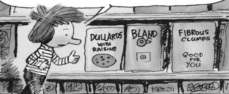

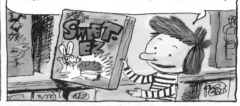

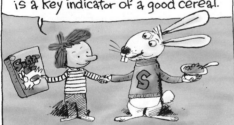

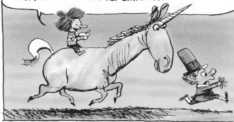

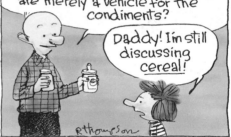

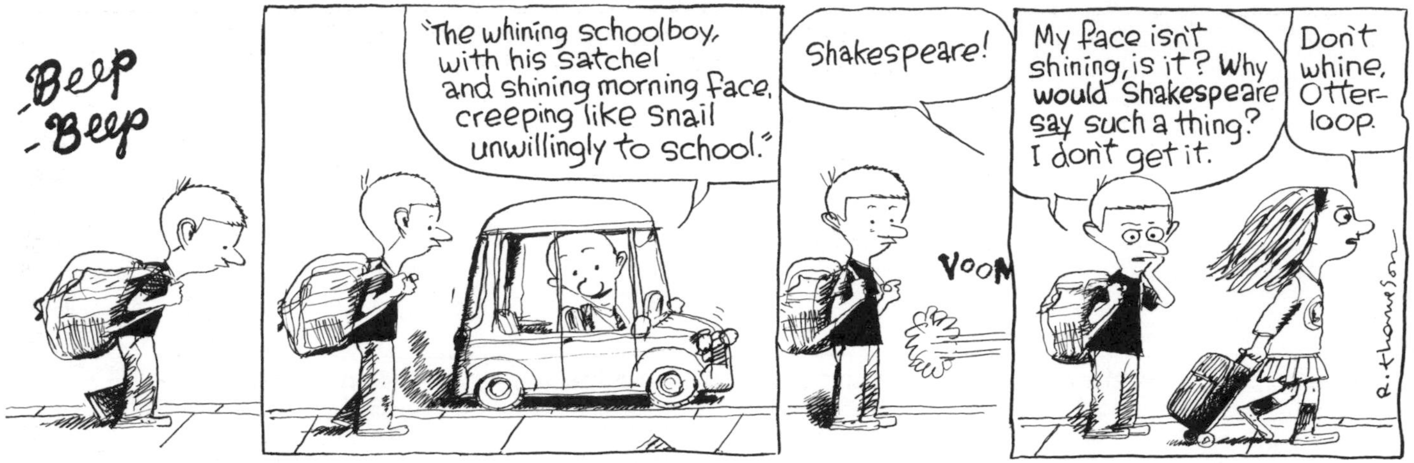

Beep
Beep
"The whining schoolboy, with his satchel and shining morning face, creeping like snail unwillingly to school."
Shakespeare!
VOOM
My face isn't shining, is it? Why would Shakespeare say such a thing? I don't get it.
Don't whine, Otterloop.

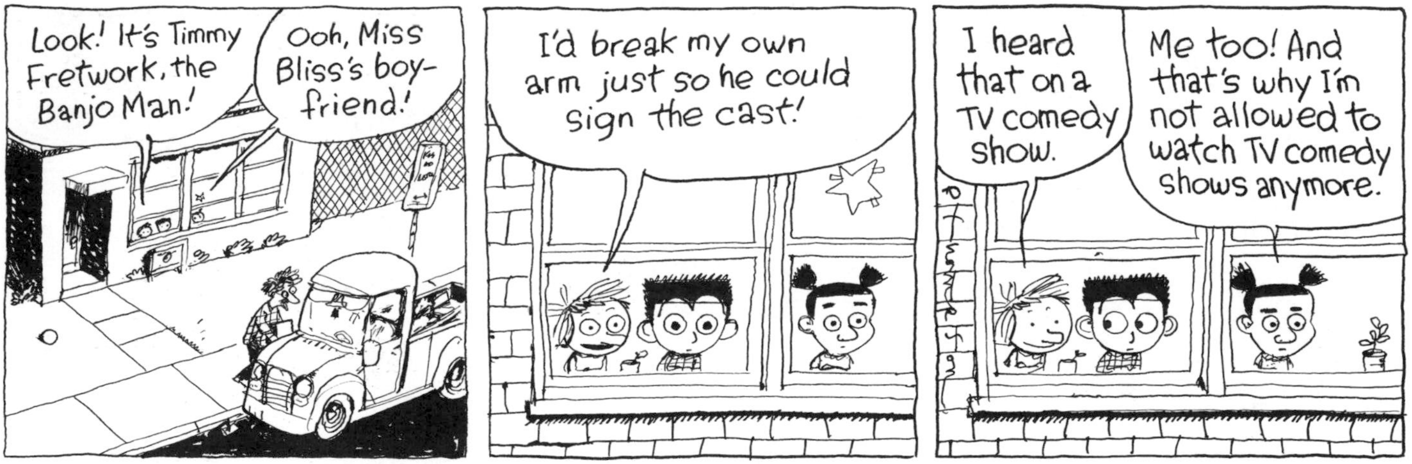

Look! It's Timmy Fretwork, the Banjo Man!
Ooh, Miss Bliss's boyfriend!
I'd break my own arm just so he could sign the cast!
I heard that on a TV comedy show.
Me too! And that's why I'm not allowed to watch TV comedy shows anymore.

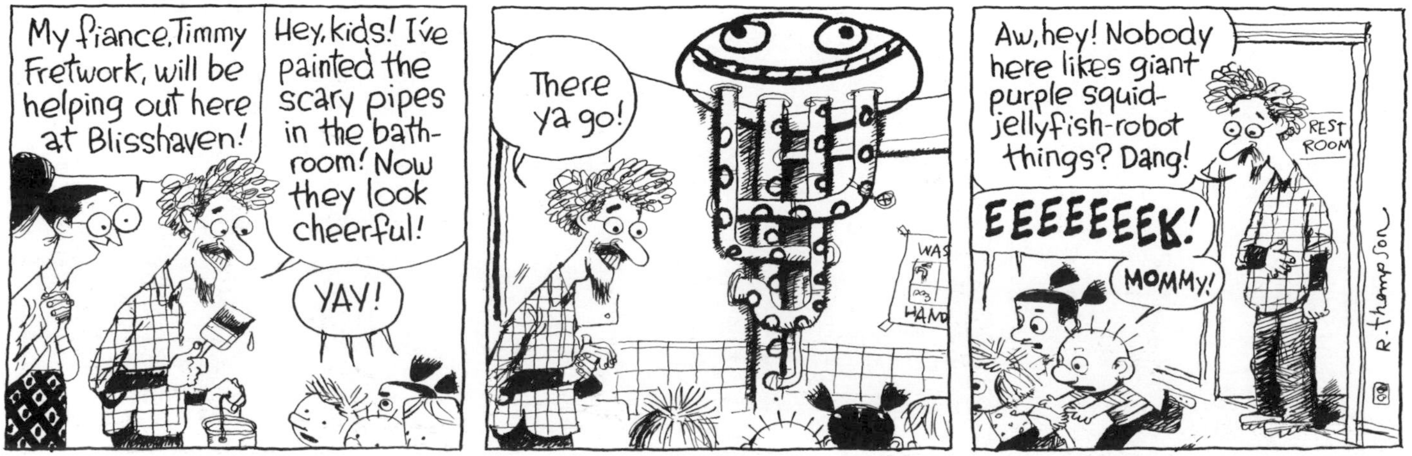

My fiance, Timmy Fretwork, will be helping out here at Blisshaven!
Hey, kids! I've painted the scary pipes in the bathroom! Now they look cheerful!
YAY!
There ya go!
Aw, hey! Nobody here likes giant purple squid-jellyfish-robot things? Dang!
REST ROOM
EEEEEEEK!
MOMMY!

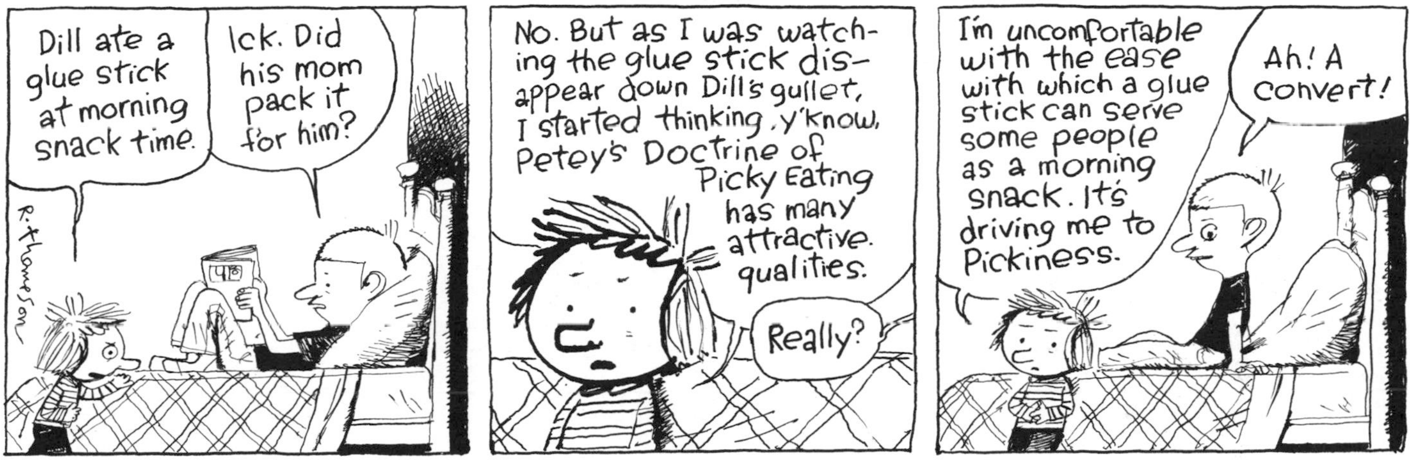
Dill ate a glue stick at morning snack time.
Ick. Did his mom pack it for him?
No. But as I was watching the glue stick disappear down Dill's gullet, I started thinking, y'know, Petey's Doctrine of Picky Eating has many attractive qualities.
Really?
I'm uncomfortable with the ease with which a glue stick can serve some people as a morning snack. It's driving me to Pickiness.
Ah! A convert!
R. Thompson

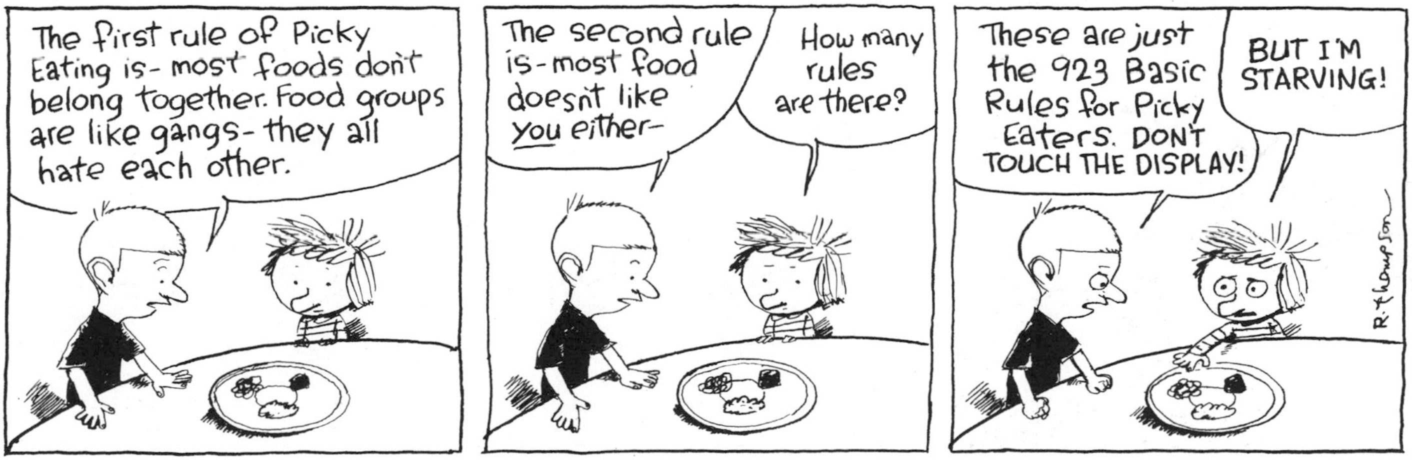
The first rule of Picky Eating is- most foods don't belong together. Food groups are like gangs- they all hate each other.
The second rule is- most food doesn't like you either-
How many rules are there?
These are just the 923 Basic Rules for Picky Eaters. DON'T TOUCH THE DISPLAY!
BUT I'M STARVING!
R. Thompson

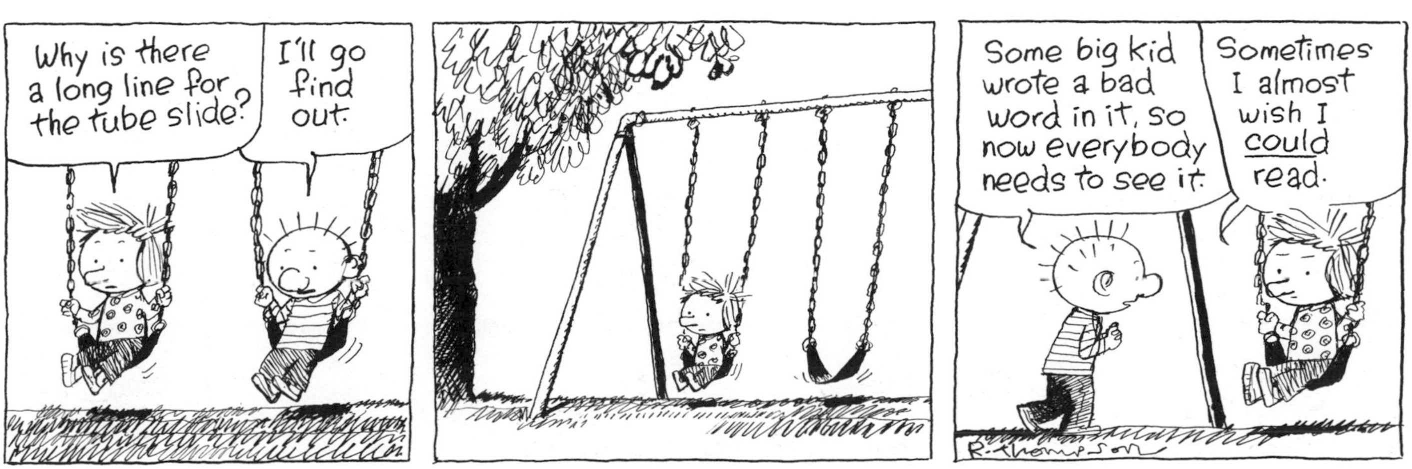
Why is there a long line for the tube slide?
I'll go find out.
Some big kid wrote a bad word in it, so now everybody needs to see it.
Sometimes I almost wish I could read.
R. Thompson

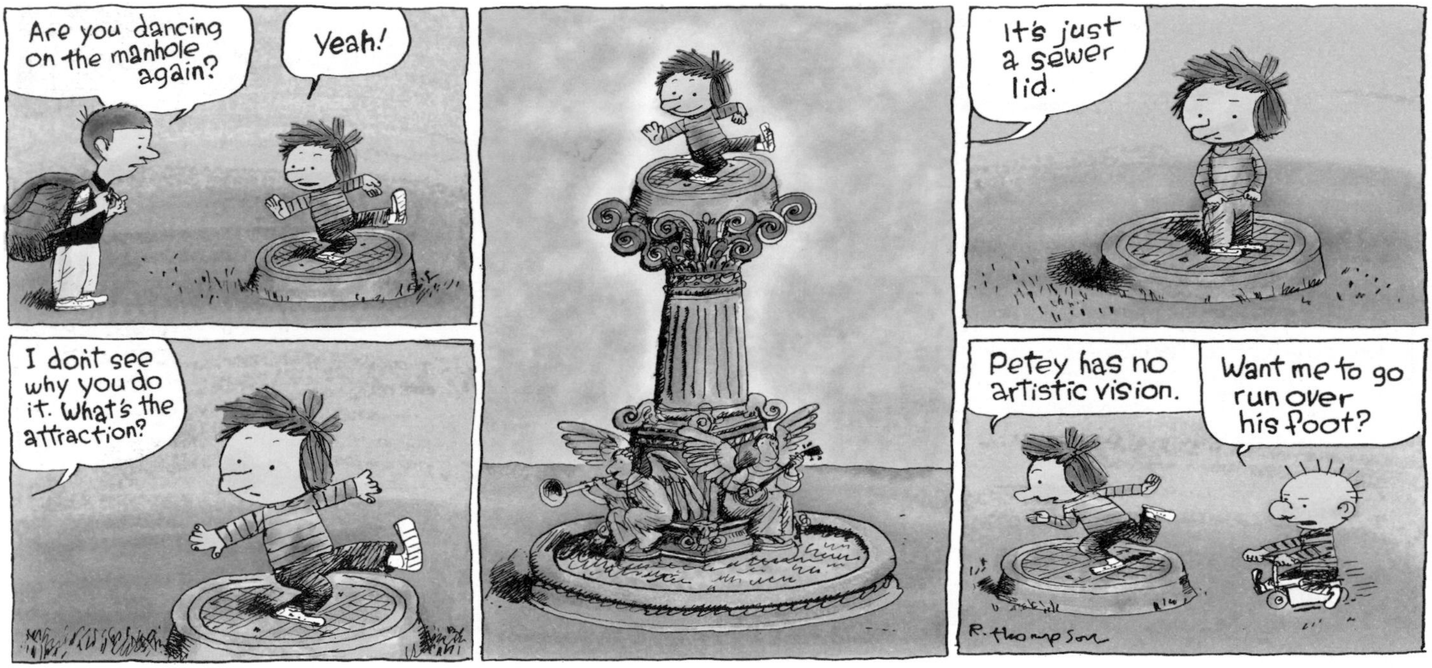
Are you dancing on the manhole again?
Yeah!
I don't see why you do it. What's the attraction?
It's just a sewer lid.
Petey has no artistic vision.
Want me to go run over his foot?
R. Thompson

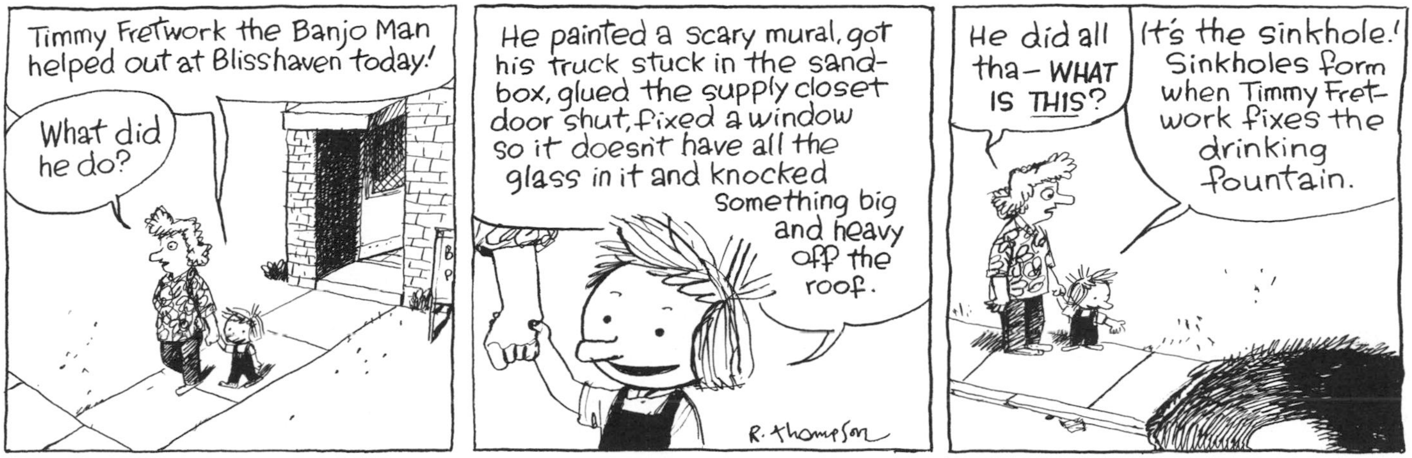
Timmy Fretwork the Banjo Man helped out at Blisshaven today!
What did he do?
He painted a scary mural, got his truck stuck in the sandbox, glued the supply closet door shut, fixed a window so it doesn't have all the glass in it and knocked something big and heavy off the roof.
R. thompson
He did all tha— WHAT IS THIS?
It's the sinkhole! Sinkholes form when Timmy Fretwork fixes the drinking fountain.

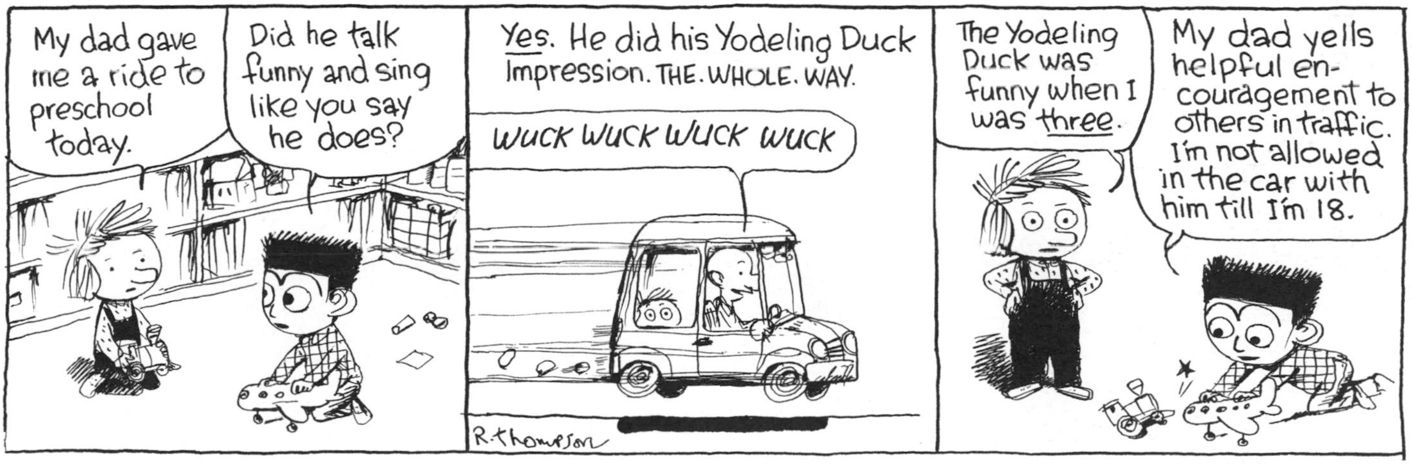
My dad gave me a ride to preschool today.
Did he talk funny and sing like you say he does?
Yes. He did his Yodeling Duck Impression. THE. WHOLE. WAY.
WUCK WUCK WUCK WUCK
R. thompson
The Yodeling Duck was funny when I was three.
My dad yells helpful encouragement to others in traffic. I'm not allowed in the car with him till I'm 18.

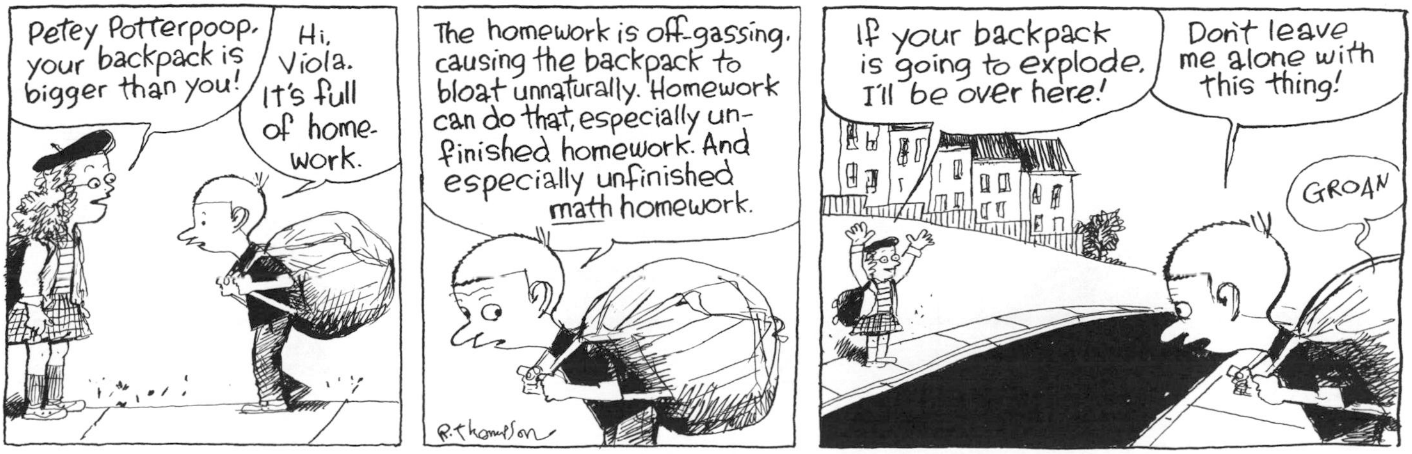
Petey Potterpoop, your backpack is bigger than you!
Hi, Viola. It's full of homework.
The homework is off-gassing, causing the backpack to bloat unnaturally. Homework can do that, especially unfinished homework. And especially unfinished math homework.
R. thompson
If your backpack is going to explode, I'll be over here!
Don't leave me alone with this thing!
GROAN

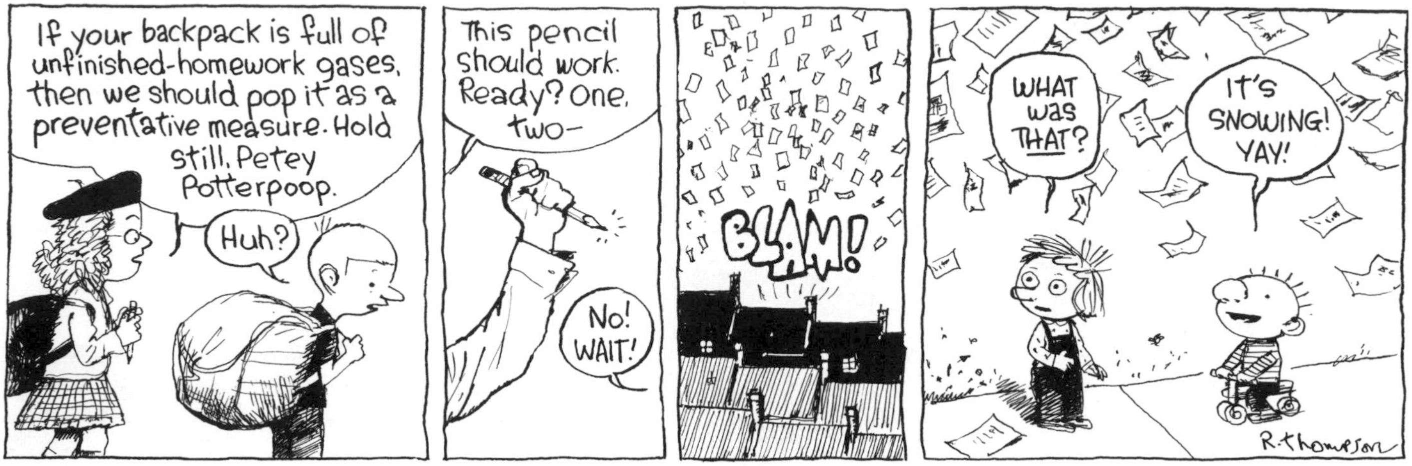
If your backpack is full of unfinished-homework gases, then we should pop it as a preventative measure. Hold still, Petey Potterpoop.
Huh?
This pencil should work. Ready? One, two–
No! WAIT!
BLAM!
WHAT was THAT?
IT'S SNOWING! YAY!
R. Thompson

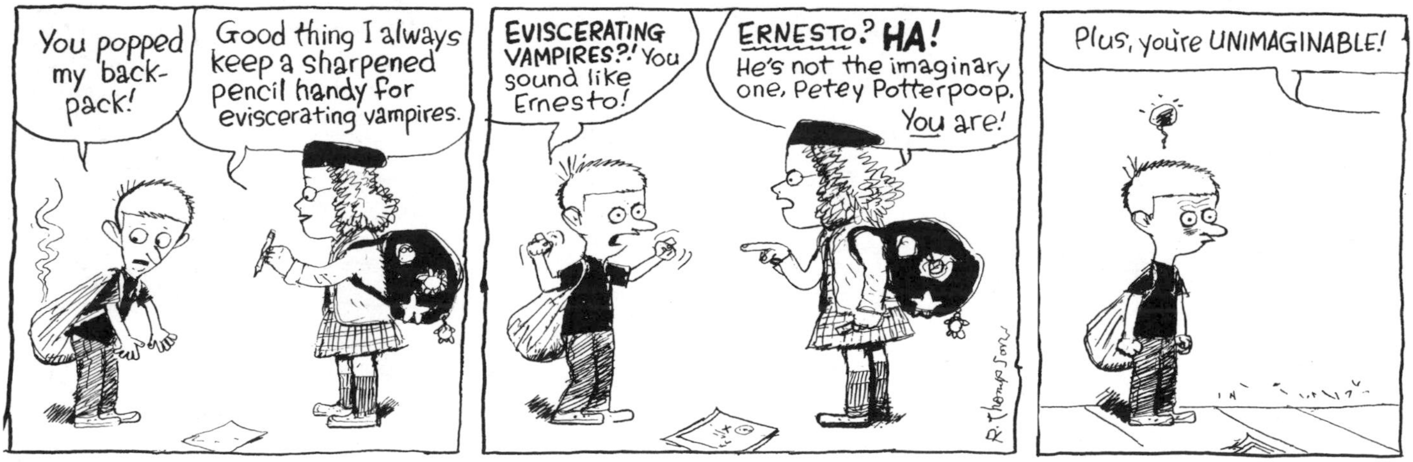
You popped my back-pack!
Good thing I always keep a sharpened pencil handy for eviscerating vampires.
EVISCERATING VAMPIRES?! You sound like Ernesto!
ERNESTO? HA! He's not the imaginary one, Petey Potterpoop. You are!
R. Thompson
Plus, you're UNIMAGINABLE!

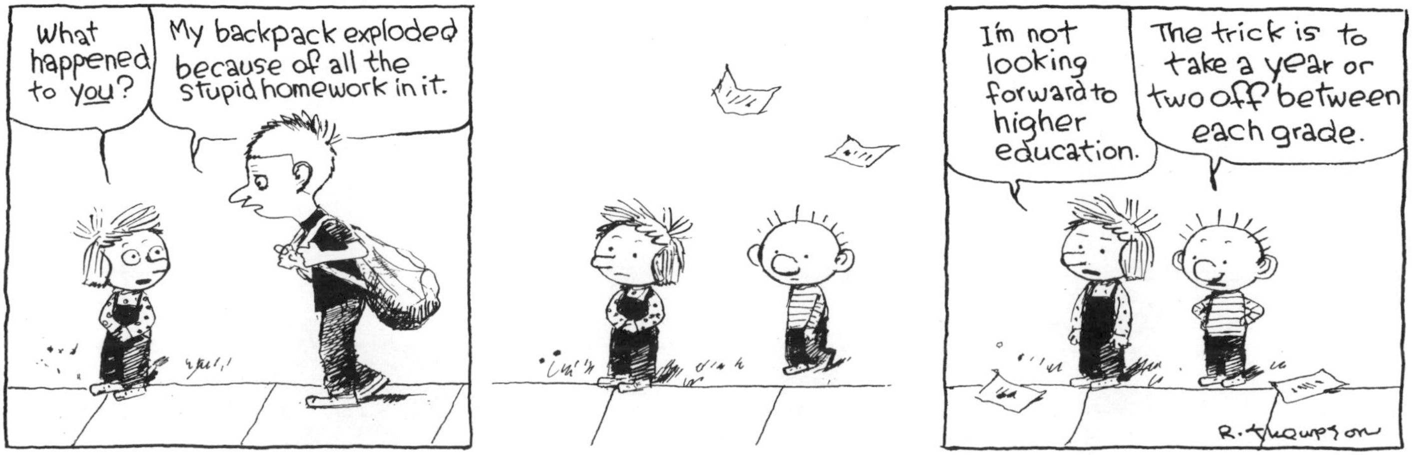
What happened to you?
My backpack exploded because of all the stupid homework in it.
I'm not looking forward to higher education.
The trick is to take a year or two off between each grade.
R. Thompson

Hey, Marcus, is your mom still making scrapbooks about you?
Yes.
It's gotten worse. She's started a blog about me called "MARCUS DE MARCO, SUPERSTAR."
EW.
It's got everything - stories, quotations, photos, stats. There's a Marcus Forum, a Marcus Art Gallery and a Marcus Mart so you can buy Marcus Wear for all ages and sizes.
There are Marcus hats, shirts, scarves, tote bags, umbrellas, soap, bath beads-
Who'd want any of that stuff?
You'd be surpri-
Hey, Marcus!
GAH.
My mom loves the bath beads and my dad wants this shirt in 5x Large! Can we do a deal?
EW.
R. Thompson

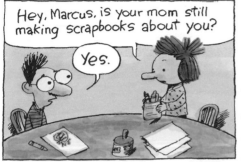

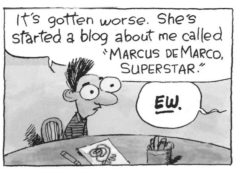

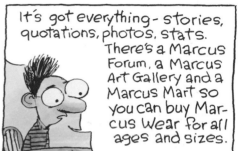

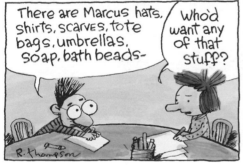

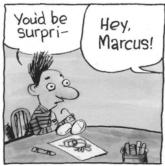

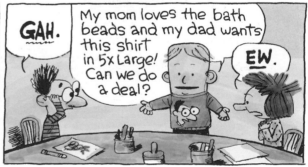